Luxury Retail
and Digital Management

Luxury Retail and Digital Management

*Developing Customer Experience
in a Digital World*

SECOND EDITION

Michel Chevalier
Michel Gutsatz

WILEY

Published by John Wiley & Sons Singapore Pte. Ltd.
1 Fusionopolis Walk, #07-01, Solaris South Tower, Singapore 138628

Edition History
John Wiley & Sons Singapore Pte. Ltd. (1e, 2012)

Other Wiley Editorial Offices

John Wiley & Sons, 111 River Street, Hoboken, NJ 07030, USA
John Wiley & Sons, The Atrium, Southern Gate, Chichester, West Sussex, P019 8SQ, United Kingdom
John Wiley & Sons (Canada) Ltd., 5353 Dundas Street West, Suite 400, Toronto, Ontario, M9B 6HB, Canada
John Wiley & Sons Australia Ltd., 42 McDougall Street, Milton, Queensland 4064, Australia
Wiley-VCH, Boschstrasse 12, D-69469 Weinheim, Germany

Library of Congress Cataloging-in-Publication Data

Names: Chevalier, Michel, author. | Gutsatz, Michel, author.
Title: Luxury retail and digital management : developing customer
    experience in a digital world / Michel Chevalier, Michel Gutsatz.
Other titles: Luxury retail management
Description: Second edition. | Solaris South Tower, Singapore : Wiley,
    [2020] | Includes bibliographical references and index.
Identifiers: LCCN 2019048771 (print) | LCCN 2019048772 (ebook) | ISBN
    9781119542339 (hardback) | ISBN 9781119542346 (adobe pdf) | ISBN
    9781119542353 (epub)
Subjects: LCSH: Luxury goods industry—Management. | Retail
    trade—Management.
Classification: LCC HD9999.L852 C34 2020 (print) | LCC HD9999.L852
    (ebook) | DDC 658.8/7—dc23
LC record available at https://lccn.loc.gov/2019048771
LC ebook record available at https://lccn.loc.gov/2019048772

Cover Design: Wiley
Cover Image: © jcarroll-images/Getty Images

Typeset in 11.5/14pt, BemboStd by SPi Global, Chennai, India.

Printed in Singapore by Markono Print Media Pte Ltd

10 9 8 7 6 5 4 3 2 1

You can have the best strategy in the world, the difference between the excellent and the incompetent is execution, execution, execution.

−Domenico deSole, former CEO Gucci

Contents

Foreword

I am convinced Michel Gusatz and Michel Chevalier are very right in writing a second edition of their comprehensive book on the retail management of luxury goods.

I see three major forces converge and reshape this area:

First, as the title of the new book suggests, *digital has taken the luxury goods industry by storm* – including its retail side. Ten years ago, you could find the vast majority of luxury brands still pushing back on digital (frequently, I heard comments like: 'the Internet is not for us', 'we want our customers to come to our stores to experience the brand and the product', 'e-commerce is for CDs and books', 'I have better things to do than setting up a website – I need to open more stores in China'). Today, everyone is bending over backwards to convince the market they have set 'digital' as their number one priority. The mere notion of luxury retail without m-commerce, e-commerce and a fully integrated digital service in-store (buy online, pick-up in-store; buy online, return in-store; order in-store for home/hotel delivery) is tantamount to the idea we should commute to the office every day on horseback. It is not just yesterday's story; it is utterly and completely obsolete. Either you have a fully developed digital retail strategy and activity, or you are not in a condition to play. Hence, the need to think through what the right digital strategy and the right digital activity should mean for the specifics of your brand and your business.

Second – and linked to the point above – *physical retail network development in luxury goods is virtually done*, at least for the foreseeable future. We have seen for a number of years that the largest luxury brands haven't added any stores to their total. Actually, most have been in 'trimming mode', reducing one or two stores here and there. A case in point is the network consolidation that has been going on in China, hand in hand with a Darwinian fight among luxury shopping malls, which has led to a shake-out and 'survival of the fittest'. When we look at who has been leading store openings in the past five years, we find two kinds: (a) up-and-coming smaller brands that have been able to 'strike gold' (Moncler, Saint Laurent, Celine, Balenciaga); (b) accessible luxury brands that have built their networks worldwide (a case in point, Michael Kors). The point here is that everyone else has been confronted with a relatively static store base and a completely new set of challenges versus the previous expansion era.

In fact, during the expansion phase, *most brands were concerned about attaining comparable standards all across the world.* Store appearance and in-store service was supposed to be of a similar level, anywhere in the world. So much so, that store blueprints and 'selling ceremony hand-books' were created. One could say, most brands used a cookie-cutter approach to store expansion. The advantage, of course, was consistency. The disadvantage – and this is becoming all too obvious today – was a risk of boring customers and failing to drive in-store traffic. Why on earth should I go and visit a store in Milan, New York or L.A., when it is virtually identical – and actually a tad smaller – than the one I have close to me in Shanghai? And why should I go to a store in the first place, when I can buy what I need online, and when I can touch and see the products while I go through the airport in their airside locations?

Brands today are confronted with a new task: how to make their stores unique and interesting enough so that customers continue to be keen to visit them – both in their hometown and when they travel. This will require a completely new approach: standardisation is out. It is time for brands to go back to the drawingboard and answer two questions. For starters: How can I make my stores different from my competitors', other than for the colour of the marble on the floor and their size? How can the new stores 'speak' about the DNA of my brand, and plastically embody it? We have seen a few brands stand out on this front – Tiffany opening a cafe in its NYC flagship with a view of Central Park is a best-in-class example of uniquely reconnecting store and brand equity. And then of course, the other question is how to make each store in my chain slightly different and interesting enough to deserve a visit. This, I believe, will demand more 'localisation' and less 'globalisation'. Striking the right balance alone demands a whole new handbook on how to manage luxury goods retail.

Third, luxury brands face today more demanding consumers. Gone are the days of lines in front of luxury flagships, and hordes of new consumers all clamouring to buy the well-known luxury icons. Today, many consumers have seen it all and bought it all. This means *innovation has become essential,* if brands want to continue to stay relevant to them. Product innovation, first and foremost. But in-store innovation too. As well as innovation in communication and client engagement. We have called this the need to 'surprise' consumers. *For luxury retail, this means that stores need to change frequently and host a whole new array of activities.* Mostly, brands have tackled this need with *pop-ups.* Far from being a 'side act', pop-ups have become a major cost line in the overall retail budget. This opens up a completely new management front: how to best locate pop-ups vs flagships, what to do in them which can be meaningful for the brand, how to create synergies with the rest of the network, whether to locate outside or inside flagships themselves. Here too is a whole new world for managers to tackle.

Luca Solca
Managing Director, Luxury Goods, Sanford C. Bernstein (Schweiz)

Introduction

What Is the Reason for This Revision?

January 2012 saw the publication of the English version of our book *Luxury Retail Management* that we had written in 2010 and 2011. Seven years later, as close observers and players in the luxury industry,[1] we realised that the industry had undergone such upheavals since then that we had to revise our book so that it remained relevant in the context of these evolutions. During this rereading, we also realised that the 2012 edition was premonitory in many respects (especially the chapters referring to the Internet and China) but it did need to be completely revamped if we wanted it to preserve its role as a reference book to be read by every specialist of luxury distribution in its English, French or Chinese versions.

We therefore decided to rewrite most of this book, structuring it around the new luxury business model – omnichannel – where the customer is placed at the core of communication and distribution channels,

---

[1] The authors are – independently of one another – involved in the perfume industry.

and of organisations. *Is*, or *should be*? As we will see while reading through these pages, this will be the major challenge for luxury brands over the next 5 years: placing the customer at the heart and building the organisation and information systems that will allow it around the customer.

It is therefore necessary to start with the client, and to do so one needs to understand the major changes that have taken place in recent years.

Change Is Accelerating: The Luxury Customer Is No Longer the Same

In their 2017 annual study on luxury, Bain & Co. showed that all the structuring trends for the industry are linked to the rise of the millennials – or Generation Y, that is, those born between 1980 and 2000 (Strauss and Howe 2000). Two figures explain the impact of this generation:

- They currently represent 38% of luxury buyers and 30% of the market (in value).
- 85% of the growth in the luxury market in 2017 was generated by them.

Their tastes, behaviour and expectations are therefore shaping the market and influencing other generations. We have identified three behaviour traits that we believe essential:

- The quest for experiences: One no longer consumes a product but lives an experience. Giving a meaning to life is an important goal and customers will look for brands that can bring them these elements of meaning. For example, customers have their own passions and are looking for brands that know how to construct a relationship around those passions.
- Involvement: The closer a brand is to these customers, the more likely they are to become its ambassadors. They want to 'live the story' of the brand and not consume it, which in turn allows them to share it – on the Internet.
- Affirming one's own identity: By choosing a personal style, luxury is a means of self-expression.

Therefore, the bricks-and-mortar and Internet boutique duo could be considered the sole epicentre of the brand, a place where the customer will live the story. All the skill of the brand would involve linking the experiences of the customer's life (their passions, communities, personal style) to the experience of the brand (services, transactions, values, the community around the brand).

For this reason, Bain urges leaders of luxury brands to make the customer their 'obsession' and to soak in the spirit of the millennials – in six steps that should be on the agenda of every head of the industry:

1. Make the history of the brand come to life through inspiring dialogues and experiences.
2. Build personalised relationships with customers.
3. Rethink the customer's itinerary by adopting a holistic view of distribution – what we hereafter call the omnichannel.
4. Understand (and decode) customers' aspirations so that they become relevant to them – which inversely means that any brand that moves further away from customer (and particularly millennial) expectations would become obsolete.
5. Develop the individualising of the product, services and messages all through the customer's life.
6. Invest in talents and skills to achieve all these goals (Gutsatz and Auguste 2015) and maintain a product-marketing approach.

In short, luxury brands – which have been developing over the last 20 years, partly through the opening of boutiques (that require considerable investment and result in an increase in turnover) – are faced with the challenge of changing their models and rebuilding on marketing and customer relations. This will lead to increasing yearly operational expenses for public relations and promotions, which will consequently weigh down their operating accounts. Luxury brands are thus at a historic turning point: they have to reinvent themselves. The 2017 figures put forward by Bain are disturbing in this respect: whereas, at the time when the luxury sector was flourishing, whether during the period of democratisation (1994/2007) or that of Chinese bulimia (2010/2014), 85 to 95% of the brands showed positive results. Since 2016, only 65% of them are profitable (and only 35% have succeeded in increasing their profitability!). The current period that one can consider the 'New Normal' will engender winners and losers.

This book is therefore our contribution towards understanding these new challenges that luxury brands have to face.

Case Study: A Striking Example: 'See Now / Buy Now'

On 4 February 2016, Burberry announced that they were implementing what proved to be a revolution in the world of fashion: *a synchronisation of the dates of the fashion shows and the availability of the new collection in their boutiques* (Amed and Abnet 2016). From September 2016 onwards, the collections were reduced to two per year, the women's and men's fashion shows were merged and products were made available in boutiques at the same time. In the wake of this change, other brands announced their intention to follow Burberry's example: Tommy Hilfiger, Tom Ford, Rebecca Minkoff, Vêtements, Mulberry, etc.

Fast forward to 24 February 2017 – Ralph Toledano, Chairman of the French Federation of Ready-to-Wear Dressmakers and Fashion Designers announced that they would not make any changes to the existing schedule, followed in quick succession by Gucci and all the Kering brands.

Christopher Bailey, then CEO and Creative Director of Burberry, justified this choice, citing the desire to draw closer to his customers: in his opinion, he did not see why products should not be available immediately or why fashion should continue to make distinctions between fall and winter and spring and summer when fashion is distributed worldwide (and concerns both hemispheres). For him, at the end of the day, all it required was only an optimisation of the processes of supply and production:

> When you break it all down, it's just a shift in your supply chain – that's the crunch. (Amed and Abnett 2016)

He could also have evoked the lower costs that such a decision implied, especially at a time when Burberry's results were poor (for the first six months of 2015 sales and profits were stable; revenue on licences declined by 13%).

But, of course, the story lies elsewhere: the big comeback of luxury *and* a new episode in the conflict between France and Italy on the one side and the English and Americans on the other.

'Several people, including designers and retailers, are complaining about the shows. Something is not functioning because of social media, people are lost', said Diane Von Furstenberg, Chairperson of the Council of Fashion Designers of America (CFDA), announcing that they were looking into the possibility of a 'See Now, Buy Now' Fashion Week (Lockwood 2015). It was, of course, an American initiative, presented as though it was done under the pressure of social media and consumers. This point is important. One may recall, for example, that during his last fashion show, Tommy Hilfiger delineated a space dedicated to 'instagrammers', to allow them to photograph the show under the best conditions possible and to publish their 'live' snapshots by Instagram (Le Luxe est Vivant 2016) and that American fashion shows are now open to the public (against an entrance fee). American fashion shows have thus become 'democratised' entertainment.

The reaction of luxury brands (showing in Paris and Milan) was immediate. They reasserted they were luxury brands practising real scarcity management. They projected themselves as 'creation driven' – thus consigning the American brands to their 'marketing-driven' image. By doing so, they categorically differentiated themselves from the American brands (and Burberry), often presented as being accessible luxury. We thus witnessed on that occasion a general repositioning of brands within the luxury industry itself.

(*continued*)

(*Continued*)

But it was not a rigid position confronting an immovable model on the part of the French and the Italians. Prada immediately made available two models of its bags that were presented during its fashion shows in its boutiques. And Karl Lagerfeld admitted that Chanel's organisation was much smarter than previously thought:

> Chanel creates six collections a year, but I just created one more – the 'capsule' collection – that we present neither to the press nor to anyone else; it only surfaces when our stores receive the presentation leaflet. But I would like to do something else – it may be too early to talk about it – a special Internet collection: 15 models that will be displayed on the Web: You see it, you order a model and you receive it immediately. (Amed 2015)

A vision much more refined than 'See Now, Buy Now'.

The Definition of Luxury

It is impossible to speak about *luxury* without attempting to define the concept. Many experts debate what the word means, apparently without having reached a consensus.

The first distinction one has to make is between luxury and fashion. For some, a brand in the textile or accessories sector starts out merely as a 'fashion' brand and becomes a 'luxury' brand only if it has achieved a certain consistency in its concept and timelessness in its collections. According to that theory, a fashion brand has to be creative and come up with new ideas, new concepts, and new products every season in order to arouse the interest of the consumer. If it creates classic models that sell year in, year out and become bestsellers that endure, its status then evolves from 'fashion' to 'luxury'. But although this distinction between a fashion brand and a luxury brand is a valid one, it is nonetheless misleading because even a fashion brand that has achieved luxury status, such as Chanel or Dior, has to come up with new models each season and present them in new ways in order to retain consumer interest.

Why Is It So Difficult to Find a Definition? The concept of luxury has varied over time. In the Middle Ages, people saw luxury as unnecessary and therefore superfluous. A luxury item was more intricate than an ordinary item used to accomplish the same function. The most striking historical example is that of Christophle, which sold tableware accessible to the petite bourgeoisie at the beginning of the nineteenth century by replacing the noble solid silver with plated silver. Up until the nineteenth century, luxury items were intended only for the 'gentry' and were a means to set themselves apart from the crowd.

Today, the term *luxury* carries a connotation that is far less negative. It is no longer considered superfluous or reserved for a small group of individuals. A new concept has emerged – the brand concept – whereby a luxury item has become an object that carries a known, credible and respected brand name. The introduction of the signature, that is, of the brand, pushes back the concept of exclusion ('It is not for everyone') and shifts the focus to the quality of the product.

Another element that may have contributed to this more positive view of the concept of luxury is the emergence of what one may call 'accessible luxury' that, in practical terms, means luxury meant for everyone. Hence, the impression that the consumer retains is that luxury products are sophisticated and expensive, of a quality clearly above average, and signed by a brand bearing a name with a strong power of attraction.

The Many Approaches to Luxury Another way to differentiate the definitions of luxury is to look at the criteria that different people may apply to distinguish one luxury product from another.

- In terms of *perception*, the consumer decides what is or is not a luxury product. Today, one would not speak of 'conspicuous waste' as Thorstein Veblen would have, but of the quality of service in a sophisticated environment.
- In terms of *production*, manufacturers decide whether or not they want their products to be part of the luxury sector. Accordingly, they

ensure that the luxury item is the product of the work of a meticulous artisan, that it is sold in a sophisticated environment and that it is promoted in a unique way, placing the focus on the brand and its own values. However, manufacturers and consumers do not necessarily agree: the management of Hugo Boss, for example, doubtlessly does everything it can to associate their brand with high-quality products sold in a relatively sophisticated environment. And taking a different approach, from the point of view of Zara's management, the focus on its exclusive network of outlets situated in the best locations in every city, and the constant flow of new models in each store, their business is akin to that of the luxury industry.

- In terms of *social and individual comportment*, sociologists would describe a luxury product as an object that allows its user to stand out from the crowd. Customers would probably speak in hedonistic terms and describe how the possession of that particular luxury item gives them personal satisfaction and genuine pleasure, perhaps reflecting the refinement of the objects they own or plan to acquire.

There is one constant underlying these various definitions: the brand itself and its own values. A product, of course, has its own technical and aesthetic characteristics – but it also carries a brand name. This brand identity should be consistent with what the product represents and should deliver added value so that its coherence is evident.

A Set of Values that Define Luxury Another approach to defining luxury is to identify the various qualities that a luxury item should include.

- The notion of *exclusivity* underlies the concept of luxury. A luxury product should be rare and not easy to acquire. It should be accessible, of course, but purchasers should have the impression that they set themselves apart by using it, that they are capable of distinguishing what makes this product so different from others or other brands, and that it reflects remarkable sophistication and taste.
- An obvious characteristic of a luxury product is, of course, its *quality*. It has to be more beautiful than another. Its guarantee should be clearly defined and generous. The packaging has to be elegant

and the object expensive, in any case more expensive than a similar mass-market product.

- Another aspect: a certain form of *hedonism*. The product should be a pleasure to own and use; it should give the owner a very personal feeling of satisfaction.
- The *brand image* is undoubtedly the crowning touch. It has to be reputed, but also unique, and different, but with features everyone recognises.

Ultimately, luxury simply boils down to a question of status. A professional in the luxury business should never forget their real job: to make customers feel they have a special status, directly or indirectly, through whatever form it takes.

In short, customers are willing to pay higher prices because, with all its features, the luxury item satisfies all their desires, emotional or symbolic, and offers them a memorable experience. That is what exclusiveness, quality, hedonism and brand image are all about.

The Various Types of Luxury   Instead of embarking on a long debate to find one common concept of luxury, it may be more practical to distinguish the different types of luxury.

- *Authentic luxury* would refer to objects that quite clearly differ from mass-market products in that they are the handiwork of skilled craftsmen. They conceivably last longer, are probably simpler to use and have a brand identity that is gratifying. A true luxury product will be timeless to some extent and the user will find pleasure in operating or using it because of the endless number of refined and carefully crafted details it has. It will definitely not be cheap, and its name will represent a great deal more than just its monetary value. It will not be so much a question of price as an object endowed with aesthetic components that will bring added emotional value to its owner.
- *Intermediate luxury* (one of the authors of this book has coined the expression '*Luxe Populi*' in his other book, see Gutsatz 2002) refers to products that have the traditional attributes of luxury in terms of creativity, statement and coherence where brand identity

is concerned, but are merely an upgraded version of traditional consumer products. They are not the product of individual craftsmanship. They position themselves in the upper-middle range on the price scale and are produced in relatively large quantities in automated factories, but their brand image is carefully cultivated and controlled.

- *Offbeat luxury* refers to products that are in fact exclusive creations that stand out very clearly from the ordinary. Ferrari is a good example: a Porsche would be an authentic luxury product; a Ferrari adds another dimension, more off-the-wall. Ferraris are produced in very limited numbers (for years Ferrari capped its annual production at 7,000 cars) and seem to assert the right to the freedom and creativity typical of Ferrari. The company does not manufacture automobiles but exclusive collectors' items, some of which will never see an ordinary country road.

  As Jean-Louis Dumas, the former Chairman of Hermès, once said: 'A luxury brand must respect three conditions: produce beautiful objects, select clients who will become individual agents of its own promotion, and decide freely and without any constraint what it wishes to do' (personal communication). There is probably no better definition of luxury.

- *Affordable luxury* may not be luxury at all, or perhaps it may just be a special category of intermediate luxury. Zara is an example of this segment: creative products that rotate very quickly, and consumers who find a psychological satisfaction in buying and using these quick-moving products. The prices are very reasonable and the brand image is carefully managed and promoted, with a well-defined long-term vision. As we will see, Zara's business model is very effective. Although, from the manufacturer's viewpoint, it employs many tools derived from the luxury sector, it is perhaps merely a form of intermediate luxury – or even simply a sophisticated and skilful mass-market brand. Zara is perhaps a poor example because most readers would say that the brand has nothing to do with the luxury sector. We do understand this point of view, but in our opinion many tools used in luxury could be used for mass-market brands. Besides, we can no doubt discern a continuum with Zara at one end and Gucci and Chanel at the other.

The Contents of This New Edition

The difference between this edition and the first one, which contained 13 descriptive chapters, is that in this one we wished to emphasise four essential factors that come into play in the management of sales outlets. We could be in fact discussing not only the luxury sector, but also all other market sectors for which stores are often the primary source of income.

It is a fact that, compared to more traditional sectors, the luxury industry has some specificities that are noteworthy: the possibility of being able to identify customers whose contact information is relatively easy to obtain and to track their purchases over several years. The same customer may also purchase products sometimes near their home or place of work, and at other times at the other end of the world while travelling for work or pleasure.

In the first part, we will be describing the main choices facing luxury brands in terms of distribution:

- Which distribution model should it adopt? (Chapter 1)
- Do we still need stores? (Chapter 2)
- What store concept should it adopt? (Chapter 3)
- How can it integrate its offline and online businesses? (Chapter 4)

In the second part, the customer will take centre stage. Luxury customers expect seamless service. They wish to be able to change from an online approach to an offline approach at any time and expect the brand to be organised enough to allow them to switch seamlessly from one method to another at any given time. There is no universally accepted term that describes this today: the term most often used in France is omnichannel; in the USA it is called ROPO ('Research Online, Purchase Offline'), i.e. search for information online (on the Internet), purchase offline (in a store), or the contrary: search for information offline (in a store), purchase online (on the Internet). In China, the term O2O ('Offline to Online') is used. In this book, we will use the term O2O – which is interchangeable (Offline to online/Online to offline/Offline to online to offline, etc.). However, O2O, which has to continuously adapt to customers switching from one system to another, requires very astute management, logistics and control systems.

We will therefore examine successively:

- How brands can place the customer at the centre of their approach and their organisation (Chapter 5).
- How brands can identify the customer and the issues around CRM (Chapter 6).
- How brands can coordinate marketing campaigns in an O2O world (Chapter 7).
- The war of the platforms (Chapter 8).

In the third part, we will delve deeper into the type of service to be provided to customers, how to build loyalty and how to ensure the quality and meticulousness of service.

This will bring us to four essential elements:

- Understanding customer behaviour (Chapter 9).
- Building customer relationships (Chapter 10).
- How to ensure customer loyalty (Chapter 11).
- Understanding how the Internet has shattered the traditional sales model (Chapter 12).

In the fourth part, we will present the more traditional and more typical elements of sales point management.

- Location of sales points (Chapter 13).
- Management of sales point staff (Chapter 14).
- The financial analysis of sales points (Chapter 15).
- Managing sales prices in global markets (Chapter 16).

In Chapter 14, we have also compiled all the information that could be useful to a luxury sales point manager or a business or sales point development manager.

In this book we have sought to answer all the questions that luxury brands have today with regard to physical distribution and to offer some ideas for reflection and a projection of what could happen in the next few years.

Part I

Important Choices in Luxury Distribution

Chapter 1

The Various Models in Luxury Distribution

Luxury today no longer sells because of rarity but on a feeling of exclusivity, which depends primarily upon the selectivity of its distribution, both physical and digital.

–Jean-Noël Kapferer[1]

From the outside, observers may believe that all luxury brands are distributed in the same way – through exclusive stores owned by the brand – and that they are able to manage them from their head offices. In fact, the reality is much more complex.

---

[1] Kapferer (2017).

Some luxury products, such as perfumes and watches, are sold for the most part in multi-brand stores that do not belong to them. These stores generally do what they think is most efficient for their multi-brand businesses and they are never easy to motivate or mobilise.

In some countries (e.g. Thailand and Vietnam) a foreign company that imports and distributes products manufactured abroad is not allowed to be a majority owner of its local subsidiary (it is only possible in China since 2018). It has to associate with a majority-holding partner that is a national of the country. So, no luxury group can, even if it initially wanted to, become the owner of all its sales outlets in the world.

Building a global network of outlets demands an enormous amount of time and money. Indeed, for a large luxury brand, having its own store in Ulaanbaatar would be wonderful, but how can it ensure that customers will find the same service there (hospitality, advice, prices and after-sales service, for example) as they receive in Paris or Milan?

Also, although Gucci or Chanel might have the means to invest in opening a store in New York, a small brand that is already struggling to make profits in its Paris store would find it much more difficult to do so.

A discussion on the sales points of luxury brands all over the world therefore involves describing all models, physical or digital, that can or should be used to present the products to customers the world over.

Direct and Indirect Distribution

Luxury brands did not start out with exclusive stores in every city in the world. Their distribution systems grew. They often opened a single store in one city (the city of origin) and then used a network of multi-brand outlets that afforded them initial exposure and international turnover. The business environment has also evolved over the last 150 years; the main store categories have changed and found their *raison d'être* and their stability.

A Historical Perspective

Retail trade is doubtlessly one of the oldest professions in the world. From the dawn of history, when people realised that they could not obtain everything they required for their own survival by themselves, they had to turn to others who were capable of searching for and gathering together the various commodities they required, and who exchanged these items for a monetary consideration. This act of selecting and gathering various goods that would be subsequently sold to others saw the emergence of the trader and retail trade.

Later, during the Middle Ages, as trade developed, merchants from the same domain often tended to cluster together in the same street. They seemed to believe that it was better to place themselves in proximity to their competitors, assuming that customers would be more likely to enter their shops, and those of their competitors as well when they went around all the shops on the street. Those that set up shop elsewhere, resolutely isolated from their peers, found themselves away from the shopping circuits and missed out on sales opportunities. Being located far away from other shops but close to residential areas was nevertheless an advantage for everyday services such as food – in other words, as convenience stores.

This distinction between proximity purchases and others has always existed and explains the differences in localising strategy. The fact that merchants from the same sector wished to group together and concentrate their pulling power is not very different from what we see today in big cities with the concentration of luxury stores in the same neighbourhood.

The foundational event worth mentioning here is the creation in 1851 of the world's first department store, Le Bon Marché, in Paris. The idea behind it was that, for the first time, ready-to-wear clothes for men and women, shoes, kitchen utensils and suchlike would all be sold together in the same store. As always, when an idea is good, it is quickly emulated and in 1856 the first American department store, Macy's, opened in New York, where it still stands now.

As time went on, the appearance and the system of presentation of the products in department stores were strongly influenced by technical innovation. In 1869, the first elevator was installed in a Parisian store, making it easy for customers to go from one floor to another, and also making it possible to present products on four or five different levels.

Yet another innovation, which dates back to 1892, influenced the cadence in all department stores in the world: the escalator. This allowed customers to go from one floor to another at their own pace, without having to wait for a lift. Escalators have thus defined the space of almost every department store today: a central well in the middle of a hall as large and impressive as possible, sometimes crowned with a dome; the escalators moving through this well, allowing customers to go from one floor to another as and when they wish. The first escalators were installed in Harrods in London in 1895.

Mitsukoshi Nihonbashi, the first Japanese department store, was opened in Tokyo in 1915.

The year 1919 is also another very important date: the first air conditioning system was installed at Abraham & Strauss in New York. Since then, department stores no longer need windows. Air conditioning does away with the need for windows for ventilation and, in some cases, for doors that open onto the street: stores could be integrated into a gallery or mall. Boutiques therefore do not need windows anymore, except, of course, as showcases for presenting products. The appearance of department store buildings remained more or less unchanged after that, much like we know them today.

In 1922, the first shopping centre, the Country Club Plaza, was opened in Kansas City and the appearance of these centres has remained virtually unchanged for the past 95 years, with very little innovation, except for the first duty-free store that opened in 1957 in Shannon Airport, Ireland.

On another plane, we should mention the appearance of the first electronic cash register in 1970 and the first optical reading device in 1975. Before these dates, it would have been difficult to imagine that every product sold in the world would one day have its own code easily decipherable by a machine.

Today's department stores, shopping malls, shopping arcades and duty-free outlets are in fact the end products of 150 years of innovation and development in distribution.

The Various Types of Sales Outlets

Wholesale and Retail Sales There are in fact two methods to present products to the consumer: having one's own store, to fully control customer relations (retail), or selling to stores that will present the products to their customers themselves (wholesale). This distinction applies, of course, to brick-and-mortar stores. The same difference also exists in the digital domain. Celine, for example, sells its shoes through their own website (retail) but also sells them on the 'Net-a-Porter' website (wholesale). In both cases, the selling price to the consumer is the same (same retail price) but in the second case (through Net-a-Porter) Celine has to pay a retail margin to the platform.

At first glance one might think that the wholesale option (through independent multi-brand outlets or online sites other than that of the brand) is simpler, because the brand would have practically nothing to do and it would not have to tie up its capital in store ownerships and stocks. But, of course, it would have to share its margin with the respective stores.

On the contrary, one might think that it is easier to sell exclusively through directly operated stores and save the entire margin. But is the brand reputed enough to attract customers and persuade them to enter their own stores? Also, is the purchase important enough to a customer to motivate him to go and buy the product directly? An example may make the issue clear: would Hermès sell more bottles of its cologne, *Eau d'Orange Verte*, if it sold this product in all the perfumeries in Paris or by reserving it exclusively for its own boutiques in Paris?

Directly Operated Stores Directly operated or independent stores seem to have priority among many brand managers.

Of course, when a brand acquires a strong power of attraction, and it disposes of sufficient financial means, it could be tempted by this system, which enables it to determine consumer reaction to a new collection or a new product early in the game. But developing a large network of directly operated stores somewhat changes the manner of functioning of a brand that creates exceptional products: it would have to become a manager of these sales points, and the priorities of the brand, its organisation and the use of its financial resources may be affected. Selling, as we will see later, is a real profession. Most luxury brands – structured around creation – did not have 'retail' skills and acquired them over time.

Partner Stores To a customer, partner stores (or TPOS – Third-Party-Operated Stores) are outwardly similar to a directly operated store: they use the same concept, the same decor and the same layout as a directly operated store and the client would not be able to tell them apart. They display the brand's products in exactly the same way as the original store in Paris or Milan, but they are managed, financed and developed by an intermediary.

The intermediary is sometimes a 'franchisee' who is interested in a particular brand that is not found in his chosen territory (Toulouse, for example, for a French brand, or why not in Astana in Kazakhstan?). The franchisee undertakes to open a store, fully respect the concept of the brand, buy a minimum quantity of the brand's products from each collection, and pay the brand a percentage of its turnover in the form of royalties (in general, 2–5%). In exchange it will be granted territorial exclusivity for the duration of the contract.

This system is widely used by national fashion brands with a 'premium' price category. They use several franchisees in the same country, each having exclusivity over a city or part of a city.

For luxury brands, the intermediary is more often an exclusive distributor in a particular country (for example, China, Japan or Russia). It will be granted territorial exclusivity and will choose, with the brand, the cities where it will be installed in priority. The exclusive distributor invests directly in the building of a network of exclusive boutiques and will be granted a long-term contract (sometimes more than 20 or 25 years). In such cases, the distributor would have to ensure the advertising and digital media presence of the brand and its public relations in the country.

Lastly, there exists a specific type of exclusive distribution, where the luxury brand operates in a country where foreigners do not have the permission to hold majority stakes in a subsidiary. The brand's management therefore decides on an exclusive distributor who will become the *majority shareholder* of the local distribution subsidiary. This majority shareholder also has to respect the guidelines of the brand in the design and decor of sales outlets, and will ensure the logistics of the brand in a particular territory. As mentioned above, in certain countries such as Kuwait, Qatar, Thailand, Vietnam and many others, a foreign shareholder cannot hold majority shares in a distribution subsidiary.

Department Stores   Traditionally, department stores were created to obtain supplies of various kinds of products, purchase them, and have the specialised staff to present them to customers at suitable counters. Department stores have therefore to accomplish a range of tasks:

- Finding and selecting products.
- Purchasing, receiving and storing of the products.
- Paying for the products, sometimes before they are received.
- Display on a counter.
- Presenting the product to customers.
- Selling and other activities by sales staff.
- Collecting the proceeds.

These, therefore, are a combination of financial, logistics, merchandising and commercial services.

Today the major luxury brands are sold in shops-in-shops. Here the department store provides the space (almost like a real estate agent), the luxury brand decorates it at its own expense, hires and trains the sales staff, provides them with a uniform and remunerates them. It selects the products that will be most suitable for that particular sales point and, in many cases, retains property rights until the day of the sale. The department store merely collects the sale proceeds, retains the retail margin and transfers the wholesale amount to its 'supplier'. Its function simply consists of:

- Providing a space
- Collecting the sales proceeds

Its role is thus relatively simpler as compared to the initial responsibility of a department store – and resembles that of a lessor of a building space.

Between these two methods of working with a department store (the new one and the traditional), there exists a third type of agreement: a 'corner' contract obtained by the brand where it disposes of a corner space, opening out to the other departments but still identifiable and convertible, with vendors paid by the brand and merchandise that is the property of the department store.

Evolution and Perspectives of the
Various Types of Sales Outlets

Evolution since 1950

In Table 1.1 we show the number of outlets and the turnover of certain luxury brands over the past 18 years. The brands chosen are: Bulgari, Cartier, Van Cleef and Arpels, Gucci, Louis Vuitton and Tiffany.

The table clearly illustrates the following facts:

- The increase of direct sales points has clearly been a major occupation and strategic issue for luxury over the last 20 years.
- Among these six brands given as examples, the total number of single-label stores increased from 922 to 1995. The management, control and human resources relating to these outlets have thus become important aspects for the management of a luxury brand.

In fact, in this progression, we see both the general evolution of the market and the emergence of big brands that are becoming increasingly stronger.

Well-known brands find it quite easy to pay very high lease rights to acquire a privileged location in a big city like Tokyo or Paris and be appealing enough to attract a very large number of clients right from the outset – the break-even point is easily attained.

For a small brand, the situation is more complex. At the beginning of its development cycle, the brand usually starts with a directly operated store and distributes its products through selected retailers, in particular, multi-brand outlets. To enter a new market, it will do so through local agents or a distribution agreement. For example, Bluebell and Dickson Poon are distributors that European brands often have recourse to when they wish to enter the Asian market.

When the brand grows, it establishes its own stores and, at the same time, switches from distribution agreements to franchises or joint ventures with its local partners. In nascent markets, like the Russian market, franchises would be the solution. For example, in December 2000,

Table 1.1 Examples of the Development of New Stores for Some Brands (Estimation)

	2000	2003	2007	2012	2018
Bulgari					
Turnover	376	759	1,019	1,100	2,800 (E)
Number of stores	126	182	207	267	300
Cartier and Van Cleef & Arpels					
Turnover	1,500	1,994	2,435	5,206	6,447
Number of stores	250	250	301	400	401
Gucci					
Turnover	1,200	1,800	2,300	3,639	6,211
Number of stores	143	174	233	429	529
Louis Vuitton					
Turnover	1,500 (E)	2,200 (E)	3,700 (E)	7,000 (E)	10,500 (E)
Number of stores	284	317	390	500	450
Tiffany					
Turnover	1,334	1,600	2,342	3,035	3,682
Number of stores	119	141	184	275	315

Notes: Turnover in € millions (annual reports or estimation/number of stores shown on Internet sites). (E) indicates estimates by the authors.

Hermès opened a 250 m² boutique in Moscow, with the help of its intermediary, JamilCo.[2] The Russian company covered the total initial investment of the project, including the construction and decoration costs of the store, while Hermès was responsible for the interior design. The two Gucci boutiques in Moscow were also managed by an intermediary, Mercury Distribution. Another interesting example is that of

---

[2] In 2011, several brands announced that they were going to change their economic model and develop in Russia by themselves. Prada announced the end of its partnership with Mercury and Hermès ended its contract with JamilCo. The luxury brands operating directly in Russia are Christian Dior, Louis Vuitton, Chanel, the Swatch Group and Hugo Boss (among others).

Club 21[3] from Singapore, distributor for Armani in the UK, the US, and Asia (Singapore, Malaysia, Thailand, Hong Kong and Australia) through franchise agreements.

Eventually, when a brand considers that it is sufficiently robust and the market is mature enough, it will buy back these franchises or its distribution joint ventures and create a wholly owned subsidiary. This has been a major trend in recent years for global brands like Gucci and Hermès, as mentioned above, and Louis Vuitton and Armani. We see here an emblematic model with Gucci – the brand that had actually initiated this business model 20 years ago under the initiative of Domenico De Sole.[4]

At the end of the day, controlling distribution relies on managing five major channels:

• Directly operated stores in the major markets (in foreign countries: through subsidiaries).
• Distributors or franchises in developing and foreign countries.
• Shops-in-shops in department stores, so as to retain full control over visual merchandising, sales and customer relations. Only very well-established brands can operate in department stores exclusively with large shops-in-shops. Other brands would have to settle for counters that would be strongly influenced by the department store itself.

---

[3] Christina Ong, the wife of the Singapore oil magnate, Ong Beng Sing, can be credited for having given London a fashion capital label in the 1990s. Club 21, her business empire, had franchises from some of the most coveted fashion brands: Giorgio Armani, Emporio Armani, Prada, Donna Karan, DKNY and Guess. Not only owner of a substantial part of London's most coveted commercial real estate, Ong had been able to intelligently attract, by other means, the modern London visitor who was eager for culture and had money to spend. She owned two of the most distinguished hotels of the capital – the Halkin opened in 1991 in Belgravia, with staff dressed by Giorgio Armani, and the trendy Metropolitan Hotel on Old Park Lane, where the staff wore navy-blue uniforms created by DKNY (*International Herald Tribune*, 15 March 1997).

[4] In this context, Gucci had a far-ranging plan: July 2001: It bought back the remaining 35% of its joint-venture with FJ Benjamin Holdings Limited in Australia. February 2001: It bought back its operations in Spain (three stores) from its intermediary. May 1998: It bought back nine stores and nine tax-free sales points from its Korean intermediary Sung Joo International Limited. April 1998: It bought back 51% of Shiatos Taiwan Co. Ltd, its intermediary in Taiwan (nine stores and one tax-free sales point).

- *Travel retail* sales outlets, because even if operating costs and margins demanded by duty-free operators are high, sales volumes are significant. However, the image of the brand and the impression of exclusivity and quality of the products may deteriorate over time if the company does not maintain sufficient control over these operations. For this reason, Gucci established its first duty-free outlet outside Italy, in Heathrow in 1999 – and extended those in Rome and Milan by 100 m²; Chanel opened its first duty-free outlets in 1999 in several terminals in Heathrow (100 m² each), but Prada, for example, took a longer time to open there.
- For watches, jewellery, perfumes, cosmetics and eyewear, more and more brands are selecting the top multi-brand stores, those that are compatible with their brand image.

Type of Distribution and Robustness of the Brand   As explained above, there is no single made-to-measure system for the distribution of luxury goods, but opportunities resulting from the level of attractiveness of a brand and its sales volumes.

Professionals easily compare brands based on the turnover per square metre generated at their sales points. When this figure is very high (say between €50,000 to €100,000 per square metre a year), opening new stores and paying their rent is not an issue. When this figure is 10 or 20 times less, it is better to work with multi-brand outlets.

That is why there is no one optimum solution for the distribution of luxury goods. It would depend on the sales volumes that can be generated at a sales outlet:

A *relatively little known brand* could have a single, directly operated point of sale in the country of origin. For the rest, it would be wise to opt for multi-brand stores. In such cases, department stores can also offer the ideal solution. They have footfalls: customers pass through the aisles of the store and are ready to buy. The brand will be presented along with other brands that are more or less appealing or well known and this creates a favourable and prestigious setting. Also, when it is displayed on a shelf, the salesperson will be paid by the department store. Of course, if the turnover of the counter is too low, the department store will not be likely to repeat the experience and the brand would have to find another distribution system.

For an *extremely small brand*, department stores – which demand a more or less minimum turnover – are not the ideal solution. In such a case, the most suitable one may be a small store which serves as a sales point but which also serves as the official address and public relations operations centre.

The Impact of the Type of Distribution on Product Policy

Although the product's qualities may have a bearing on the ideal distribution model, conversely, a chosen distribution model imposes an appropriate product policy.

Indirect and direct distribution channels require very different marketing strategies, as we can see in Table 1.2.

For indirect distribution, it is not practical to have a range that is too extensive. It would be far better to launch a single product that will have enough impact to succeed. However, when a brand relies on single-brand stores, it has to offer a fairly wide range so that each customer entering the store can find the product that corresponds to what he or she is looking for.

The key for a given brand in a multi-brand perfumery store is to have a single flagship product that customers look for and can easily identify. In a single-brand store, however, the same product may not necessarily appeal to all customers; it risks overshadowing other products that target specific segments of the market.

Distribution channels, direct or indirect, require different kinds of advertising and promotional support. In the indirect circuit, advertising in the mass media is a priority to convince the consumer – who is faced with a wide choice of products in each store – that brand X is more

Table 1.2   The Differences Between Direct and Indirect Distribution Models

	Indirect distribution Non-exclusive boutiques	Direct distribution Exclusive boutiques
Product line	Limited	Wide
Product objective	Flagship product	Part of a larger whole
Advertising and promotion	Pull the product	Push the product
Flexibility of prices	Wide	Limited
Relationship with the client	Limited	Strong (CRM)
Logistics requirements	Limited	Imperative

desirable, more modern, more prestigious or simply more suitable than others. In the direct circuit, advertising in the mainstream media may be necessary to draw customers to the store, but the difference hinges on the efforts made by the sales team that has to use its powers of persuasion and its own sales arguments.

In the indirect circuit, the customer, faced with a multi-brand offer, uses price as a criterion of selection. In the direct circuit, the customer may not buy the product if he finds the price excessive, but this will not be the criterion for choosing from a range of products falling within a price range that he considers reasonable.

In the direct circuit, a strong personal link between the consumer and the brand should be created over time through customer relationship management (CRM). Customers will have to be identified, their names and addresses recorded, as also their preferences and purchasing patterns. It is then possible to develop a strong relationship and organise promotional offers designed specifically for them. In an indirect circuit, most customers are anonymous and unidentified, making it difficult to establish special relationships between them and a given brand, the client being only one amongst others to whom offers are presented.

The requirements in terms of logistics are also quite different from one system to the other. In the indirect circuit, the intermediary often assumes responsibility for a part of the logistics, such as storage and deliveries to each sales outlet. In the direct circuit, these tasks are the sole responsibility of the owner of the brand.

There is a tendency to consider the direct system more efficient than the indirect system.

Case Study: The Ralph Lauren Case

The example of Ralph Lauren, however, is a counter-example. His results demonstrate the strengths of the indirect system.

The company's management talks about a 'flexible integrated model' that includes direct distribution, indirect distribution and franchises. With annual sales close to €5.3 billion and a net profit of €140 million in 2018, Ralph Lauren attains a

(continued)

(Continued)

profitability comparable to that of major brands, which is really not a bad performance for a first-generation brand still headed by its founder. This business model relies on an integrated approach to advertising and marketing, but in commercial matters, each region has a combination of directly operated and franchised stores, sometimes supervised by local distributors, sometimes directly. Turnover can be broken down into 55% for indirect channel sales, 40% for direct channel sales and 5% from royalties from licences, but what is not insignificant is that only 23% of total operating profit comes from directly operated sales points.

Ralph Lauren has 8,611 indirect retail outlets in the United States and Canada. However, there are only 120 in Japan. In fact, for Ralph Lauren, the indirect segment includes 11,000 sales points. In the direct distribution segment, Ralph Lauren handles 153 stores (134 in North America and 19 in Europe) and 158 factory outlets.

Ralph Lauren has recourse to licences for perfumes (L'Oréal), eyewear (EssilorLuxottica) and watches (Richemont) as well as for custom-made menswear (Dealers), men's underwear and pyjamas (Hanes) and sportswear Chaps (both from PVH Group).

Its management relies on exclusive distributors to manage their indirect distribution in many countries such as Japan, Korea, Hong Kong, China and Singapore, as well as Colombia, Ecuador, Peru, Bolivia, and other countries in Central America and the Caribbean.

The method Ralph Lauren offers is a diversified approach to luxury. Of course, all its products end up in stores, but not necessarily in sales points directly managed by the brand. The management uses the indirect distribution channel, but also has distribution contracts with local partners and licensed operators to constantly improve the quality of their product presentations and the viability of their global growth model.

What is important is to understand that each situation corresponds to an adapted and evolving distribution policy and that each policy has its own advantages and disadvantages.

Advantages and Disadvantages of the Various Distribution Channels

Even if the most powerful brands grow strongly using integrated direct distribution, one should certainly not make this system the only variable in the luxury industry. Everything depends on the size of the company, its financial resources, and its prospects. A significant difference between the systems relates to their financial aspects.

Margins and Distribution Costs

The important difference between these systems is that in the case of integrated distribution, the brand sells at the retail price and benefits from the full margin. However, when it sells indirectly, for example through a multi-brand retailer or a department store, it has to pay a retail margin of 40% or 50% of the selling price to them. The difference between the different types of retailers and its impact on management appears in Table 1.3. For example, if a Chanel store is owned by the company and if its annual sales are €500,000 before taxes, it keeps the full amount. If, on the contrary, it generates the same turnover through a department store, it would have to pay a margin of €200,000 or €250,000 to the department store, reducing its turnover to the same extent. The computation of their different impact on the cost and price structure appears in Table 1.4.

At first glance, a directly operated store seems the most judicious model, but the store would have the responsibility of organising sales, managing unsold stocks, paying the wages of sales staff, and most importantly, paying the rent.

Fixed Costs and Variable Costs   The big difference when a brand has its own network of shops is that it is responsible for paying fixed costs (rents and salaries), whereas if it worked with franchisees, it would only

Table 1.3   The Relative Advantages and Disadvantages of the Various Distribution Channels

	Advantages	**Disadvantages**
Directly operated boutiques	Enhancing of the brand's image Presentation and merchandising of the whole range	Capital invested in key money Easy profitability for flagship stores but difficult to achieve for stores in cities with limited potential
Franchises	Development of the presence and knowledge about the brand Presentation of the whole range	Loss of control over the image
Shops-in-shops in department stores	Enhancing of the brand's image Development of the presence and knowledge about the brand Presentation of the whole range	
Multi-brand boutiques	Enhancing of the brand's image	Limited presentation of the range No control over the brand image
Independent retailers	Development of the knowledge about the brand	Segmented presentation Loss of control over the brand image (except if there is a strict selection)
Corners in department stores	Development of the knowledge about the brand Increased rotation	Segmented presentation Loss of control over the brand image in certain department stores
✱ Travel retail	High frequentation Increased rotation New customers	Loss of control over the brand image in multi-brand sales points and airport galleries

Table 1.4 Calculation of the Margin According to the Distribution System

	Directly operated store	Store belonging to a third party	Store serviced by a distributor
Retail price	€100	€100	€100
Wholesale price		€50	€50
Margin of exclusive distributor			€20
Invoicing price for the company	€100	€50	€30

have to set aside a margin for them. The impact of the different levels of fixed costs on profitability is computed in Table 1.5.

One could also elaborate on this demonstration further: for a really low turnover, the department store system, where the vendor has to be paid, can turn out to be more expensive than renting a small shop in a modest location with a very low rent, where the seller can also carry out other tasks (accounting, for example) and lighten the burden on the final results.

The message in this chapter is clear: there is no one distribution structure that is more efficient than another. Everything depends on the dimension of the brand and its prospects. Everything also depends on the products themselves. If it is easier to analyse fashion and accessories, the exercise is more complex for watches or perfumes, for example, where

Table 1.5 Impact of Fixed and Variable Costs on Profitability

	Turnover of €5,000,000 per annum			Turnover of €1,000,000 per annum		
	Directly operated store	Department store	Multi-brand store	Directly operated store	Department store	Multi-brand store
Sales figures	€5,000,000	€5,000,000	€5,000,000	€1,000,000	€1,000,000	€1,000,000
Retail margin		€2,500,000	€2,500,000	€500,000	€500,000	€500,000
Wholesale figures		€2,500,000	€2,500,000		€500,000	€500,000
Rent	− €1,000,000			− €1,000,000		
Salaries	− €200,000	− €200,000		− €100,000	− €100,000	
Margin before production costs	€3,800,000	€2,300,000	€2,500,000	− €600,000	€400,000	€500,000

customers often prefer going to a store if they wish to compare products from several different brands before making their choice.

In this first chapter, we have said very little about digital sales. It is not an oversight. Our aim, above all, is to make you, the reader, aware of the diversity and the complexity of the subject and to convince you that there are several ways of organising the distribution of luxury products. In the following pages, we will explain that even very strong brands do not limit themselves to a single system of sales outlets but know how to adapt to all systems according to the country, according to local legislation, according to traditions. In this regard, digital distribution, or the quest for perfect continuity between digital distribution and physical distribution, only makes the issue more complex.

To recap:

- *The management of luxury goods* has shifted from a phase where most of the effort was focused on creation, craftsmanship and manufacturing to a phase where physical and digital distribution and management of sales outlets are an everyday concern.
- *Product presentation to end-customers* is organised both directly and indirectly and each of these two activities contributes to the brand's vitality and development.
- *Department stores*, just like multi-brand stores, can in some cases, and during certain phases of the development of the brand, be loyal and important allies.
- *An economic analysis of the sales points* (which will be presented in Chapter 16) ~~is essential for evaluating the advantages~~ and disadvantages ~~of each of the aspects he analysed~~

LV. – only does Marketing and Branding.

Similar to Supplement businesses.

OEM Makes everything So all brands need to do is to source the best OEM.

Chapter 2

Do Luxury Products Still Sell in Stores?

If you control your distribution, you control your image.

−Bernard Arnault[1]

T he question: 'Are luxury products still being sold in stores?' as it appears in the title, seems to have an obvious answer. Of course, yes! For these products are intended for the end customer, and apart from cases where they are delivered directly to their doorsteps, they have had to obtain them somewhere, and so, one would imagine, this would be from a shop.

---

[1] Levine (1997).

The question could also be asked differently: Does the client buy his product in a store belonging to the brand, or belonging to an independent intermediary who can apply its own criteria of performance and quality? Or, formulated in another way, does he buy his product in a multi-brand store or, on the contrary, at a sales point dedicated exclusively to the brand?

We should also distinguish between two different situations: when a client buys a Cartier watch from Galeries Lafayette, he knows he is making a purchase at a sales outlet that does not belong to Cartier, but if he makes the same purchase at an exclusive and single-brand Cartier outlet in Bangkok, he feels like he is 'at Cartier's', when he is in fact at an exclusive distributor of the brand for Thailand. Americans have a simple way of distinguishing these two cases, as we explained in Chapter 1. They speak of either *Directly Operated Stores (DOS)*, i.e. a store 'directly managed by the brand', or *Third-Party-Operated Stores (TPOS)*, i.e. stores managed by a third party. This very useful distinction is not always clear, because some brands, in their annual reports, consider their 'shops-in-shops' in department stores as DOS (since the sales staff are their own employees) while others call them TPOS because it is the department store that provides the space, collects the payment, retains its margin and, sometimes, owns the stock.

Whatever the definition used, what is certain is that today a brand like Chanel, well known especially for fashion and accessories, considers itself a retailer and is very strongly involved in the search for appropriate locations, in the design of its stores and in the daily management of these stores. In a way, Chanel's managers have become retailers, and in the teams, specialists in management of sales points are 'on an upswing'.

At first glance, it could be said that between 1960 and today the functions of luxury business managers increasingly resemble those of an international retailer, managing stores all over the world, and ensuring the designing and production of products adapted to its customers. We will show in this chapter how this evolution has been categorised.

And to complicate things even more, another phenomenon has grown over the last 20 years: the DIGITALISATION of the economy and the physical distribution of products. Some luxury companies that had direct contact with 'end-user' customers have developed online sales

Table 2.1 Evolution of Turnover of a Fashion Brand[a] According to the Different Systems of Distribution

	1960	1990	2010	2025
Single-brand stores	20%	50%	65%	55%
Independent multi-brand stores (including department stores)	80%	50%	30%	20%
Digital sales	0%	0%	5%	25%
Total	100%	100%	100%	100%

[a]This evolution is completely different in the beauty or watchmaking industries, for example.
Source: Authors' estimates.

platforms that have proven to be very effective. Today, it is estimated that these digital sales to end customers (direct or indirect) represent 10% of the turnover of a luxury business (such as major fashion brands) and could reach 25% in 2025.

Table 2.1 retraces the estimated evolution of sales channels of a fashion brand since 1960, with a projection up to 2025.

We notice here the sharp decrease in sales in the multi-brand circuit (and the evolution of department stores that rapidly made the choice to reserve spaces for major brands in the form of 'shops-in-shops') and lastly, the growth in digital sales.

The development of digital shopping will force luxury brands to review their distribution channels.

The Owner Becomes a Retailer as Well

Traditional Division of Functions

Until the 1950s or 1960s, a fashion brand usually had only one retail outlet in the world – the original store – that was not yet called a 'flagship'. Dior had only one sales outlet on Avenue Montaigne, and Chanel had its boutique on Rue Cambon. As for Bulgari, it had its original boutique in Rome. At the time, to buy a jewel from Bulgari, one simply had to travel all the way to the boutique in Rome. In fact, especially for fashion, international distribution was quite structured. Dior sold its clothes in certain large department stores in New York, but elsewhere in the United States, it sold its dress patterns, which were, in fact, purchased by American women who had their usual dressmakers tailor the model for them.

From that time, Dior wished to establish a stronger commercial presence abroad and granted authorisations, with 'master-licences' and 'sublicensing' structures in the United States and Japan. Chanel, on the contrary, never did wish to develop that aspect of the business.

Business operations focused on the management of the Parisian sales outlet and the building of a network of international partners consisting of foreign department stores or multi-brand boutiques which shared a very specific view of fashion. The work consisted mainly of running this network of foreign distributors, and in the case where licences were also given, providing them with designs and models, verifying prototypes and manufacturing and supervising the business activities that ensued from it.

In the fashion business, the work already centred on the Creative Director, who spoke to journalists and organised fashion shows in a number of major cities around the world.

The Growth of Franchisees and Distributors   In the 1980s, the franchise system grew rapidly. It allowed a brand to outsource the opening and management of a single-brand retail outlet, incorporating the concept and design of the main store, in a country or city where exclusivity would be guaranteed to the sales outlet. For example, this system permitted the extremely rapid growth of a well-known mass brand, Benetton, which opened franchises in cities the world over, and which, at its peak, opened one store every day.

But for major brands, and especially for luxury brands, it was difficult to manage the consistency of sales and marketing activities in a partic-ular territory under the franchise system. In addition, franchisees that invested in a single store often had limited financial resources and could not always follow through by opening two, three, or five stores in their territory as and when the brand grew. Hence the advantage of exclusive distributors who usually have the administrative, human and financial means and who could open 10 to 30 sales points rapidly, organise their supply professionally and control the quality of the service provided in these stores while at the same time developing the appropriate advertising and marketing presence.

This distribution system is still one of the most rapid and efficient today. It is recommended in major countries or where access is complex. A strong and diversified presence can be quickly established.

Another system that had been considerably important during this period was the department store. These stores have been able to promote the shop-in-shop concept, that is to say, they provide a location where a brand will be able to recreate its individual concept with its own colours, logo and distinctive decoration. The brand is free to create the decor that suits it.

Shops-in-shops are in fact another form of franchising, described above, where a brand can be installed rapidly in a city or country. Which brand has not dreamed of a shop-in-shop at Bergdorf Goodman or at Sak's Fifth Avenue in New York? It is in the realm of possibility if the performance of the brand in Paris or London is encouraging and if its project for establishing itself in the United States is realistic.

Over the last 30 to 40 years, franchises and department stores have played a vital role in the international development of brands. As for distributors who played a significant role during this period, they continue to play it today, and are often indispensable.

Selecting the Stakeholders

Since the 2000s, department stores have not been able to continue as drivers in the growth of luxury brands, probably because the latter wished to open a larger number of outlets than they could offer. Also, the growth rate of luxury brands (between 8 and 10% per year) is much more rapid than that of department stores (1 to 2%) and they had to bypass them to maintain their pace of development.

This acceleration in growth was partly achieved by the creation of wholly owned subsidiaries in the principal priority countries, or by setting up joint ventures with the best distributors.

Gradually, as we explained earlier, the tendency has been to boost sales in the sales points controlled by or belonging to brands (the so-called 'Directly Operated Stores'), and jewellery brands such as Cartier, for example – which had claimed, a few years ago, that 50% of its turnover came from its 'retail' outlets (directly operated sales points) and 50% from 'wholesale' (sales to multi-brand retailers) – moved to a turnover that was largely generated by its own boutiques. Richemont announced that 63% of its sales came from retail in 2018, as against 50% in 2011.

- Increasing sales from owned retails.

The Establishing of Online Systems

From the year 2000 onwards, luxury brands began asking themselves which online system would be the best for development.

The first hesitancy related to the system itself: should the site be ① a multi-brand site (an emulation of a luxury department store, which could have easily been developed in France by Printemps or Galeries Lafayette), or on the contrary, should a separate site be created for each particular brand?   ②

Around that time, it was not easy to perceive that the creation of an online brand-specific merchant site would not entail huge costs and that 'hosting sites', which the end consumer did not know, could handle the IT and logistics management of their sales very well.

We saw, in a first phase, the development of several groups such as Yoox and Net-a-Porter.com (now merged into a single group: Ynap, which belongs to Richemeont) that fast-tracked the implementation of their online business. However, in the long run we would have to ask ourselves another question: If the logistics are so simple, what more does a multi-brand site bring in terms of satisfaction, convenience or ease than Chanel's or Cartier's own sites?

In concrete terms, the added value of a multi-brand site may stem from, for example:

- Lower prices
- Items from earlier collections or those on sale
- Exclusive models

But this added value also has disadvantages and, if it is absolutely necessary to lower prices to get rid of a stock with prices too high for a product, why not do so on one's own site?

One after the other, mega brands such as Louis Vuitton and Hermès decided to go online. At the beginning, they did it separately and independently of their traditional outlets, but with prices adjusted according to the customer's country of residence and the customs duties applicable. And sales grew.

It is estimated that today the major luxury brands earn 5 to 10% of their turnover through their sites, which is not such a bad result (the equivalent of a large flagship store, they claimed, and today, it is much higher). Gucci, for example, saw its digital business reach €270 million in 2017.

For a long time, other brands like Hermès were less ambitious. Their online catalogue specialised in gifts and easy-to-purchase articles (ties, scarves, bracelets, for example). What we see today is that, with a few exceptions, the online department is kept separate from business operations at sales points and merely acts as an adjunct.

As we will see later on in this book, a further step still has to be taken: to make digital business an integral part of each of these brands, and to remove all obstructions, allowing the customer to go seamlessly from his search for information, his trial fittings, his purchases and his after-sales service on the Internet site to any boutique or sales point of the brand, and to do so seamlessly.

Different Situations According to the Different Luxury Segments

So far, we have discussed luxury in broad terms, almost always citing fashion and accessories, sometimes jewellery, to track the evolution of practices that have moved relatively quickly from wholesale to multi-brand retailers, from developing sales points to selling online. In fact, in parallel with this evolution, we also perceive here an increasingly important prominence given to single-brand stores, which is accompanied by a strong diversification of the offer.

The Starting Point

Until the 1990s, it can be said that, depending on the sector, having some directly operated mono-brand stores was more or less the norm.

In perfumery and cosmetics, it seemed that there was only one solution, selling wholesale to several multi-brand perfumeries. In certain countries, these multi-brands were essentially department stores and accounted for more than 50% of turnover.

This was the case in the United States, of course, but also in Japan, Great Britain, Mexico, Canada, Australia and a few others. In these countries, the perfumery department is situated on the ground floor of department stores and sales take place in 'cubicles' with the name and the logo of the brand (such is the case with Dior, Chanel, Estée Lauder, Yves Saint-Laurent, Armani, Ralph Lauren, Gucci and some others). For a brand to have a cubicle in its name, it would need to have a large turnover, which was generally possible for brands that developed not only alcoholic perfumery but also make-up and skincare products.

In other countries, such as Italy, France, Russia and often in South America, perfumes were sold through the many neighbourhood perfumeries.

To visit and serve these numerous sales outlets, the brands needed to have a large sales force in each country which could visit and stimulate sales in these stores. The same could be said for wines and spirits that were also sold exclusively through multi-brand stores. Incidentally, one should also not forget a second sales network catering to restaurants, cafes and nightclubs.

At that time, watches were only sold at retailers or multi-brand department stores and it would not have seemed very logical for watch brands to open single-brand stores.

One perceived that jewellery and watch brands had a distribution system that was adapted to watches. For brands such as Cartier, whose watchmaking turnover was very high, they were sold both in the directly operated stores of the brand and through a large number of independent jewellers. For brands such as Tiffany and Van Cleef & Arpels, not primarily known as watchmakers, they were almost exclusively sold through single-brand stores or department store shops-in-shops.

And how about pens and other writing instruments? These were sold exclusively in department stores and at stationers. At that time, four major brands shared the premium market: Montblanc, Parker, Schaeffer and Waterman, and they were all sold exclusively through multi-brand stores. In 1991 Montblanc decided to create single-brand stores, the first of which opened in Hong Kong. This gave the brand both the opportunity and the obligation to diversify its product offering in watches, followed by men's leather goods, jewellery, and women's leather goods. Today, the other three pen brands are not doing that well. For its part, Montblanc has a turnover of €760 million and an impressive operating profit. Converting to a distribution system consisting of several single-brand stores together with a diversification of its product offer appears to have been successful.

The Case of Wines and Spirits

For alcohols, the need to distribute through separate channels (supermarkets, but also cafes and restaurants, not forgetting specialist shops) complicates matters. Experts of this sector divide this market into two segments: the 'on-premises' segment for alcohol consumed on the spot, i.e. in restaurants, bars and clubs, and alcohol consumed 'off-premises', that is to say, away from the sales point, meaning at home, and these outlets are usually supermarkets or grocery stores or neighbourhood wine stores.

With a few exceptions, the wines and spirits business will continue in multi-brand outlets. It is the only luxury sector that is distributed at major food outlets and discount stores. When Carrefour organises a wine fair, this company is able to sell an impressive number of bottles. They have the clientele: hypermarket buyers. They have logistics: car parks and caddies. They have selling and buying power to obtain good purchase prices, and it would be difficult to replicate this.

Watch Manufacturers and Niche Perfumers Are Creating Single-Brand Outlets

Like Montblanc, some other watch brands have also created mono-brand stores. The first one, Ebel, had opened stores in South Asia, the first one being in Hong Kong circa 1990. But the turnover was not what was expected and the company went through a difficult time. In mainland China, first Omega and then Rolex opened dozens of outlets while selling in multi-brand stores as well. This was a lucky move for Omega, which acquired an enviable position in that country. The trend now in watchmaking still favours multi-brand stores.

The Breguet brand, for its part, followed a different strategy. It opened single-brand stores in a number of major capital cities such as Paris, London and Moscow, usually very well located, which served as a showroom for multi-brand retailers, a showcase for public relations operations, and additionally as sales points.

The Growth of Niche Perfumery

Over the past 40 years, many entrepreneurs in the perfume business decided that, unlike mainstream perfumery, they would launch niche perfumes, often two to four times more expensive than those found in department stores, and sell them in unique single-brand outlets without any advertising budget. The idea was to place the emphasis exclusively on perfume and its fragrance by offering knowledgeable and interested consumers unique perfumes in an atmosphere where an 'expert' in perfumery talked to 'other experts in perfumery'.

The first brands of niche fragrances, such as *Le Jardin Retrouvé* (1975), *L'Artisan Parfumeur* (1976) and *Annick Goutal* (1984), were the trailblazers, but these brands were quickly snatched up – *L'Artisan Parfumeur* by the Puig Group, *Annick Goutal* by the Korean, Amore Pacific. After that there was *Jo Malone* and *Editions Frederic Malle* that were both acquired by Estée Lauder Companies. The year 2006 alone saw the creation of several niche brands: *État Libre d'Orange*, *Le Labo*, *Byredo*, *Escentric Molecules*. Every luxury group seemed to be positioning itself in this rapidly growing segment. L'Oréal thus bought *Atelier Cologne* (2017), LVMH bought *Francis Kurkdjian* (2017) and in 2018. The Estée Lauder Companies added *By Kilian* to its portfolio of niche brands. Finally, having understood the potential of niche perfumery, recently luxury brands have developed product collections at prices that are significantly higher than their standard perfume ranges. One thus saw the emergence of *Les Exclusifs de Chanel*, *Dior Collection Privée*, *Le Vestiaire des Parfums* from Yves Saint Laurent, Armani Privé, Maison Lancôme Collection, Louis Vuitton, etc.

This segment of the perfumery sector is growing rapidly, around 25% per year, and introduces a completely new distribution mode for the product category. Today, we estimate that if we include the brands of perfumes belonging to large groups but sold – for a large part of their turnover – in single-brand boutiques, and the niche versions of well-known brands, the sector's turnover attained over €3 billion in 2018.

The Future of Multi-Brand Stores

Independence is always good.

The more luxury brands anchor themselves, increase their product offerings and progress, the less they are obliged to accede to the demands of multi-brand stores. This seems to indicate that multi-brand stores are at risk of seeing the brands with the highest turnover volumes leave, and will be left with only newcomers that are more difficult to sell and without real pulling power.

The Department Store Examples

In the first edition of this book, written in 2011, we devoted around 15 pages to department stores and remarked that they were experiencing serious financial difficulties, especially in the United States and Japan, leading to mergers or takeovers. In the United States, we mentioned the merger between Macy's, May, and Bloomingdale's and in Japan the mergers between Mitsukoshi, Isetan and Marui on one side, and Seibu and Sogo on the other. In this second edition, we have decided to confine ourselves to only providing an overview. What interests us here is to see how these sales points could grow in the years to come.

At the beginning of this chapter and in the preceding chapter, we described how department stores have moved from the stage of selection and purchasing of merchandise to that of managing and renting of space for brands already known and respected elsewhere. This does not prevent them from developing and promoting their own brands – for example, at the Bon Marché in Paris, the Balthazar menswear brand is located in prime spots and has ever-wider and more innovative collections.

But the future doubtlessly also depends on the development of wider offers and new products. Here, department stores have a big advantage. They are able to draw customers and attract significant footfalls, and can thus offer a physical connection between these 'visitors' and promising new brands.

Also, department stores are often found in 'enchanting' locations – in the historical centre of a city, or in the pedestrian zone of a suburb. That is the now-or-never opportunity to create vibrant areas of activity and experiences, maybe with restaurants, museums and theatres.

Also, their new metier as managers of commercial spaces for luxury or fashion brands could persuade them to develop shopping centres reserved for these brands.

The Crisis Facing Department Stores   Since our first edition, the situation of department stores has not improved much. In their new role as commercial space managers, they are competing with the growth of shopping centres devoted exclusively to luxury brands, like the large number that exists in China. With prestigious locations but often expensive, they find it difficult to follow population movement to the outskirts of cities and open profitable and prestigious stores outside city centres.

In Table 2.2, one will notice that there are three groups that are weakening – J.C. Penney's, and the two major Japanese groups, Isetan Mitsukoshi and Takashimaya; two groups with low growth – Macy's and Le Printemps; and three fast-growing groups, which have revised their objectives.

In the case of Galeries Lafayette, it is certain that at least the BHV and doubtlessly La Redoute have been integrated into its accounts. The main

Table 2.2   Performance of Various Department Store Chains (Turnover in € Billions)

	2010	2017
Galeries Lafayette	3.0	4.5
Harrods	0.58	2.2
Isetan Mitsukoshi	11.7	10.1
J.C. Penney's	12.9	10.8
Macy's	19.0	21.6
Nordstrom	6.1	13.0
Printemps	1.3	1.5
Takashimaya	7.2	6.9

Source: Annual reports or authors' estimates.

reason for buying La Redoute is to familiarise the group with digital activities, which seems rather judicious. Also, the 8 stores located abroad (some 20 are planned by 2025) probably contributed to the growth of the group. The Champs-Elysées store, opened in May 2019, should also provide another source of long-term growth.

The other two fast-growing stores, Harrods and Nordstrom, have seen their businesses change dramatically. Today, for example, Nordstrom has 117 department stores, and 216 'Price Nordstrom Racks' where the type of business is significantly different because these are essentially stock clearance and discount stores. The Nordstrom case is interesting. This chain from Seattle, which is very well placed in the western United States, opened its first department store in New York on 13 September 2018. It began with a store for men, then, on the opposite side, a store for women to be completed in September 2019. At a time when many US department stores are closing down their New York branches, a family-owned group comes along with force and enthusiasm, establishing itself on the basis of a remarkable history of growth.

Some professionals draw on the weaker sales figures of many US chains to explain the decline of US department stores. The closure, in the fall of 2018, of Henri Bendel's specialty department store is also not very encouraging. It is true that life is not always easy for this type of store, but we can also say that this distribution system that had undoubtedly overdeveloped in the United States (with 5,000 department stores, while France has only 92) had become too commonplace. The increase in discount stores is also not a factor that would give customers the desire to revisit even the most luxurious American department stores in the city centre.

News about other department stores is not very good either. In Germany, Kaufhof and Karstadt had to merge. The English chain, House of Fraser, has declared itself insolvent and its main competitor, John Lewis, has seen its early 2018 profits decrease by 99%!

Coming back to international developments, while observing the internationalisation of the luxury and fashion industries, many of these department stores have failed to step out of their country of origin and to take root abroad. Apart from Selfridges and maybe Debenhams, the major American, Japanese and European <u>brands have had a hard time establishing themselves overseas</u>. We often see brands that quit countries, for example, Sears (Spain, Chile and Brazil) and Daimaru (Hong Kong and Singapore).

The success of department stores abroad presupposes conditions that are particularly difficult to group together: (1) local residents originating from the country of the brand or who have lived in a country where the brand is already established; (2) reputable fashion brands from the brand name's country that can sign exclusive contracts and are not bound by prior contracts with department stores within the country; and (3) a brand that can build on the lifestyle and fashion conventions of the country, or home decor that may interest consumers in this or that new country.

Too often, although department stores are able to hold their own in their country or city of origin, they find it difficult to bring enough novelty and creativity to a new country.

Multi-Brand Chains in Perfumery and Cosmetics

Alongside small individual perfumeries, four empires were created: the first is Sephora, which enjoys a strong position in Europe, the United States and Asia, and whose turnover in 2018 exceeds €8 billion. Sephora distributes major perfume brands and selective cosmetics, but also creates its own products under its brand name, which are estimated to represent 24% of operating profits. The second is Marionnaud, linked to the Asian chain Watson's, which is dominant in China and whose consolidated turnover for all its operations reached €15 million.

The third, Ulta Beauty, created in the United States in 1990 and with 1,074 points of sale in the country (with an average floor space of 1,000 m^2) and a turnover of €5.2 billion in 2017, is also a major operator. This group probably has a higher turnover than Sephora in the American continent and has a concept that is more open: care centres in each store, and also a range of products encompassing both selective and mass perfumery products. The fourth, Douglas, is well known especially in Germany, Eastern Europe, Italy, France, Spain and Poland where sales reached €3 billion.

Generally, these groups now deal in almost all the major brands of perfumes and cosmetics, but they also develop their own ranges of make-up and skincare which, for some of them, represent a significant part of their turnover.

Multi-Brand Fashion Stores

Some of the multi-brand fashion stores were very famous at a certain period, such as Victoire and Colette in Paris and Corso Como in Milan. Colette had a single sales outlet in Paris of about 400 or 500 m² where it offered exclusive fashion products. The store was always crowded and customers would come there regularly, without always having the intention of buying anything specific. The Colette boutique, situated between the Place Vendôme and Palais Royal, became a reason to go out for a walk. Visitors looked for specially woven Lacoste polo shirts with a red crocodile, or Ralph Lauren shirts with a Polo player twice as large as the standard logo. In fact, customers come looking for fashion items, expensive, but which could not be found anywhere else. The owner of Colette, Ms Colette Rousseaux, retired on 1 January 2018. She had opened the store in 1997 and it had been the favourite haunt of fashion victims for 20 years.

The winning formula for a store of this type seems to be that it should be a place that one can browse in, with a flow of new or exclusive products, or small souvenirs that would make original gifts. The exclusive sale of Louis Vuitton sneakers will certainly be remembered as one of the exceptional events the store has organised.

Also, worth mentioning are the Joyce boutiques in Hong Kong. Joyce is a chain of fashion stores, founded by Ms Joyce Ma, that wished to bring its customers new designer brands that have every chance of growing quickly because they have something new or original. Joyce went through difficult times in 2008 and it was acquired by the Lane Crawford chain, which took advantage of this acquisition to give itself an image of a specialist in highly sophisticated fashion.

The lesson one can draw from examples like Colette and Joyce is that there is a place for stores that are able to detect new trends in fashion and bring a wide variety of products, often original or exclusive, to their customers, although one may ask the question of their durability and their development. The closing of Colette, like the relative failure of Corso Como franchises in China, shows that these concepts are closely linked with their creators.

The Special Case of Travel Retail

Travel retail turnover amounted to €57 billion in 2017, broken down to about 36% for perfumes and cosmetics (€24.5 billion) and 17% for wines and spirits (€11.4 billion). This type of business, of course, almost always consists of 'indirect sales' and without the likelihood of digital growth since the products have to be purchased physically within a well-defined area, usually duty-free, and have to go through customs control when leaving an aircraft or a ship crossing international borders.

A list of the twelve busiest airports includes four in the United States (Atlanta, Los Angeles, Chicago and Dallas) and four in Asia (Beijing, Tokyo, Hong Kong and Shanghai), while Asia leads the volume of luxury goods sold (44.4% of duty free sales), followed by Europe (29.9% of travel retail sales) and only 16.5% in America. This is explained no doubt by the fact that in the United States the vast majority of flights are domestic.

The airports with the highest travel retail revenues are Seoul (€1.8 billion), Dubai (€1.6 billion) and Singapore (€1.5 billion), followed by two European airports: London Heathrow and Paris Roissy. As one can see, a large airport generates a far higher turnover than that of a very well-established and renowned department store.

Airports rarely manage these 'travel retail' sales points themselves. They organise auctions and sign concession contracts with the operator who will guarantee them the highest possible commission. These are generally long-term contracts (often 5 to 7 years) and the concession holder undertakes to guarantee a commission (generally between 40 and 55% of turnover to the airport). This has two consequences:

- The first is that the commissions paid are often the primary source of revenue for the airport, even ahead of the landing, parking and takeoff fees for aircraft that airlines pay.

- The second is that to be able to pay such high commissions and win auction bids, operators have to be able to generate a very large volume of sales to obtain attractive prices and discounts from perfumers, wine and spirit producers or fashion accessories manufacturers. At the end of the day, the manufacturers are the ones who will get short-changed.

These 'travel retail' operators are often European (Dufry, Aelia Lagardère, DFS and Heinemann) and generally operate in specific regions of the world: DFS, which belongs to LVMH, works mainly in Asia and the Pacific; Heinemann, a family-owned company based in Hamburg, is very active in all Eastern European countries; Dufry is very well established on the American continent.

In general, sales teams that sell to travel retail operators are not allocated geographically. In the majority of cases, they manage all these customers through an exclusive sales force.

Travel retail sales represent a very significant turnover for brands. They are also very important for the visibility they provide and the opportunity for distributing their products in new territories.

To recap:

- *The role of retail outlets for the luxury goods* industry has changed dramatically and even several times over the past fifty or sixty years. With the arrival of the digital world, a new revolution has occurred and will bring about a new change.
- *Today, it is not the future of retail outlets that is in question,* but the way they will fit into a larger omnichannel system.
- *Although digital sales are low today (10%),* we expect that they will reach 25% by 2025. When these digital sales reach 25%, it will not mean that physical stores will be irrelevant. They would simply have to be planned so as to allow consumers to benefit from an omnichannel service at all times, with seamless continuity from one system to another, never having the impression that one of their interlocutors

seemed to privilege one system over another. To make this possible, it is important that employees, collaborators or intermediaries outside the company feel it is never in their best interests to propose one system over another.

- *Today, there are external interlocutors* for physical business activities. There are others for digital activities. Eventually the division of direct commercial business and indirect commercial business may change, but no luxury business will ever be able to integrate the totality of its international activities.

- *Every one of the current intermediaries in the luxury goods distribution chain*, from department stores, independent franchisees, exclusive distributors in a given territory, to digital commerce specialists, will see their business activities evolve, but they will all have to define a new corporate goal and to increase the added value they offer today to customers and brand managers.

Chapter 3

Concept and Design of a Luxury Boutique

The customer must simultaneously identify the brand worldwide, and still be surprised when entering a store.

—Christian Blanckaert[1]

L uxury brands reinvented themselves the day they discovered they had to sell not only to distributors but also directly in their own stores. This led them to develop new skills, including store

---

[1] Blanckaert (2007, p. 69).

39

concept and design. We will examine this point, crucial for the sale of luxury goods, under four key headings:

- *The concept of the boutique*: the boutique has to, by its concept, interpret the vision of the brand. One has to understand the role of the brand's vision before looking at the specificities of store design.
- *The design of the boutique*: this is all about understanding both the layout of the store and the importance of its show windows.
- *Visual merchandising* is an art which luxury brands have mastered, because it allows customers to perceive the aesthetic specificities of the brand.
- *The design of the e-commerce site*: even more than for brick-and-mortar stores, the notion of design is essential to attract online clientele.

Relaunching a Brand: The Urgency for a New Concept of Boutiques

When Domenico De Sole became CEO of Gucci in May 1994, one of his first decisions was to redesign its boutiques:

> In December 1994, within six weeks, all the stores around the world were 'Milanised', that is, redesigned, based on the model of the Milan store. Minor changes, inexpensive, but which had a major impact.

When Gucci acquired Yves Saint Laurent in November 1999, the very first thing it did was to develop the store network and revise the design of the usual layout of the stores. The prototype of the new YSL boutiques, designed by Tom Ford and the architect William Sofield, opened in 2000 at the Bellagio in Las Vegas, a second in New York, and the flagship boutique on Madison Avenue in September 2001. The number of boutiques, 15 at the time of the acquisition of the brand, grew to 30 a year later, and to 42 years later. In 2010, YSL had 78 boutiques worldwide and 184 in 2017.

When Gucci acquired Bottega Veneta in February 2001, the brand had 19 stores. The first flagship boutique, new version, opened in

December 2001 on Madison Avenue. Six additional boutiques – in Paris, Milan, London, San Jose, Costa Mesa and Chicago (which moved to a more prestigious venue in the Hyatt) – and eight boutiques in Japan were opened in 2002, in addition to the complete renovation of the existing stores, all in one year. This means that in the two years following the acquisition, Bottega Veneta renovated all its stores and doubled their number! In 2010 – nine years later – the brand had 148 stores. In 2018 the number had risen to 270.

When Alessandro Michele took the helm of Gucci's creative department in January 2015 and Marco Bizzari was appointed CEO, two of their first decisions were to revamp the concept of the Gucci boutiques (the first renovated store was opened in September 2015 in Milan), and to rethink all the points of contact between the brand and its customers in order to bring them into line with the new creative vision of the brand (advertisements, website, customer testimonials, press relations, events, social media, catalogues, etc.), *and* show windows, packaging, and visual merchandising.

Case Study: How Giorgio Armani's 'Vision of the World' Nurtures the Design of Its Stores

My fashion is in tune with our world. I see my job as a mission: I must not produce anything superfluous, I must show the way, create differences.

For me, it is essential to eliminate the irrelevant, at work, at home, even in my social life. Everything must have a meaning and be in harmony with its environment. The woman wearing Armani is a refined creature whose elegance stems from within rather than from revealing her bosom; she moves with grace in a men's jacket. (*Elle,* 18 November 1991)

(*continued*)

(*Continued*)

There are three fundamental elements in Giorgio Armani's worldview:

1. *Blending*: Intermingling realities. 'Today's fashion plays on many levels of reality – women dress in so many different ways. So, there cannot be only one trend, you have to mix them up' (*Harper's Bazaar*, September 1996). Mixing styles: 'There is no longer one trend but a mingling of trends' (*Elle Décoration*, 1989). complexity .

2. *Contrasts*: Contrast of sensibilities within the same person: 'I think that today the most attractive man is the one who ironically accepts a certain feeling of insecurity and is not afraid to show it ... I imagine him also as tender, free to express his feelings, his emotions, to be shy, and all this constitutes a vital and precious part of his personality.' Divergences between the sexes in fashion: 'She wanted a men's jacket with a silk satin t-shirt underneath – a very strange mix at the time' (*Harper's Bazaar*, 1996). 'An elegant woman knows how to play with opposites, to combine contrasts ... '

3. *Harmony*: 'Luxury today is no longer a question of showing your power to others. It's more of a life in harmony. To be in harmony with oneself, with one's clothes; harmony should exist at home and in places where one likes to be. Yes, harmony should be the link between everything; it's my philosophy' (*Elle* Germany, September 1991).

Giorgio Armani opposes the woman-who-is-herself to the woman-who-shows-herself. Having a preference for the former, he considers that the clothes he designs should highlight her personality, help her to be in harmony. Her colours should express serenity; as her body moves, her clothes should be designed to move with her. He wished to dress people who are actors of their own lives and see themselves as free and autonomous. As Giorgio Armani himself says in one of the aforementioned articles: 'To impose a fashion, whatever it is, means to have no respect for the person who wears your creations. Personally, I do the opposite. My goal is simple: to help people to distil, to refine their own style through my clothes and to avoid transforming them into fashion victims' (*Elle*, 18 November 1991).

He applies this philosophy by combining fabrics ('I did not invent any form, only the way to mix fabrics and shapes in very original combinations: leather and georgette, white silk and coarse tweed'; *Madame Figaro*, 19 September 1992); using neutral colours ('Combining two beiges is something that seems subtle to me'; *Elle*, 24 April 1995); eliminating all that is superfluous ('Less is more'); juxtaposing the spots of interest in his stores ('I wanted a music corner, newspapers, and a small restaurant, I would have liked to have an art gallery too. It must be a place where people meet'; *Marie Claire*, February 1998) with a conception of space ('A district of the city dedicated exclusively to fashion is the worst thing'; *Marie Claire*, February 1998).

This explains why the Armani stores are a mixture of beige and grey tones, why the Armani Casa stores are harmonies of brown and beige and why the Emporio Armani store in Paris was the first to open a restaurant, the Armani Café, which has been autonomous since 2016 and exists independently of the boutique with its own entrance on the Boulevard Saint Germain. All the brand's store concepts are consistent with the brand's vision.

The Concept of the Boutique: Applying the Brand's Vision

The primary focus for luxury brands is to ensure that its vision is successfully and consistently implemented everywhere (see the four poles of a brand's vision in Figure 3.1). To understand the impact this has on

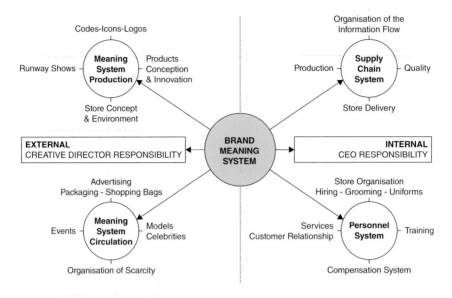

Figure 3.1   The Four Poles of a Brand's Vision

the brand's visual merchandising strategy, we suggest breaking down the actions of a luxury brand into four main components:

- *Creating a brand vision:* This is where the continuous flow of ideas and images that embody the brand's vision (or the vision of the creator, if he is still controlling it) is generated. Important examples are the fashion shows, the products themselves, the concept of the boutique and, of course, the codes and iconography of the brand (its logo, its iconic products, its institutional colours). This explains the crucial importance of the design of the stores themselves, because it is there (together with the e-commerce website) that the daily encounter between the brand and the customer takes place.
- *Spreading the brand vision:* Once created, the vision of the brand must be conveyed, transmitted, put into circulation. A key element for this circulation is, of course, advertising, but also packaging, bags, the use of a 'face' (someone who is consistent with the brand, not someone chosen because it is the man or woman of the moment!), the important events organised by the brand – an anniversary, a launch, an exhibition. An example we have in mind are the various strategies

that luxury brands use to impart information to Chinese customers about the brand's history and legacy, such as the *Louis Vuitton Retrospective* in Shanghai in 2010 and presenting of the *Made by Hermès* artisans around the world showcasing the know-how and quality of the brand's products – 'Hermès hors les murs'.[2] Like the diffusion of its vision, production is the direct responsibility of the *brand's creative director*, and is carried into effect at the store level by visual merchandisers who work in the retail image department (see the case study showing Bally's organisational chart in Figure 3.4 below). Artistic control is handled by this team at the brand's head office where a standard layout of products is defined and where the store window visuals are created. They may even compose original music for diffusion in the boutique.[3]

- *The supply chain*: Once the brand vision has been defined and announced, the entire supply chain has to be organised in a consistent manner, in line with that vision. This means, for example, that new products advertised should be delivered to the boutique *before* the public hears about them, not after. If not, sales are lost and the image of the brand is adversely affected.

Example

One of the authors witnessed this type of brand damage when he was HR Director at *Bally*. At a meeting of the management committee, the Creative Director was agitated: 'Where are the new shopping bags? We have redesigned the entire identity of the brand. We have a new concept for the stores. We have a

(continued)

---

[2] https://www.hermes.com/fr/fr/story/131226-hors-les-murs-lyon/

[3] Tom Ford, the designer of Gucci and Yves Saint Laurent, while preparing the opening of the YSL shop in New York in December 2000: 'He moved a white stool, he was concerned that customers could get hurt if the handrail of the staircase had rough edges and he drew a small mark on the volume knob of the stereo so that the music level corresponded to the mood he wanted' (Hirschberg 2001).

(*Continued*)

new packaging but the new shopping bags are not in the stores. Where are they?'

No one knew!

A few days later, while visiting a warehouse, he sees huge cartons on the floor. 'What is this?', he asks the logistics manager. 'The shopping bags.' 'But we are looking for them everywhere! Why are they not in the store?' 'Because I do not have their code – you know I cannot ship anything without a code! And the IT department tells me they have so much work lately that they do not have the time to generate codes for free articles!' (Welcome to the world of day-to-day management glitches that disrupt the consistency of a brand!)

Today such a problem could be solved by using a company like Infinity Global, which takes charge of ordering and delivering all merchandising materials of a big brand to its stores. The *raison d'être* of these companies is to handle deliveries to the brand's stores worldwide in a timely fashion.

• *The human resources system*: All this requires personnel. The construction of a luxury brand frequently needs people with the right skills, the organisation of a boutique in line with the image of the brand, and a clear-cut definition of the type of customer relationship that the brand wishes to establish. The two latter points come under the direct responsibility of the CEO and his management teams.

Case Study: Luxury and Expertise Displayed in China's Boutiques

In 2010, in partnership with the French Chamber of Commerce, Hong Kong hosted an event called 'Boutique Boulevard: So Lush, So Central', a gathering of luxury brands in Hong Kong.

From 14 to 23 May, the most famous brands organised a series of encounters with professionals in the luxury business who were able to display their know–how to their many fans in Hong Kong, and share their exceptional world with them.

The event began with an evening reserved for the happy few in Hong Kong's most vibrant area, the Central District. The itinerary wound through the neighbourhood, linking the various shopping malls dedicated to luxury, allowing guests to wander from one store to another to discover:

- A perfume workshop (*'Scent & Sensibility'*) presented by Guerlain and led by one of the creators of *L'Instant by Guerlain*, Ms Sylvaine Delacourte, who explained why and how one should wear a perfume.
- A workshop dedicated to the art of the (double) shave, presented by Angel Gonzales, barber from the prestigious Mandarin Oriental.
- Information and advice offered by the highly esteemed French sommelier, Pierre Legrandois.
- Fashion presentations and workshops with advice on fashion and etiquette offered by a number of brands, from Dunhill and Tiffany to Armani, Cartier, Gucci and Louis Vuitton.

The event also echoed the 'Savoir Faire' exhibition organised that same year from 30 April to 2 May by Dior in Hong Kong for its new Rosewood jewellery collection. Organised for the first time in Paris the year before, this exhibition helped to highlight these unique pieces of jewellery as an expression of Dior's expertise and creative passion.

Encouraged by the success of the Paris event, the brand sent three jewellers to Hong Kong to demonstrate their expertise and present the new Rosewood collection designed by Victoire de Castellane, which included 13 jewels that paid tribute to

(continued)

(*Continued*)

Christian Dior's favourite flowers: the roses of his garden in Milly-la-Forêt.

In the same style, Montblanc organised an exhibition presenting the historical and artisanal dimension of the brand in Shanghai in April 2014 and Hermès showcased its artisans in a travelling world exhibition, 'Le Festival des Métiers', that became 'Hermès hors les Murs' (Hermès beyond the walls).

Where does the obsession that luxury brands seem to have for this type of event spring from? What benefits do they gain?

This type of 'seduction operation', which presents the know-how of the most prestigious brands, is very popular in Asia. Indeed, with the growing number of newly affluent Chinese, luxury brands are trying to transmit values on which their reputation in Europe is based to their current and future customers. These values, this know-how, this expertise and the demonstrations of the meticulous handiwork of their most qualified artisans affirm their legitimacy – and the prices charged by the big luxury houses.

The display of manufacturing processes, the immersion in history and the discovery of the world of the brand go hand in hand. Once customers are satisfied that the product is well made and of high quality, they have to be persuaded to adhere to the image of the brand and what it reflects. This process takes longer than a simple act of seduction, but if it succeeds, customer loyalty will flow from it and customers will be convinced that they have placed their trust in a high-quality brand that closely reflects their own values.

In addition, organising marketing operations of this scale can also attract considerable media coverage and make cities like Hong Kong, Shanghai or Seoul meeting points for luxury in Asia. In fact, China and Hong Kong are, in general, keenly interested in spectacular promotional events that create a buzz. In an environment where showing one's best side always matters, luxury brands in Asia generally try to be more imaginative than their neighbours and constantly strive to raise the bar even higher for these events – Chanel (Cruise, Autumn 2010), Dior (Spring–Summer 2013) and Louis Vuitton (Fall–Winter 2012–2013) had, for example, presented their collections on the Bund in Shanghai.

Although luxury brands do not always attract customers in the immediate aftermath of these events, they will still initiate the process in some of them. Visitors who come out of curiosity, and who may not be the brand's core target audience, are no less likely to be fascinated by the brand universe and become its clients as soon as they are able to. This preliminary approach to a clientele less familiar with luxury also helps to demystify the approach to some of these famous brands, which can often be perceived as intimidating.

Recently some brands initiated a new model of exhibitions cum pop-up stores: Diptyque had a very successful exhibition in Shanghai in April 2019 showing 50 years of history of the brand, where visitors could also buy the products of the brand. Not only were visitors queuing to visit but sales were very important. This is a perfect example of how to build both brand awareness and sales.

Store Formats: Closed or Open?

Traditionally, the boutique of a luxury brand was an enclosed shop into which one entered through a glass door. In fact, the best way to preserve the exclusivity of the brand was to limit access to the store. However, we see that this ancient format has changed significantly and we find three different formats today – from the most enclosed to the most open – all of which have significantly different types of access to the brand:

- A boxed-in store window, with no view of the interior of the store, and a door that opens only upon request: this is the traditional format of watch and jewellery stores – much like the green marble format that Cartier used in most of its stores until the 2000s. One of them still stands on Rue de la Paix in Paris.

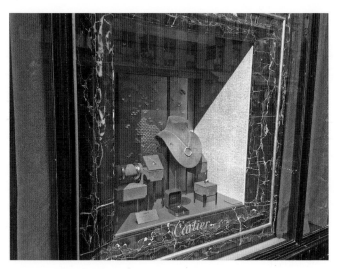

Photo: © Michel Gutsatz.

- An open show window, presenting the products against a remov-
able backdrop that gives a partial view of the interior of the store.
This format has become the standard for luxury stores in the fashion
and leather goods sector, and more recently perfume (see the Balenciaga, Burberry and Diptyque showcases below). Jewellery brands
may sometimes use this style – such as Cartier and its 'slate' shop
on rue du Faubourg Saint-Honoré in Paris. This is the format one
would link to the period of democratisation of luxury: the customer
should be able to see the entire store and therefore understand that
the product offered is much wider than that displayed in the window.

Photos: © Michel Gutsatz.

- An open, transparent storefront that allows the customer to see the entire store from the outside and access it without crossing thresholds. This is the case in many beauty shops (like Sephora) and most shops in shopping malls.

Photo: © Michel Gutsatz

Each of these different formats will engender a different type of relationship between the customer and the brand, and will depend very much on the degree of proximity between the customer and the brand (see Table 3.1) and as Alfred Taubman (2007) once said, each of them will generate a different level of 'threshold resistance'. 'Threshold resistance is what keeps your customer from opening the door and

Table 3.1   Shop Format and Brand–Client Relationship

	Regular customers	**Non-regular customers**
Closed show window	They will feel at ease, protected from the rest of the world in a very select environment	They will not feel welcome and probably would not even push open the door of the store.
Open show window		A good compromise to encourage non-regular customers to enter.
Half-open show window		They will feel more comfortable, being able to foresee what awaits them inside.

coming in over your threshold. I think we can reduce that with a better design.'

The democratisation of luxury also means that potential customers, who are not brand insiders, should be able to access it without feeling excluded or intimidated. The open window format is therefore far more apt for new customers.

There is also a fourth store concept, the (fully) open store, which does its utmost to be welcoming to uninitiated customers. There is no door or showcases to hinder their entrance. Two examples of these stores are:

- Almost all airport boutiques follow this concept. People can enter them freely without having to go through a door. All studies show that this facilitates access to luxury brands for uninitiated customers. Even jewellers like Cartier and Bulgari opt for the open store format at their airport outlets.
- Sephora, specialists in the distribution of perfumes and cosmetics, has chosen this format. Their flagship store on the Champs-Elysées is a perfect example. It is interesting to compare it to the conventional Guerlain perfumery boutique located just 50 metres down the avenue, particularly since the situation has changed significantly since the writing of the first edition of this book.

Example

In 2012: The two storefronts are approximately the same size but crossing the threshold of the Guerlain store is intimidating. Firstly, there is the heavy door behind which there is a security guard; the entrance is flanked by two traditional store windows through which the customer perceives that it is a rather small store with four vendors inside. The overall impression is very intimidating.

Sephora, on the other hand, has an entrance fully open to the avenue, with a gentle slope leading towards the interior of the store. The security guard's presence is very discreet and there is a steady flow of customers going in and out. There is no barrier at the entrance (see Figure 3.2). The outcome is that customers who were too intimidated to enter the Guerlain store find their way to Sephora next door, and probably buy their Guerlain perfumes and cosmetics at Sephora!

Figure 3.2 The Sephora Storefront
Photos: Michel Gutsatz.

Figure 3.3 The Guerlain Storefront
Photo: Michel Gutsatz.

Fast-forward to 2018: Guerlain's brand managers (who probably read our book!) decided to take advantage of the space between Sephora and their boutique when it became vacant to install their Atelier Guerlain Parfumeur boutique, which fully opens onto the Champs Elysées (see Figure 3.3).

Customising Boutiques and Flagships

The major credo for all luxury brands is that their stores around the world should resemble each other so as to create a unique brand image that customers will recognise immediately. Prada was the perfect example for a long time: the total-control syndrome developed by the brand led it to apply the same format not only to their stores (mint-green paint and glazed carpets) but also to their offices.

This strategy changed in the early years of the twenty-first century – especially with regard to flagship stores. Brands that considered themselves strong decided to change their approach and Prada, as usual, was a trailblazer in this area. In 1999, they enlisted Rem Koolhaas for three projects: a new 2,250 m^2 store in the former Guggenheim Soho area in New York; the designing of the 2,000 m^2 store in Los Angeles, and the 4,300 m^2 store in San Francisco. Other architects, Herzog and de Meuron, who gained fame thanks to the Tate Modern project in London, among others, redesigned the Tokyo store, as well as the offices of Prada in New York and the head office of the Tuscan factory. 'This is an exceptional project', Miuccia Prada said in a WWD interview:

> We believe that many brands now have stores that look alike—and that's just boring. We wanted to develop an experimental store. We wanted to ask, 'What does shopping mean?' We understand that customers today enjoy shopping, that it's become a way to socialize and communicate.

Prada then introduced a new concept, which they called 'epicentre stores', that has since become a general trend among all luxury brands in the form of flagship stores. These are the stores whose role is to contribute to the definition of the brand by displaying the ostentation, the space and the opulence that a luxury brand is capable of. As Rem Koolhaas said:

> The risk in numbers is repetition. Each new store decreases the overall aura and helps create a sense of familiarity. The risk associated with scale is the Standard Bearer Syndrome: a megalomaniac accumulation of obviousness, which tends to efface whatever remains of the elements of surprise and mystery related to the brand, and to imprison it in an identity 'carved in stone'. But growth can also be an opportunity for redefining a brand, by introducing two types of stores – the typical and the unique – the epicentre store becomes a brand renewal mechanism by going against the tide and by shaking up any preconceived notion of what Prada is, does, or will be. The epicentre store functions as a conceptual showcase: a means of proclaiming its future direction, which gives a positive image to the larger mass of regular stores. (Bertelli 2001)

Typically, flagship stores may be five to eight times larger than regular stores, cover a larger area than the traditional ground floor, and include other elements than a simple store. The Chanel flagship in Ginza, Tokyo, which opened in 2005, has 10 levels. According to a report by the *Architectural Record*:

> 'Functioning as a 21st-century branding billboard, the building is a conceptual rendering of a classic Chanel tweed,' says principal architect Peter Marino. 'The design team's primary objective was to create a contemporary, iconic architectural expression of the Chanel ethos. At 215 feet, the building is the tallest in the upscale Ginza shopping district. The 10-story building comprises a three-level Chanel retail boutique, a fourth-floor exhibition and concert space, rental offices on the upper floors, a gourmet restaurant on the penthouse level, and a multifunction rooftop garden terrace'. (Weathersby 2005, p. 204)

A marketing director interviewed about flagship stores once said:

> The rules of luxury are clear. Space, and what is referred to as 'extravagant use of free space' defines a luxury experience. By having commercially inactive spaces, we send a signal of exclusivity, luxury and extravagance that is the very core of luxury. (Moore et al. 2010)

These unique spaces can also help the brand build its reputation through a clever combination:

- Historical buildings: this allows part of the building's history to blend in with the history of the brand itself. The most striking example, and the first of its kind, was Ralph Lauren's acquisition of the Rhinelander House in 1986. This 2,000 m² flagship belonged to an elite New York family at the beginning of the twentieth century. Creating a store in which the original elements as well as paintings and furniture were preserved gave the brand a distinctive stamp that proved its legitimacy – that of a WASP (White Anglo Saxon Protestant) lifestyle. The Ralph Lauren head office on Madison Avenue also reinforced its legitimacy: the lobby in mahogany reminds one of (according to the architect who carried out the project) the first-class lounge on the *Normandy*.

- Famous architects: 'Luxury brands are the new patrons of architecture – we have succeeded Popes and royalty!'[4] Since the early 2000s, all the major luxury brands have worked with the big names in architecture, both because this has a positive impact on the image of the brand and because this gives them an innovative momentum by capitalising on the creativity of the architect. Peter Marino works for Chanel, Dior, Louis Vuitton and Zegna; Massimiliano Fuksas designed the Armani stores in New York, Tokyo and Hong Kong.

The years 2017 and 2018 saw the upturn in the building of flagship stores that are increasingly large and impressive. To name but a few: Louis Vuitton has opened a superb 3,500 m² boutique on the Place Vendôme in Paris; Hermès installed itself in the 920 m² Prince Building in Hong Kong (after opening a fifth Maison Hermes boutique of 1,200 m² in Shanghai in 2014); Chanel has replaced its first Ginza store in Tokyo with a new building of more than 1,000 m², and plans to open six new flagship boutiques (including its completely renovated boutique on Rue Cambon in Paris).

- Developing the image of the brand implies having excellent relations with the press, and the fashion press in particular. The flagship stores play a role here, which is best understood by examining this fascinating counter-example: a distributor explained that when their flagship store in London closed (due to unsustainable operating costs), the fashion press no longer covered the brand, and this had a negative impact, according to the company, on the turnover of their other outlets:

The press needs to link a location to a brand. When we closed our store, it was as if we had been deleted from the reporters' minds. It was amazing: it did not matter what we did, we just did not matter to them anymore. We had to quickly reverse our decision because the impact of non-coverage by the media is simply terrible for a luxury brand's turnover. (Moore et al. 2010)

---

[4] Head of a luxury brand, cited by Moore et al. (2010).

These flagship stores have yet another role: they support the relationship that the brand has with its other distributors. The existence of a new store concept – created by a famous architect – can act as a fulcrum when the brand wants its partners and distributors to upgrade their stores, and can also serve as a showcase for recruiting and retaining intermediaries:

> It is very clear to us that a flagship has an important role to play in the development of wholesale sales. When we opened a flagship in Shanghai, the impact on our wholesale sales was incredible. If we renovate our flagships, we know that because of it, we will also attract more than a hundred new intermediaries. (Moore et al. 2010)

A flagship store is where the brand trains its franchisees and provides information on new collections and the launch of new product lines; it is the place where it discloses its new merchandising strategy to intermediaries who will also have to adopt it at one point or another.

Flagship boutiques and new store concepts are therefore at the core of the very complex relationship between a brand, its customers, its distributors and the press. The decision to launch a new store concept or to invest in a flagship store costs a lot, but the spin-offs are there: you should never gauge an investment of this type on the basis of turnover alone![5]

As Scott Fellows, former Creative Director of Bally, once said to one of the authors:

> Why do you think I choose to put red or blue shoes in the men's window? Because this will attract customers to the store, and they will leave with a pair of black or brown shoes!

In the art of selling effectively, show windows play a very important role: it is the first visual contact between the customer and the brand and its products. Shop windows can stop passers-by in their tracks and draw them into the store.

---

[5] This phenomenon does not concern only the luxury sector. When Starbucks opened its new flagship store, The Roastery, in Shanghai in 2017, the brand saw sales in standard Starbucks stores grow by 20–30%.

Example

One day, one of the authors was walking around the Soho neighbourhood in New York when his eyes were drawn to an empty show window. On the other side of the street, facing him, was another shop that seemed to have an empty show window as well. It was quite the opposite of everything he imagined in terms of visual merchandising, so he decided to cross the street. As he approached, the interior of the store gradually became visible, and once he reached the window, he had a clear view of the interior of the store! This is a fascinating example of how a brand, in the early 2000s, mastered the intricacies of the relationship a window can establish with a passerby: *Issey Miyake's Pleats Please* used a new glass technology to surprise and draw attention to the brand and its products.

A few years later (towards the end of 2005), Abercrombie & Fitch reinvented the absence of a show window: all the store windows of its new flagship store on Fifth Avenue were closed. There were no products on display. There were more than 10 windows – a valuable asset in such an expensive location – and they had been closed off. Instead, customers were drawn to the entrance of the store by the music that emanated from it.

The show window is where emotion is born.

How many luxury brands – apart from their flagship stores – create show windows that reinforce the image of the brand and strengthen their emotional connection with their customers? Too few.

How many brands use their store windows to enlighten customers, to impart an understanding of the brand? One of the authors was quite surprised to see recently, in Bally's store window on New Bond Street, photographs of shoe models created by the brand in the nineteenth and early twentieth centuries. The message came through, loud and clear, in a matter of seconds.

How many brands do what the Bonwit Teller department stores did in the 1930s: entrust the designing of their store windows to artists? And among them Salvador Dali, Man Ray and Marcel Duchamp? And Andy Warhol in the 1950s?

Most brands use their windows only for displaying products. Luxury brands should not have to say anything to their customers or passers-by. They should use their show windows to display their uniqueness and build a strong emotional relationship. This is exactly what Hermès did with the extraordinary creations of Leila Menchari (who decorated its show windows from 1978 to 2013 – now replaced by Antoine Platteau, a leading decorator in French cinema) and what Paul Smith is doing in most of his boutiques; that is what Dior succeeded in doing when John Galliano arrived and completely revamped the brand's image (the windows of Avenue Montaigne contained 'scandalous' images of Gisele Bundchen): creating emotion, to stimulate the viewer's desire to enter and participate in this story.

Visual Merchandising and the Institutional Image of the Brand

Store windows are an important part of the brand's visual merchandising. Luxury brands have transformed what was once a distinctive feature of department stores into a key element for their corporate brand image. They learned that every detail counts and that specialised teams – visual merchandisers – are essential to implement, at the store level, the artistic orientations decided at the head office.

The best way to understand this is to examine a case that one of the authors knew as an insider at Bally, when a new organisational chart was implemented in 2000, drawing inspiration from American department stores.

Case Study: Organisational Chart of the Retail Image Department at Bally

The retail image management team included both a global team and regional teams, responsible for implementing in each store the guidelines of the company decided at the international level.

(continued)

(Continued)

The global team was placed directly under the supervision of the Creative Director and called the Retail Image Management (see Figure 3.4). It consisted of:

- A coordinator of global visual merchandising.
- Four visual merchandising specialists for directly operated stores.
- A show window designer for directly operated stores.
- A visual merchandising coordinator for wholesalers and travel retail shops.
- Four visual merchandising specialists/designers for Europe.
- Four visual merchandising specialists/designers for Asia and the US.

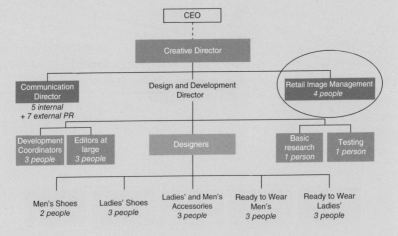

Figure 3.4   Retail Image Management – Bally's Organisational Chart
Source: Chevalier and Mazzalovo (2015).

We perceive the importance of window decoration, thanks to the presence in this team of a visual merchandising specialist who concentrated entirely on show windows.

When revisiting a store, visual merchandisers (VMs) have to ensure that store managers are implementing their guidelines. They therefore need detailed guidelines. The document shown in Figure 3.5 is an example of a grid filled by central visual merchandisers after a visit to the store.

Country	France	City		Paris	
Store	Étoile	Date		14.03.01	
Store Manager		Store V Manager			
Regional Manager		Divisional Manager			
VM Representative					

	Pilot Store				Non-Pilot

	1	2	3	4	5
	Very Poor	Poor	Acceptable	Good	Excellent
General condition of the store					
Display					
Impact					
Men's department					
Women's department					
Upkeep					
Staff attire					
Help from staff					

Total Score: 27/40

Feedback of the Manager on the current state of the store (if pertinent):

	Very Poor	Poor	Acceptable	Good	Excellent
Photos taken		Before	After	Before and after	

Figure 3.5 Working Document for Visual Merchandising – Bally

(continued)

(*Continued*)

A month later, the VM revisited the store and his comments show that the local team had understood his visual guidelines:

Remarks of the VM
- The set-up of the store is good.
- The blocks ordered during our previous visit were delivered.
- We reviewed the layout, which improves the number of presentation options.
- X was a great help and we would like her to be the VM for this store.

The Prada epicentres boutiques and all the brand's flagship stores are examples of 'Wow!' stores. But are they anything other than the manifestation of attempts by one brand to impress other brands? Could they not be seen as another step in an escalation of concerted efforts aimed at regaining the declining attention of customers? Koolhaas versus Gehry (who built the Louis Vuitton Foundation that opened in Paris in 2014), or Marino versus Future Systems, might be just expensive avatars of the brand war. Isn't the customer just a hostage to an 'upward spiral whose movement tends to eliminate the customer himself from the equation – to end up being nothing more than artistic directors speaking to other artistic directors and designers to designers. The client has become more and more a spectator of these circus games rather than their focal point?'[6] Our take here is that the attention lavishly dedicated by luxury brands on concepts and visual merchandising in their stores – however important they may be, as we have seen – should not be the be-all and end-all. When the focus is no longer on the quality of service, the customer will be sidelined, except to remark how impressed he is with a store that, in the end, is nothing but a decor.

---

[6] Simon Doonan, Barney's former Artistic Director, New York, https://www.salon.com/2001/06/26/retail_redesign/.

To recap:

- *Luxury brands* have turned into retailers over the last 30 years, and the choice of an architectural concept is of particular importance for a brand's identity.
- *Shop formats* are evolving into larger and more open spaces, so as to remove any barriers to entry.
- *The show window* is a privileged means of expression of the brand – where emotion should be created with a very strong impact on the client/prospective client.

Chapter 4

Online, Offline or O2O?

The founding principle of NET-A-PORTER.COM was, and remains, to create a balance between content and commerce.

–Natalie Massenet

The Internet has become a major channel of distribution and/or communication for luxury brands that have chosen to invest in it – but their attitude towards the web has not always been easy. This chapter takes us through the twists and turns of the love/hate relationship that luxury brands have with modern communication technologies. We will use a defining event as a starting block: How did Yoox .com and its business model change the point of view of luxury brands on e-commerce?

If we wish to understand the cultural difference that exists between luxury and the Internet, we need to go back a few years to trace the evolution of this love/hate relationship. We will then come back to the

current situation, where the Internet is used both as a means of communication and as a vector for e-commerce, a situation that will certainly
continue to evolve in the years to come. We will also try and explain the
complexities of digital marketing and lay out seven guidelines that any
brand should respect on the Internet and social networks when it wishes
to develop its online business.

From Yoox.com to the Merger with NET-A-PORTER.com

During the 2009 Milan Fashion Week, one person created a sensation:
Federico Marchetti, the CEO of Yoox, who was given pride of place in
the first row for all the shows.

How did he merit such an honour? Because Federico Marchetti had
transformed Yoox into a key player in the luxury sector, with a total
income of €214 million in 2010, €524 million in 2014, which reached
€2.1 billion in 2017 after the merger with NET-A-PORTER.com.

A brief history of Yoox will give us an idea of the innovative business
model he set up.

Yoox was launched in 2000, and was one of the first discount
Internet outlets, offering Italian luxury and fashion brands a means to
dispose of their unsold stocks from previous seasons through an elegant
virtual portal. Its logistics was designed to offer customers a service
worthy of the brands themselves. In its first phase, Yoox positioned
itself as a reference for e-discount, the key element of its business model
being that Yoox only pays its suppliers after the sale is concluded – and
therefore did not have to bear warehousing costs.

In a second phase, Yoox established a *differentiation strategy*: offering
creations from young designers, and also objects and books. Two important aspects characterised this new offer: the merchandise was sold at its
normal price (without discount), capitalising heavily on the 'Made in
Italy' image. 'Our soul is Italian', said Federico Marchetti. In this second phase, Yoox positioned itself as a key player in the fashion sector,
abandoning its 'everything is on sale' image.

After acquiring an expertise in e-commerce, Yoox outsourced two important functions: the stocking and packaging of products ('pick and pack') were entrusted to Norbert Dentressangle, and delivery to UPS.

Yoox realised that it had the much sought-after know-how when luxury brands started (finally) to study the question of selling online. To do so, they had to find an independent and professional operator, which happened to be Yoox Services, a subsidiary of Yoox. Marni, the e-commerce website, was launched in 2006, soon followed by others carrying, like it, the words 'Powered by YOOX': Emporio Armani, Diesel, Dolce & Gabbana, Jil Sander, Valentino, Bally, Dsquared, Miss Sixty, National Costume, Emilio Pucci, Stone Island and CP.

Yoox also created a Masters in e-Fashion at MIP, the Politecnico di Milano business school, with scholarships funded by Armani. Yoox also grew, building on its privileged relationships with brands in the service of a real training strategy in the areas of brand management and e-commerce.

The yoox.com website is an excellent example of a modern e-commerce site, with information, runway videos and exclusives, as well as an eco-design section, Yooxigen. It only lacks the 'Community' dimension to be comprehensive.

This business model has been successful because it is built around four strategic operational advantages:

- *A comprehensive and integrated e-commerce offer* – this is a concrete (and new) expertise that luxury brands did not know how to instinctively employ, and which requires specially trained cadres.
- *Confidence built around a customer–supplier relationship* – and a thorough knowledge of each brand's sales.
- *Use of a technology fully controlled in-house* – RFID chips to reference products, proprietary e-business software, a design studio, etc.
- *The image of being experts in fashion, and in discount* – everyone being able to find what they are looking for: well-known brands at discounted prices, private labels, exclusives, vintage, and so on.

In 2012 Yoox created a joint venture with Kering in charge of e-commerce for all Kering brands (except Gucci). Since then, Yoox has positioned itself as an e-commerce operator for a significant number of luxury brands (more than 30 except for Kering).

But the story of Yoox took on a new dimension in March 2015: Yoox and Richemont, reference shareholder of NET-A-PORTER since 2010, announced the merger of the two companies and the constitution of the Yoox-NET-A-PORTER Group, which posted a turnover of €1.7 billion for 2015 (27 million unique visitors on their sites each month) and 2.1 billion in 2017. Richemont holds 50% of the shares and 25% of voting rights.

It had been five years after Richemont acquired NET-A-PORTER and the analysts had welcomed this move as proof of the coming of awareness of one of the major luxury groups of the importance of digital. But all through the five years, the group's brands, as also all the luxury watch and jewellery brands, continued to be laggards in the 'Internet' class – way behind beauty brands and car brands. In 2013 the American think-tank L2 wrote:

> Watches and Jewellery product pages largely disappoint. Although half offer close-up images, only a third present multiple angles, just a quarter provide interactive content and less than a fifth have tools to compare between several options. (L2, 2013)

February 2018 marked a major turning point in this evolution: Richemont announced the acquisition of the entire capital of Yoox and the control of YNAP. Awareness has grown and within two years, all the Richemont watchmaking and jewellery brands (such as Cartier, Baume & Mercier, Piaget and IWC, and also those other than Richemont like the LVMH brands Zenith and Tag Heuer, and independent brands like Tiffany and Chopard) joined this new distribution channel, as Figure 4.1 shows.

What happened? The increasing power of the parallel market on the Internet in recent years (like the 'daigu' phenomenon in China, which we will discuss in Chapter 7) has hit hard the (too) comfortable position of a sector exclusively focused on physical distribution (offline), and for which the Internet was, at best, an attractive showcase. Traditional luxury brands woke up and have become aware that they were way behind in this respect. Just as the Swatch Group was for several years the only supplier available to source the mechanisms for watch brands, will

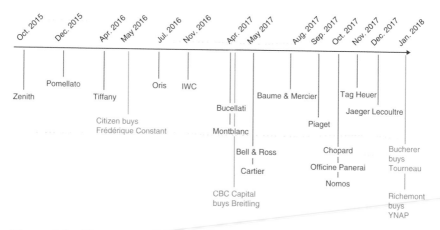

Figure 4.1 The Creation of Partnerships YNAP and Acquisitions in Jewellers–Watchmakers

Richemont (through the Yoox–NET-A-PORTER Group) become the indispensable gateway for some luxury brands in matters of e-commerce?

Case Study: The Farfetch Example

Do you know Lauren Santo Domingo? Previously Chief Editor of *Vogue*, she founded Modus Operandi, which is the first 'pre-tailer' site, in 2011 – a place where consumers can pre-order all styles spotted at fashion shows. Modus Operandi raised US$165 million in funding at the end of 2017.

Do you know 'The Real Real'? This is an Internet marketplace selling (authenticated) second-hand items. Founded in 2011, it raised US$173 million in funding in 2017 and has just opened its first store in New York.

New luxury platforms are growing rapidly on the Internet, and investors abound. But the most interesting and most

(continued)

(*Continued*)

developed among them currently is doubtlessly Farfetch. The initial idea of José Neves in 2008 was very simple. There are many luxury multi-brand boutiques in the world that would like to expand their customer base and have online sales tools much more sophisticated than those they would have (eventually). Farfetch provides them with an answer: it is a platform for communication between these multi-brand boutiques (which present their offer) and global customers looking for exceptional products. The shop has both sophisticated sales tools (such as an app and secure connections) and access to a customer database. Farfetch charges a commission on each sale (about 25%), the shop taking care of shipments (and returns). The stock therefore remains in the store, which is no longer satisfied to simply post its offer online: the more advanced buy a function of the new clientele they reach as well (and Farfetch can represent up to 45% of their sales). The site had 524 stores in December 2018 from more than 40 countries and offered products from more than 200 different brands. Farfetch handles the merchandising to ensure a unique and homogeneous 'look'. Specifically, customers have access to products, without their being linked to a particular store. The link is only made at the time of purchase. However, the platform allows for 'click and collect', offers same-day deliveries in more than ten cities and allows a customer to return a product to an outlet other than the one where it was purchased. The model has significantly evolved, the brands themselves integrating the platform in 2015 (more than 75 luxury brands were present on Farfetch at the end of 2016 and Burberry joined it in 2018). Farfetch is now, with a turnover of more than €700 million, a key player in luxury sales on the Internet – combining both single-brand and multi-brand sales channels on a single platform.

The Farfetch business model has evolved further, through its entry into China in 2018. To better master the specificities of the Chinese market, it started by buying out a digital marketing agency, Curiosity China. This enables Farfetch to offer to brands wishing to enter China (thus broadening its brand offer) a completely new set of expertise: e-commerce solutions, data and advertising solutions, e-crm solutions and digital marketing solutions. This is taking them very close to what YNAP has been offering to most of their clients. When one notices that this is being done with the help of Tencent while YNAP is partnering with Alibaba to enter China, we now have all the clues in hand: Farfetch is setting itself up as a major competitor to YNAP today in China and we can imagine in the future worldwide.

Farfetch's shareholding has also expanded. Beyond investment funds, we find Conde Nast, JD.com (since 2017 – which opened up the Chinese market and allows it to benefit from the logistical expertise of JD – they recently merged Farfetch China with Toplife, the luxury mall of JD.com) and Chanel since 2018 (without selling its collections directly on Farfetch). The partnership between Chanel (which still does not sell online) and Farfetch allows the brand to offer its customers who have downloaded the Farfetch app to be identified when they enter the store and benefit from tailor-made service based on their purchase history. Hence, Farfetch enables Chanel to benefit from its technological know-how to meet the expectations of its connected customers.

The latest undertaking is the announcement of the opening of Farfetch physical stores: 'Store of the Future'. The technological tools that are put in place are at the service of the customer *and* for the collection of data – customer identification (via a universal identifier), digital mirrors to make all the products sought by the customers available, a mobile payment system (like Apple's), and an RFID chip system to identify the products the customer is looking at. One of the goals is to free vendors from inventory management and administrative tasks, enabling them

(continued)

(*Continued*)

to focus on service. Farfetch is planning a network of 1,000 'Stores of the Future' opened by partners (current or other partner stores) to which Farfetch offers its technology (to make it a hub of luxury service) in exchange for data collection (these partners will also be able to supplement the technological offer with new apps), a real ecosystem of partners. As José Neves says: 'Data is currency and I expect something back ... once you get a customer to share her data, it's gold dust' (Kansara 2017).

A Brief History of the Love/Hate Relationship that Luxury Brands Have with the Internet

In the luxury industry, the example of yoox.com was a catalyst. Luxury brands used it as a motive to start thinking about their online strategies, centred on the same question: When, in the last 20 years, their strategy was structured around a business model that included full control of their distribution, why would they be ready to entrust the very promising distribution channel to the hands of external operators? Why should they not also control the e-commerce margins so that their profitability remained at very high levels (see Chapter 16)? Given the increasing cost of CAPEX driven by the need to open new and attractive stores in places with higher and higher rents, why deny itself the opportunity to earn money through a distribution channel whose costs are significantly lower than those of a store?

But this would have only been possible if the luxury brand itself acquired this new know-how – that of e-business – just as it had, over the years, acquired that of traditional business. That is why luxury groups launched a hunt for e-business talent:

- The Richemont group, which had acquired www.NET-A-PORTER.com in 2010, considered one of the best e-business companies in the fashion sector, ended by taking over full control of the Yoox-NET-A-PORTER group.

- Kering created a joint-venture with Yoox (in 2012) for six of its brands (Bottega Veneta, Saint Laurent, Balenciaga, Brioni, Alexander McQueen, Stella McCartney). Kering handles the creation of e-commerce sites, the management of these sites, web marketing, CRM and customer relations.
- LVMH developed one of the best e-commerce sites in its brand portfolio – sephora.com – and between 2000 and 2009 it was the owner of e-luxury.com, the first ever luxury multi-brand e-website in the luxury business. It allowed it to acquire extensive experience in Internet and online commerce. Following this, it created 24sevres.com (in June 2017), the digital platform of the Bon Marché, but while reading the presentation brochure of the 24sèvres card it is difficult to find a reference to the website, as if online and offline coexisted but were compartmentalised. Finally, a digital division (Digital Atelier) was created in 2015 with Ian Rogers (from Apple) at the helm, whose goal it was to create a true digital culture within the group.
- Chanel resisted digital for a long time, then signed a partnership and invested (in 2018) in Farfetch (see our Farfetch case study above). Farfetch offers a range of digital services, new experiences (including a customer experience in augmented reality) and customer services in 190 Chanel boutiques across the world.

We see that, actually, the digital rush in luxury really began around 2015 – only a few years ago!

In concrete terms, it was about becoming aware that the traditional luxury model will no longer be effective in the medium term. Thus, there are two views of this world that are very different at work: that of the luxury industry – which one can divide into three periods (before 2000–2005, from 2005 to 2015, and since 2015) – and five phases, each one corresponding to the different roles assigned to the brand's website.

Before 2000–2005 (Depending on the Brand)

At the beginning of this century, luxury brands considered the Internet as something alien, because they believed that the Internet and luxury were built around very different cultures (see Figure 4.2).

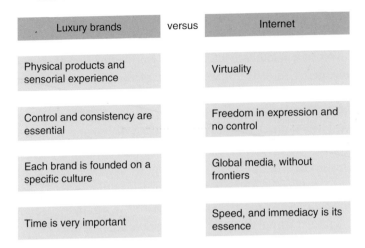

Figure 4.2   Cultural Comparison of the Internet and Luxury Brands

At least two factors – the <u>question of virtuality and of control</u> – played a determining role in the love/hate relationship between luxury brands and the web, and these points are essential in understanding the four main phases that this relationship went through.

Let us get the question of virtuality out of the way: if the essence of a luxury product is to be able to 'feel' and 'touch' it, sales and marketing directors can be led to believe that luxury can only be bought in a store, that a customer has to touch and feel the product and that the presence of a vendor is essential. These aspects are, no doubt, important, but not essential: consumer studies (we will come back later to this point) have shown that consumers of luxury are quite eclectic and are willing to buy any luxury item through the web as long as the site is sufficiently attractive and functional.[1] Over the years their argument lost its validity because the apprehension was elsewhere: marketers and luxury brand executives all feared (and still fear) that <u>a strong virtual presence without their control would endanger their brand – because control would lie in the hands of the Internet users, which is true.</u>

---

[1] Luxury brands have taken this into account by providing extraordinary photographic quality in their Web photos, 360-degree images, virtual models, and so on, turning the Internet experience into something unique – something that sometimes has no equivalent in the store.

Because of this apprehension, the Internet found itself playing four roles – as we see through some very interesting studies by L2, an online think-tank dedicated to observing, analysing and gauging the relationship between luxury and the web. Seventy-two brands were analysed in their 2010 report (and it has since added more reports by category and by country).

It is during this period – 2000 to 2005 – that we see that there were luxury brands managing without a website. Their roles could be defined thus:

Original role: Internet was ignored and the brand did not have a website. Prada's website was known for several years for displaying only a home page saying: 'Opening Soon'. It created a site dedicated to perfumes only at the end of 2005, and as for the main site, it opened only in 2007.

Between 2005 and 2015: Brands Shared a Compartmentalised Vision, Where the Website Was 'Like a Glorified Flagship Store'

The brands then went through three more phases – all of which were marked by an organisational vision where e-commerce was either outsourced (as to Yoox by most Italian brands) or created in-house and integrated into the sales department. In the first case, the e-commerce marketing was entrusted to the partner, the brand retaining the 'boutique' marketing, with a disconnection between the two. In the second case digital communication (and social media) were attached to the communications and sales of the marketing department – and worked in parallel. Here we see a compartmentalisation of the organisation into which the customer was not integrated.

It is during this period that the Internet site assumed three new roles:

Role 1: An institutional site. This was the type of site where a brand would present its DNA, its history, events and collections without ever having contact with its customers. Online, they were kept at a distance by luxury brands whose relationship with the web was 'aristocratic', top-down: 'Venerate our brand'. L2 found that only 39 of the 72 brands studied in 2010 had an e-commerce site (32 in 2009). Almost half of all luxury brands were still at this stage of their online development, although they were present on social networks.

Role 2: The e-commerce site. Once the Internet was recognised as a full-fledged distribution channel, the brands included an e-commerce site in their institutional site (this is where operators like yoox.com came into play). More than half of all luxury brands are at this stage of their online development (see the Hermès case study below) today. Brands that sell online are more likely to have a presence on multiple platforms, bring together a larger community, and interact more frequently with their fans and followers. Brands in e-commerce are also better digital marketers and are more likely to use e-mail and sponsored search results to drive traffic to their sites and boutiques (L2, 2010).

Role 3: The Internet, a network where commerce, communication and presence on social networks combine. All the luxury brands that had become familiar with the Internet had, of course, boarded the social media train. They all had Facebook pages, Twitter accounts, applications on the iPhone and iPad. Ninety percent of brands studied by L2 were on Facebook in 2010 (against 79% in 2009), 48% were on Twitter, 55% on YouTube and 39% offered apps for smartphones. Although they increased the points of contact, brands did not get to know their customers; they did not interact with them. They always controlled the relationship and the message – and often their presence in social media left something to be desired, as we will see later.

Since 2015: The Fundamental Challenge for Brands Is to Place the Customer at the Centre

The powerful upsurge in Chinese customers (who now account for 32% of global luxury sales according to Bain; see d'Arpizio and Levato 2018) and awareness of the importance of the millennial generation has turned the brand world on its head. Both share a common characteristic, that of being 'digital natives'. Phone in hand they travel through the world and their lives, sharing experiences and shopping with their friends. Moving effortlessly from the virtual to the real, experts in a customer journey combining many sources of information and potential points of sale (single-brand, multi-brand, online, offline, etc.), trusting only their peers, they raise a fundamental question for luxury brands: is it possible to move from an 'aristocratic' top-down view of the brand (characteristic of the two previous epochs) to a 'democratic' vision where the main approach is that of dialogue?

This has an immediate organisational significance: How can a customer journey, customer service, a satisfactory customer experience be organised without placing the customer at the hub of the mechanism?

Brands are running a race against time in this respect, though looking at where they started, they show a significant margin of progress. A study conducted in 2015 by Exane BNP Paribas and ContactLab (2016a) in the United States was revealing.

Even if the authors observed an improvement of 25% over the past year between online and offline performances for 30 luxury brands, the overall result is distressing (see Figure 4.3). At most, 6 brands enable clients to collect an order placed through the Internet from a store, and 16 allow them to return a product bought on the Internet to the store. We are still far from the offline/online integration sought by customers.

It is to overcome these shortcomings that Yoox-NET-A-PORTER is positioning its omnichannel offer (see Figure 4.4). It offers their customers three levels of e-commerce delivery, the most elaborate of which they call the 'fully-integrated omnichannel', which offers the customer a seamless experience between boutique and Internet ('seamless online-offline brand experience') offering the customer a range of nine services, and to the brand, all the customer data ('single view of the customer') gathered in one place.

Then arises the next battle: that of customer data. As Farfetch's CMO John Veichmanis says,

Data is the new currency. (Milnes 2017)

Of course, every brand working with YNAP has all the data relating to its own customers, but YNAP has the data of all the customers of the 50 brands it works with – a real goldmine, which we will dwell on in Chapter 6 on CRM.

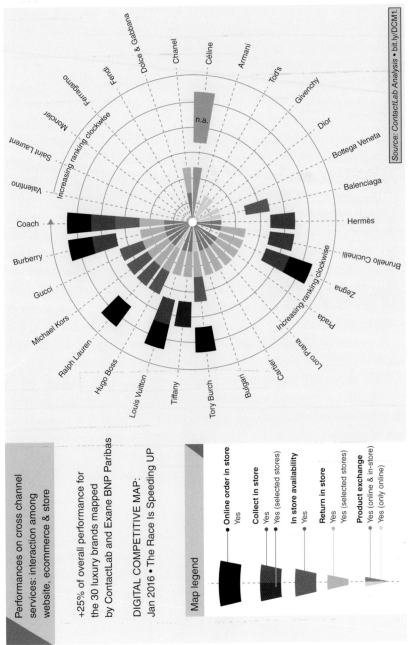

Figure 4.3 Luxury Brands' Performance in an Omnichannel System (New York, 2016)

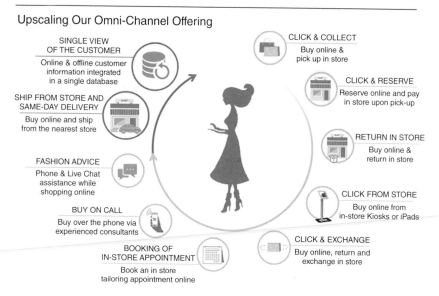

Upscaling Our Omni-Channel Offering

SINGLE VIEW
OF THE CUSTOMER
Online & offline customer
information integrated
in a single database

CLICK & COLLECT
Buy online &
pick up in store

CLICK & RESERVE
Reserve online and pay
in store upon pick-up

SHIP FROM STORE AND
SAME-DAY DELIVERY
Buy online and ship
from the nearest store

RETURN IN STORE
Buy online &
return in store

FASHION ADVICE
Phone & Live Chat
assistance while
shopping online

CLICK FROM STORE
Buy online from
in-store Kiosks or iPads

BUY ON CALL
Buy over the phone via
experienced consultants

CLICK & EXCHANGE
Buy online, return and
exchange in store

BOOKING OF
IN-STORE APPOINTMENT
Book an in store
tailoring appointment online

Figure 4.4   The Yoox-NET-A-PORTER Offer
Source: YNAP IPO.

We can therefore add a fifth role attributed to the Internet to L2's first four:

Role 5: Selling and building an omnichannel experience. Luxury brands have finally realised the importance of the Internet in a customer's journey. It therefore becomes essential to build customer relationships across all possible channels of distribution and communication – providing the customer with a unique brand experience. Information systems are to be reconstructed around a single customer database and a single CRM. The brand then builds a real ecosystem where sales and communication are permanently interconnected. The e-commerce site then becomes what it should be: a place for selling. The best example is the new 'hub' type organisation set up by Gucci (Kering's only major brand outside the scope of the JV with YNAP) since 2016 as shown in Figure 4.5 (Gucci 2016).

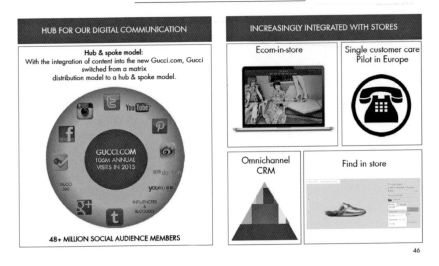

Figure 4.5   Gucci's Omnichannel Strategy

The battle to establish a customer-centric structure is therefore underway, but a preliminary analysis of the Internet strategies of luxury brands leads us to two important conclusions:

- Luxury brands have to integrate their communication and distribution circuits.
- The Internet and social networks are nothing more than tools at the service of a client relationship strategy.

Case Study: Evolution in Website Design in Luxury: The Hermès Example

The recent changes in the hermes.com website is a perfect example of the evolution that we described above, moving from a conception centred on the image of the brand to one that is centred on selling.

Creating a website consistent with the image of the brand

Luxury brands have to make important choices when they reach the e-commerce stage to create a website that is fully consistent with brand values and image. The 'top of the class' here was undeniably Hermès.

Hermès is a brand that knows how to take its time – it launched its e-commerce site only in 2008. The site is a wonderful reflection of the brand's intelligence. From the outset, the home page sets out the fundamental elements of the brand's aesthetics, each of which is a reference to the 'global vision' (ethics) of the brand.

- An off-centre logo, slightly slanted. Here, where so many brands have a tendency of displaying large, almost aggressive logos, Hermes chooses to be discreet.
- The use of drawings and writing: Hermès is a brand that attaches importance to the handmade, to the gesture – that of the artisan and that of the designer.
- An impression both romantic and unconventional: Hermès touches the imagination of its customer.
- The use of the colour orange and the orange box, emblems of the brand.
- The discreet dashed lines one can see on all the pages (used to separate the divisions on the web pages) – the saddle stitch – symbol of its core business.

The next page shows the coach and the coach driver who has descended from the coach to deliver your purchases and in doing so leads us into the world of Hermès. You will discover the meaning of the word *sabrer* ('cut/slice with a sword'), and the work of the *sabreuse* (machine used in treating sheepskin), the symphony of tools; you are invited to thrill at the sight of the Hermès diary of the Baroness Nica of Koenigswarter, to discover

(continued)

(*Continued*)

the small tricycle of Napoleon III, part of the Émile Hermès collection, and well, much more. The site offers a poignant and exceptional stroll through the world of artisans, materials and anecdotes of the brand.

As we navigate towards the store, escorted by a forest of links that open as the mouse moves over the page, we discover sketches, inscriptions and products presented in a staggered manner.

The site is a real feast for the senses. It captivates the eye as well as the ear. The brand expresses its vision of the world, its ethics as well as its aesthetics. Its products are well presented; the act of purchasing is a natural outcome of the emotion felt when browsing the site – even if the range of products sold online is quite limited (and some might even find this frustrating).

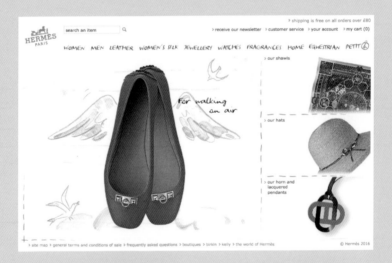

2017/2018: Creation of a new dedicated sales site

In 2017 when presenting the 2016 accounts, Axel Dumas announced a new website and stated that he preferred to 'bet on online sales rather than on a new institutional site'.

He said he wished to optimise it to offer his customers a unique experience: 'To better restore the magic of *Hermès*, we decided to create a site in which people can lose themselves. Result: people really do lose themselves'.

The new hermes.com website, tested in the USA, was extended in early 2018 to cover all of Europe. The difference is striking: an online sales site (as there are many) where the brand codes are barely noticeable, but where navigation is optimised (with the left column where one can select prices, categories, sought after products – like that of Sephora). References to the brand exist but are far less numerous: the customer should not 'get lost' outside the prime objective – buying. The brand will continue to tell its story and establish a conversation with its customers elsewhere, via app or social media.

The Hermès case illustrates our point. Luxury brands have evolved considerably over the last decade and today they have integrated the Internet into their strategies. However, the pressure of the major multi-brand platforms will be felt more and more, and the stakes will now revolve around the customer experience and the control of customer data.

To recap:

- *Luxury brands*, after having neglected the role of the Internet for a long time, have now made it an essential part of their distribution and communication strategy.
- *Large luxury groups* have positioned themselves on Internet sales platforms and made them an essential strategic element.
- *The challenge for the coming years* will be to place the customer at the centre – and therefore to design a new customer experience: the customer should be able to move from one point of contact of the brand to another seamlessly.

Part II

Know and Understand
the Client

Chapter 5

Putting the Customer Back in the Centre

Go into the store and look at what people are doing.

—Paco Underhill[1]

Even though most brands – confronted with the new medium that is the Internet – have built their online presence by the superposition of layers, one over the other, the time has now come for luxury brands to thoroughly revamp their business model on the Web.

Over the last ten years, luxury brands have developed an online presence that is very much in line with their organisation and their standard

[1] Underhill (2008).

business models, to which two or more independent, or almost independent, layers have been added:

- A 'sales' layer comprising boutiques, shops-in-shops in department stores, travel retail stores, online sales sites, and indirect distribution.
- A 'communications' layer, consisting of institutional communication, customer relationship management (CRM), a presence on social networks, and a presence on mobile apps. All these are simple tools that should be placed at the service of a global (and omnichannel) client relationship strategy.

The typical organisational chart of a luxury brand separates sales from marketing and sometimes even communication, which is the responsibility of the Creative Director. Unfortunately, this causes difficulties in creating an integrated client relationship strategy across all the services – instead of an accumulation of four strategies: communications + CRM + Internet + sales.

Running contrary to the culture that serves as reference, based on the brand and its values, we advocate a complete about-turn. We believe that, to be able to meet the demands of their most connected customers, luxury brands will have to refocus and rebuild their digital business model, making the most influential player of the twenty-first century – the customer – its starting block. This, of course, means that the entire value chain has to be rethought.

The traditional value chain (see Figure 5.1) flows from the inside towards the outside: the brand identifies its core competences, draws its business model from it, then identifies its offer, chooses its distribution channels and, finally, goes to meet its customers.

The new value chain (see Figure 5.2) flows from the outside towards the inside: the brand starts by identifying and segmenting its main customer base and their needs, defines the brand experience it wishes to share with them, and only then structures its offer and its business model.

This means that building a specific and identifiable customer relationship becomes an important issue for each brand. Let us see how this can be done.

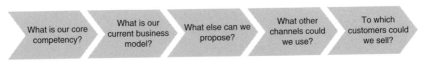

Figure 5.1   The Traditional Value Chain

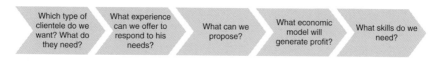

Figure 5.2   The New Value Chain

Building a relationship between a brand and its customers follows five key phases:

1. Attract
2. Approach
3. Sustain
4. Learn
5. Bond

Each phase calls for specific levers that will help build and sustain the relationship. Figure 5.3 shows how almost all these levers tell the same

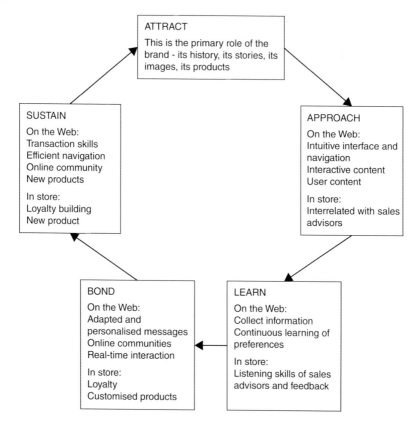

Figure 5.3   The Various Levers in a Customer Relationship

story: stores and the Internet have to be viewed as a whole because they are complementary.

Looking at It from the Customers' Side: Why Have They Logged On and How Do They Use the Internet?

All recent studies on behaviour patterns (or customer journeys) of Internet users show that they:

- Log on to the Internet to search for information.
- Then navigate to forums, focusing on their subjects of interest.
- And end up contacting people with whom they share interests and passions.

    Conclusion: people have passions and they follow their threads on the net, where they end up sharing them with other Internet users – the Web is a world of communities (and in China even more than elsewhere!). There are Facebook groups of wine lovers, perfume enthusiasts, watch aficionados, and the like.

A member's commitment to a community will depend on two factors:

- The relationship that the person builds with the core online activity of the community: the more this activity is central to the image that the individual has of himself, the more likely he is to seek and appreciate belonging to that community.
- The intensity of the social relations that the individual maintains with other members of the community.

One can distinguish four types of community members,[2] as shown in Figure 5.4.

---

[2] Kozinets (1999). This pioneering article on online communities is still a work of reference for studies on consumer behaviour.

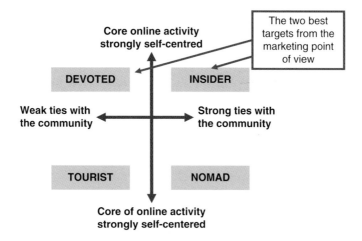

Figure 5.4   The Four Profiles of Members of a Community

Case Study: The Examples of Krug and Sephora

These stories are old by Internet years, or even brand existence, but they are still immensely inspiring. Every luxury brand should meditate on them to understand the potential of the Web for building client relationships.

Introducing the Krugists

In late 1998, Remy Krug, CEO of Champagne Krug, was invited for a cyber champagne tasting by the *Wine Spectator*. He said to one of the authors, 'It is my daughter's idea, but I don't think it's a good one. Champagne is meant to be shared!'

To his enormous surprise, hundreds of Krug fans logged on – with a bottle of Krug – sometimes alone, sometimes in a group, ready to welcome him, ready to share with him their knowledge and passion for the brand and its products. 'It was a unique experience', he said later.

The Web is full of emotions.

(continued)

(*Continued*)

Introducing the Sephora-coolics

Sephora opened its first American boutique in Soho in July 1998.

In December 1998, on the site of Alt Fashion, people asked: 'When will Sephora come to Minneapolis? I'm a Sephora-coolic!'

One invents new words only when one wishes to express something important: coining a new word shows the type of relationship people have with a brand or a seller.

The Web is full of emotions.

The Seven Rules of the Internet and Social Networks

Luxury brands wishing to harness the potential of the Internet and social networks should put these seven fundamental rules into practice.

Two-way

Rule 1: Internet and social networks are a space for dialogue, for conversations between a brand and its customers It takes two to hold a conversation. The Internet should be used to create a non-commercial dialogue with customers, on topics such as tips and advice, in forums and through other online services. This is one of the best ways to create a sense of belonging.

Example

The Huggies forum does not sell diapers. It gives free advice, offers a virtual assistant to help decorate a baby's room, offers counsel on how to manage contractions, how to massage a baby, and offers a space for reselling used baby items.

Rule 2: Accept a loss of control   Social media is based on mutual commitment. The brand should therefore accept reciprocity in exchanging information, share content with its customers, and accept criticism. In building a relationship with customers, brands should learn from case examples: 'That's what happened'/'This is how we solved this problem or how we did that'. This helps to build credibility.

Example

When they decided to revamp their image on the Internet, the World Economic Forum leaders in Davos posted photos and videos from their huge database on Flickr and YouTube. Some of them were misappropriated immediately – in particular by political opponents of some of the leaders represented, but this only helped to increase the credibility of the Forum.

Rule 3: Know your customers   This is a key point: most brands have created a segmentation of their customers based too often on demographics or sales indicators (and there are still some prestigious brands that consider customer segmentation as a tool reserved for mass market brands!). Best practices, however, recommend that such segmentation should be more multi-layered and take the level of commitment or investment of customers vis-à-vis the brand into account.

Example

Lego's customer base consists of five segments:

- Included households – all households likely to buy a Lego product.
- Active households – those who purchased a Lego product within the last 12 months.
- The connected community – those who actively connect to the brand by visiting their website or store (about half of active households). When an active household connects with the brand, the average expenditure increases threefold.

(continued)

(*Continued*)

- The 1:1 community – Lego Club members, adults registered as fans or as users of the online catalogue (about half of the connected community provide their personal data). When an active household becomes a 1:1, the average expenditure increases fivefold.
- The big users – partners of the Lego universe, these fans are also involved in the designing of new products, for example.

This shows that spending increases as consumers move up the pyramid – and the involvement of the brand is different in each segment.

This segmentation is even more productive when it is approached from the point of view of 'buyer personas': the brand creates standard profiles of its customers by identifying each one with the help of behavioural data. In it one finds, in addition to the usual demographic profile, their remarks about the brand and its category, what they feel, what they do, their expectations and desires, their consumption profile, their 'pain points', keywords that correspond to them.[3]

Rule 4: Measure, measure, measure Pure players on the Internet have developed this rule, which, surprisingly, is new to the industry: always measure the results of any action. One launches a project (a game, e-mail campaign, etc.) and can see rapidly whether it is working. The results can be measured (Google Analytics and Facebook Ads Manager provide tools for this purpose). If the project does not attain the expected goals, it is discontinued, or certain elements are modified (what digital marketers call *A/B Testing*): the subject title of the e-mail is changed, a button for an action is moved, etc.[4]

---

[3] Heinze et al. (2016). See also Chapter 11 in this book.

[4] A/B Testing is a procedure used in marketing that enables one to measure the impact of a modification of the version of a variable on the achieving of a given objective (click, validation, filling of a form, etc.). Strictly speaking, an A/B Test allows one to text two variations of the variable; an A/B/C Test, three versions, and so on. https://www.definitions-marketing.com/definition/a-b-test/

Most brands with an online business use management tools, such as, for example, *Net Promoter Scores* (NPS), that allow it to compute the promoters (e.g. brand supporters) as compared to detractors (those who have complaints about the brand). This is very important. Most brands only calculate the overall satisfaction rate and are pleased with rates above 85%. However, all studies show that for an indicator to be useful, it should measure both the approval rate *and* the disapproval rate, for an appraisal of both the rate of retention and the recommendations to be drawn: What is the level of customer loyalty and does it promote (or undermine) the brand among other customers?

Example

Lego uses NPS to measure the brand's capacity to promote differentiated referral rates. Four dimensions are taken into account: product experience (immediate purchase), online experience, in-store experience and customer service experience.

Rule 5: Form a dedicated digital team Method: the brand must form an efficient team internally with the ability to connect transversally between services and organisational 'silos'. One could even imagine the grouping together of all digital tasks (e-commerce, digital databases and digital marketing) instead of dividing them between marketing and communications (as in YNAP). Digital marketing itself requires multiple skills that consist not only of graphics (how to create beautiful images, superb videos, tell beautiful stories, etc.). It should also know how to:

- Identify customer segments and construct personas (Rule 3).
- Manage Facebook ads (and build the e-commerce site accordingly).
- Manage e-mailing campaigns according to customer segments.
- Carry out A/B testing.
- Analyse and measure all actions taken (Rule 4).
- Maintain a dialogue with clients.

Additionally, digital marketing needs a constant flux of content (images, videos, gifs, events, etc.) that has to be disseminated throughout all channels. As a consequence, luxury brands should create a Content Production Department (and not necessarily outsource it to agencies) that will be the hub of all the marketing strategy of the brand.

When it comes to anything that relates to the Internet, some basic rules should be observed:

- Respond swiftly.
- Join the conversation.
- Maintain the dynamism and interest of the channels.
- Expand the digital footprint.
- Create communication channels and prepare for any eventual crisis (which *will happen*).

This requires real investment on the part of the company. Employees should themselves be active in social networks; it is also essential to recruit a professional *community manager*. He or she will be an ambassador of the brand, clearly in charge of its image – especially during times of crisis.

Example

On Kenneth Cole's twitter account, a tweet, signed by the creator himself (or, at least, 'an authorised person') on 3 February 2011 read: 'Millions of protesters at #Cairo. Rumour has it that they learned that our new spring collection was available at http://bit.ly/KCairo-KC.'

This happened right in the middle of the Egyptian uprising. Tens of thousands of protesters rallied every day in Tahrir Square to demand a real democracy – and in the midst of these events, the American fashion brand was trying to appropriate the movement to promote its own message. This tweet spread like wildfire around the Internet, eliciting messages of sharp criticism as well as approval. The virtual world was suddenly divided: on one side, those who found the tweet in very bad taste, criticising the irresponsibility of the brand, and on the other, fans (especially American), who found the message amusing and reaffirmed their loyalty to the brand.

Kenneth Cole, after saying (rather half-heartedly) that he did not want to offend the Egyptians, finally published an apology (just as discreet) on Facebook.

Rule 6: Social networks by themselves do not sell A report from Knowledge Networks (2009) gave advertisers, marketers and researchers a clearer picture of the motivations and approaches of social media users (excluding bloggers) in the United States:

- 83% of Internet users (aged 13 to 54) spend time on social networks – 47% of them on a weekly basis.
- Less than 5% of regular users of these networks seek advice for taking decisions about their purchases.
- Only 16% of users say they are more likely to buy products from companies that communicate through these networks.

Rule 7: Luxury brands should have a cohesive view of their physical and digital businesses Social media should be an integral part of a global strategy to develop brand awareness, the image of the brand, customer relationships and, finally, to *sell*.

The Internet is not just about having an institutional website, an online store, a blog, a Twitter account, a Facebook page, a YouTube account, sending e-mails or other electronic messages. It consists of using it all in an integrated manner. All brand initiatives should be integrated, carry the seal of the brand, and be consistent.

Luxury brands need to realise that their 'digital playground' (to use Exane BNP Paribas's expression) will only grow and should be perceived as a whole (see Figure 5.5).

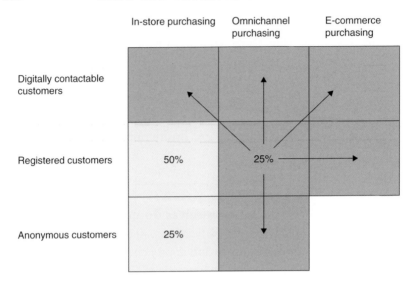

Figure 5.5   The Digital Playground

When we separate customers into three segments: 'digitally con-tactable' (customers who have given their e-mail addresses to the brand), 'registered' (customers who have given their first names, surnames and addresses to the brand) and 'anonymous' customers, we see that the rev-enues generated through the 'digital playground' – that is to say, all customers who at one time or another are in digital contact with the brand – represented 25% of sales in 2014 and will grow to 50% in 2020 (see Figure 5.6). Having an integrated view of its business activities is therefore essential for a luxury brand.

This leads us to a preliminary conclusion that is credible: today, for a brand, the notion of *integrating the various channels of distribution and communication* is crucial.

A McKinsey (2009) study, 'The Promises of Multi-Channel Retail-ing', reinforces this idea by recalling some essential facts and offering some ideas:

- *Fact*: In the United States, only 25% of department stores, 40% of retailers and 60% of fashion specialists regained their pre-crisis growth rates five years after the 2001 recession. No brand today can afford to wait that long.

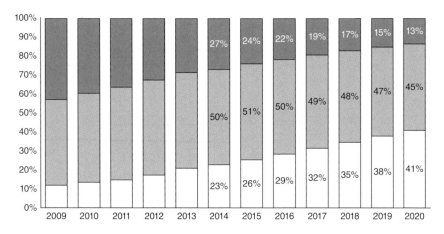

Figure 5.6 Percentage of Revenue from Customers that One Contacts by E-mail

Legend: (Dark grey) Anonymous customers; *(Light grey)* Known and registered customers; *(White)* Customers that can be contacted by e-mail. *Source:* ContactLab simulation (Exane BNP Paribas and ContactLab 2015a).

- *A fact that is too often ignored*: Consumers who buy through multiple distribution channels spend far more than those who use only one channel. The example of fashion is particularly enlightening: The ratios range from 1 to 5.
- *Why are so many brands not at the level?* Because they believe that the integration of distribution channels means duplicating the 'shop/magazine' concept on the Internet, or that creating an extract of the sales catalogue (which only reproduces what one finds in the store) and multiplying the availability of products will lead the consumer to buy more. This is a huge mistake: every channel is unique. Each one should correspond to a specific offer that complements the other channels, by the offer of services, available information and awareness of consumer expectations.

For brands, the future of the Internet is therefore based on a strategy led by the president (the question of accountability for such a strategy is clearly posed – but how many presidents of luxury brands are 'denizens' of the Web, an organisation in which distribution and communication are closely linked), and on the use of multiple channels, including mobile phones?

Case Study: When Will Brands Grasp the 'Social' Aspect of Social Networks?

Even though it is old by Internet years, this study is indicative of the attitude that brands often have towards social media.

In a 2010 study by A.T. Kearney (Singer, Mathews and Heggie 2010) of the top 50 global brands (according to Interbrand), 1,115 Facebook posts were analysed, with 60,750 responses from amongst the top 45 brands, representing a total of 70,016,541 fans.

The results were fascinating:

- Five of these brands were not present on Facebook.
- Seven – including Gucci and Louis Vuitton (they have made huge progress since then!) – only permitted dialogues initiated by the brand.
- Only one of them offered fans access to an open Facebook wall. The first 45 chose to restrict clients and fans to a (filtered) selection of institutional publications.

This means that these brands (including luxury brands) were using social media as a variation of traditional marketing – a unidirectional communication channel – which is totally irrelevant in the digital world.

But that was not all.

Eighty-nine percent of customers' messages on Facebook went unanswered – 'Gucci, for example, has not given any response in the past three months' (Singer, Mathews and Heggie 2010) – and only 11 brands answered more than one message!

Whenever brands did respond, only 15% of their responses invited the user to continue the dialogue. Which can be translated as: 'We recognise your presence, but, please, stop bothering us!' This is clearly not a conversation and has nothing to do with an enriching dialogue. This also meant that most brands did not really want to bond with their customers or learn from them. We are therefore very far from reaching the five points described above, and there is still a lot of room for improvement.

Once again, we notice not only the fear of a loss of control, but also something we could call 'marketing sluggishness': 71% of the messages published by companies are promotional – offering discount coupons, gifts and other benefits.

On the other hand, the 5% of messages that engaged in a real conversation between the company and the consumer were extremely instructive. They showed that there are three main techniques – all of them involving emotional links – that work:

- Invoking nostalgia via remembered products and brand history.
- Engaging in a conversation on the product, seeking consumer evaluation and their opinion on new colours, new fragrances, new products.
- Rallying around common causes.

Rethink the Brand's Internet Strategy

In Chapter 3 we described the five phases that luxury brands went through during the elaboration of their Internet strategies. One study (Wetpaint & Altimeter Group 2009) suggests separating it into four strategies, depending on the client relationship (top-down, or dialogue) and the strategy of the channel chosen by the brand (mono-channel or multi-channel), as illustrated in Figure 5.7. Two main factors therefore shape these strategies: the type of client relationship that the company wishes to build (Top-down? Dialogue?) and the choice of a channel strategy (Mono-channel? Multi-channel?).

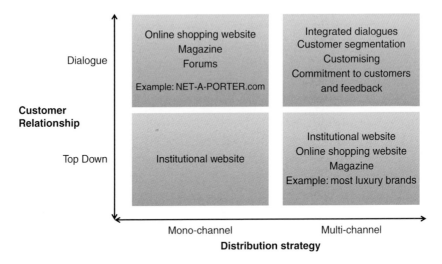

Figure 5.7   Client Strategy Matrix

Today, most luxury brands still implement multi-channel and top-down strategies. What the study shows is that the 'north-east' strategy (multi-channel plus dialogue – what today we would call omnichannel and customer experience), drawn from a profile with a high level of involvement, generates higher revenue growth (plus 18% vs only 10% for others), higher gross margins (15% vs a minor 3%) and higher net margins (4% vs negative margins) than all other strategies. The conclusion we draw is that while this strategy is difficult to implement – because it asks the brand to reinvent itself and rethink its organisation – it is the most rewarding economically. *All this argues for the establishment of a valid omnichannel strategy centred on customer experience.*

The study of Exane BNP Paribas is an argument in that direction. It finds that, on average:

- In 2014, 'digitally contactable' luxury customers spent 16% more in boutiques than 'store-registered' customers.
- Omnichannel customers spend 50% more over the year than customers who buy exclusively in 'boutiques'.

This brings us to our second important deduction: *luxury brands must first define and structure their customer relationship strategy, because it is the cornerstone of all Internet strategies.*

As the Exane BNP Paribas team forecasts in their outlook for 2020[5]:

We expect that luxury will be entirely different in 2020. We anticipate that:

- Luxury brands will get to know virtually all of their clients by name. Forty-five percent will be registered in their databases, and 41% will be contactable by e-mail. This will therefore represent almost 90% of clients.
- Separating the digital and the physical luxury will make no sense – the omnichannel will represent 80% of sales.
- Digital processing will define success or failure for luxury brands. "Digital Playground Sales" (sales to O2O clients – Offline to Online / Online to Offline) will represent 50% of sales, purely e-commerce sales (clients who purchase exclusively online) will double, even triple, and grow to 12–18% of sales.[6]

To recap:

- *The anonymous client is vanishing.* He accounts for no more than 10% of luxury goods sales in single-brand outlets. A well-organised brand knows its customers and has, at the least, their contact details, but very often their Internet addresses as well. It is up to the brand to define how it can optimise this tool.
- *Sales activities should be merged* (shops, shops-in-shops, travel retail and digital sales) with marketing activities (CRM, social media) to have an effective global omnichannel strategy.
- *The veritable levers of customer relationships* are the Internet messages intended for them, but also those that they receive from their friends or the posts that spread on social networks.
- *Letting the customers talk to each other,* letting them express themselves and share their impressions, is to accept losing control. But the brand should take care not to intervene, except, of course, if comments become extreme or unethical.

---

[5] See Chapter 7.
[6] Which leaves approximately 32 to 38% of sales to clients who buy exclusively in boutiques.

Chapter 6

Customer Identification and CRM

Your most dissatisfied customers are your biggest source of learning.

—Bill Gates[1]

The better one knows one's customers' tastes, the easier it is to persuade them. It is therefore important to know them as personally as possible. The more one can identify the overall profiles of the customers who visit one sales point or another, the better one can cater to their needs. For example, if Koreans visit a store very

---

[1] *Forbes*, 4 March 2014.

frequently, it would make sense, if possible, to have a vendor who speaks Korean. If a store has a young clientele, it is better to have a young sales staff. The brand should therefore have a database as comprehensive as possible.

This database is created together with the key performance indicators (KPIs) that each store should elaborate to ensure the smooth follow-up of operations. These are:

- The attraction rate: Number of passers-by who enter the shop, compared to the number of people who walk by. This indicator is important in a shopping centre, for example, and helps to determine whether the brand corresponds, more or less, to the clientele of the centre.
- The conversion rate: Number of customers who make purchases as against the number of customers entering the store.
- The number of customers that enter the boutique daily.
- The average ticket.
- It may also include: Turnover generated by fashion products and turnover from accessories.

In a properly managed boutique, the store manager could enter the number of passers-by (counted physically or using a camera), and the number of people entering the store, on a computer. Or the cashier or security guard, if the store has one, can be entrusted with this task. If not, they can be counted with the help of an indoor camera. Other data is available on the computer and the five KPIs listed above can be systematically displayed on the screen.

This, however, is only the basic data. What more information can one obtain about these customers? That is the subject we shall discuss in this chapter.

Here, we shall discuss how to organise and use a customer database. Luxury brands that sell a significant percentage of their production in their own boutiques or in stores they control have direct contact with their customers. They create well-organised and efficient databases from the outset. Some ten years ago, they recruited specialists, often from the hotel industry, to create them.

Managing the Customer Database

Customer records have always existed, and in the beginning, cashiers or store managers collected and entered information in large ledgers. That changed when cash registers were connected to a central computer and it was possible to update the purchase history of each customer daily and automatically.

Today, the major luxury brands have 'comprehensive' databases with lists ranging from five million to ten million customers. For example, a brand with 500 stores worldwide could have 10,000 individual buyers identified by store, of which a very large number (perhaps half) actually make only one purchase per year.

In their book published in 1997, that is, before the 'data revolution', Andrew Wileman and Michael Jary defined what they considered the 'customer database of a brand'.

In Table 6.1, we see that 21% of customers (3% divided by 14%) represent 68% of the turnover. The goal is therefore to know and understand these customers well and make them the main focus of promotional and advertising campaigns. One should also note that 71% are occasional customers (and most likely will make only one purchase) while generating 20% of the turnover. Brands have therefore to attain a twofold objective:

- Attract 'loyal' customers back to the store – especially at a time when loyalty to a particular brand is flagging.
- Constantly renew occasional customers (since they only buy once per year).

The value of a database depends on the quality of the information collected and organised: name and address, and if possible, date of birth (if the person presented an identity card or passport at the time of payment). If the date of birth is not known, the vendor could make a rough estimate (15–30, 30–45, 45–60, above 60 years) keeping in mind that it is difficult for Westerners to estimate the age of Asians, and probably vice versa.

Online boutiques also try to guess a customer's age from their name. There is a probability that a name corresponds to a particular age group. In France, for example, Kevin was a popular name for children born

Table 6.1   Targeting the Customer Base

	Percentage of the population (%)	Percentage of invoices (%)	Percentage of turnover (%)
Very faithful customers	1	30	40
Faithful customers (2nd group)	2	25	28
Sales customers	1	15	12
Occasional customers	10	30	20
Non-customers	86		
Total	100	100	100

Source: Based on data from Wileman and Jary (1997).

between 1988 and 1995. In any case, one can try to draw conclusions from an analysis of the products purchased.

Today the software available (for instance MailChimp for e-mailing) have algorithms to estimate the age of consumers. But to be effective, a database should be organised according to purchasing behaviour criteria.

Marketing Data

Basic Marketing Data

Are the Fashion Products Purchased 'Classic' or 'Trendy'?   To use this information, the software only has to identify the products that are the 'trendiest' and the most 'classic'. The database will then automatically assign a 'classic' or 'trendy' profile to the customer. When a customer enters a store, one would imagine that the vendor will try to determine to which category they belong by the way they are dressed, but exact statistical information can be useful for marketing teams that would be able to create catalogues specially tailored to these profiles and sent to targeted clients.

Purchases by Men and Purchases by Women   These findings based on the type of purchases seem to match the customer's gender. Women usually buy women's fashion products for themselves and men follow the same behaviour pattern.

But some women may buy products, mainly gifts, from an essentially male brand. Some male customers, on the contrary, may purchase products almost exclusively for gifts. This differentiation is not anodyne, and offers clues for targeted promotional campaigns.

It may also be important to know if the person buying a gift comes to the store with the receiver of the gift or buys it on their own.

Various Categories of Purchases Depending on the range of products sold, it may be useful to distinguish, for example, between customers who only buy clothes and others who only buy accessories.

This criterion could even help to identify the customer's nationality. For example, Japanese customers may prefer the women's ready-to-wear collection of a brand and almost never buy its accessories. On the other hand, Germans or Russians shop only for accessories. One can easily imagine how this precise and quantified information could be useful for marketing teams, which could then adapt advertising campaigns or promotional drives accordingly.

Customers Who Purchase Current Collections or During Sales Some customers only buy from the new collections and never buy during sales. Others, on the contrary, almost always buy during the sales. It is therefore evident that information about the boutique's activities should be sent to each category of customer on different dates. At first glance, customers who buy during sales may seem to be of little interest and unprofitable, but in fact, they also serve a purpose. This is a group of customers that is critical for the business. For example, they could be invited to 'private sales' before the sales open in the stores.

And customers buying at the beginning of the season could be invited to a preview of the collection a few days before it goes to the stores.

Of course, most customers probably buy both at the beginning of the season and during sales. But it can be useful to determine whether their purchases at normal prices represent 75%, 50% or 25% of the total.

Customer Data at the Sales Outlet

Purchase Amount over a Given Period This criterion is, of course, a complement to that of the average invoice and the frequency of purchase. The given figure could be compared to the turnover of the boutique, enabling the manager to determine, for example, that the top 50 customers represent 15% of this amount.

We will discuss the commercial utility of the database later on, but knowing this purchase amount encourages vendors to better recognise and get to know these 50 customers.

One would think the most logical purchasing calculation period would be yearly, which would, of course, have the advantage of corresponding directly to the financial year of the company. However, to be able to observe the evolution of average invoice or purchasing frequency, fashion companies often use a calculation period of 2 years.

Purchasing Frequency Three criteria – average invoice, total purchase over the year, and purchasing frequency– complement each other. One needs only two of these criteria to obtain the third one. However, purchasing frequency is very important for estimating the date of the next visit of a customer who has just left the boutique.

This criterion provides valuable insight regarding the number of visits to the boutique per year (or rather, the number of purchases per year). This is another manner in which vendors could differentiate the customers in front of them.

These customers can be grouped according to the average time gap between two visits (or visits to two boutiques) of the brand:

- Between 1 and 45 days
- Between 46 and 90 days
- Between 91 and 180 days
- Between 181 and 365 days
- Between 366 and 730 days

This criterion also helps to differentiate between customers whose visits to the boutique have increased and those that have decreased. In both cases, tailored promotional campaigns can be implemented.

The frequency of purchase will, of course, depend on the category: the purchase of skin care products or make-up will be much more frequent than the purchase of perfumes, for example.

Time Gap Between Purchases   At first glance, this criterion seems to overlap purchasing frequency. For example, some buyers buy every 45 or 90 days. Subtracting the number of days since the last purchase from the frequency of purchase gives the number of customers whose visits are overdue. If it shows they are late by 20, 45 or 90 days, would it not be worthwhile to call them or send them a short personal note?

In the case of supermarkets, 15-day gaps between visits may be normal. In the case of a fashion store, if there is a delay of more than 180 days, that is to say, spanning a whole collection, does that mean that the last collection did not please the customers?

In all cases, this criterion can give vendors a considerable advantage and help them maintain permanent contact with their best customers, forgetting no one.

Vendor Performance Data

Number of Articles per Invoice   This is a criterion that is somewhat of an 'obsession' among store managers. They look at the criterion for each vendor to establish a list of the best performers. This criterion can also be crosschecked against the size of the store. The bigger it is, the better the opportunity to present the entire range, hence, a higher possibility of multiple purchases.

A vendor who averages 1.4 items per invoice is undoubtedly more convincing and more imaginative than one who has an average of 1.1. But we could also look only at the average invoice, which is a different concept, and probably in a slightly different way of looking at it.

To come back to the consumer, who is the *raison d'être* of this database, the customer who buys two or three articles per visit is certainly someone who is important and who deserves to be encouraged.

Average Invoice   The average invoice is a criterion that one focuses on as soon as a provisional budget is drawn up for a new store: the number of customers expected given the population in the catchment area, and its average income level. The average invoice criterion helps to make a projection of the turnover expected and to weigh it against fixed costs such as rent and salaries. The calculation of the break-even point becomes easier: this is the sum of the fixed costs for a given period, which should be equal to the gross profit margin in the corresponding turnover period. This turnover break-even point is then divided by the average invoice to obtain the number of customers needed per month.

Is this number of customers budgeted per month realistic, given the brand's experience in its recent establishments, its knowledge of the catchment area and the exact location of the store?

How Can One Recognise a Client?

The First Visit

When a customer enters the store for the first time, or if one does not recollect them, the customer should be 'sized up' very discreetly. Firstly, their age and standard of living, which is sometimes revealed by clothing, jewellery, watches, and bags, in the case of a woman. However, one should be cautious, because appearances can sometimes be misleading. One may recall, for example, what happened to Ms Oprah Winfrey, the great American celebrity and journalist who was not allowed to enter Hermès on a Saturday night at closing time. The security officers, who did not recognise her, judged her on the basis of her ripped jeans and somewhat 'grungy' look.

Jewellery is not always a foolproof indicator. A very old expensive watch is not the same as a brand-new Rolex or, in another situation, a Swatch. A woman who carries a Hermès bag probably also owns a bag from Longchamp or another brand, but the fact that she carries sometimes one and sometimes the other is not unambiguous either.

Similarly, a man can often be recognised by his tie, if he wears one. The colours preferred by tie wearers can differ according to nationalities. North Americans often prefer bright colours while Europeans are more conventional in their tastes.

Nothing is foolproof, of course, and without rushing to conclusions, vendors should be trained in observation and eye for detail.

Today, observation can be reinforced by software. For example, when customers come to a store together, an app can listen to the language they speak with each other and link it to the language and nationality of clients who had come, for example, the previous week. If one notices that many Chinese or Ukrainians visit the store, it would be advantageous if a vendor who spoke their language were part of the sales team. Following the same logic, when a brand has several stores in Paris or Hong Kong, for example, vendors speaking the language of the country should be appointed in the locations where they are mostly needed.

This attentive listening could also serve another purpose. Positive or negative remarks on the products, preferred colours and colours actually purchased, or opinions on prices can be recorded, of course anonymously, and then synthesised or compared to those of the previous year.

And then, when he decides to buy, the customer approaches the cashier. If he does not pay in cash (so with a cheque or a credit card), his name is displayed. All that remains is to politely ask him for his details, and in almost all cases clients are willing to provide them.

Some stores propose store cards with attractive offers. Employees ask their customers to fill in the details or fill them out themselves. Others prefer that the details be filled in by the cashier directly on the computer. This is also the perfect moment to ask for a phone number and e-mail address.

In the employee evaluation criteria, some brands use a 'capture rate' or a 'digital accuracy' rate. The latter refers to the percentage of customers in a store whose complete addresses the employee has obtained. The practice is becoming more and more formalised.

When the Client Returns to the Store

What changes everything in the feeling of the relationship between a brand and its customers is when they are recognised, and addressed by name, if possible, when they visit the store a second time.

Vendors have always taken pains to remember the names of their customers. They have made a habit of noting them down in a little note-book,[2] maybe even with a description of a (positive) physical trait which serves as a practical cue card. They also note down anecdotes that can serve as conversation starters in the future. The idea is, of course, to

---

[2] See our explanation on *Clienteling* in Chapter 10.

show the customers that they are appreciated and that you are sincerely interested in them.

Today, facial recognition software is used in countries where it is permitted. This helps to augment the number of cases where the client is recognised and received as someone important.[3] Used with tact and discretion, this system greatly improves the welcoming quality of a boutique.

In fact, if the customer could be identified when they enter the shop using the location service of their mobile phone, this would be even easier. Their contact information and, if possible, purchase history with regard to the brand would be immediately available. Technically, it is possible to access this information, and when 'Google glasses' existed, the information could have been displayed on the small screen of the vendor's glasses. Technically, this information can be accessed, but the laws of each country will have to decide if this system respects privacy regulations.

It is important to understand that recognising a customer when they enter a store is a great advantage. The vendor is then able to advise them, having in mind previous purchases and what they reveal of the customer's tastes.

This information should be available instantly. If it can be accessed only when the customer is paying with a cheque or credit card, it is not very useful.

What is certain is that between face recognition software, identification at the entrance of a store using the geolocation app of a mobile phone, and as a last resort, identification at checkout, obtaining complete information about regular customers will become more and more common.

What is also certain is that being greeted by name when entering a shop or a restaurant is definitely a gratifying experience: 'Good evening, M/Ms So-and-so!' It is a little easier in restaurants because people have to give their names when booking a table. Before dinnertime, the floor manager could look at the names of those who have booked, and re-verify their preferences and special requirements, making the

---

[3] Some companies offer software that will use 11 points to define one's face and will guarantee that the actual picture of the customer is not stored in the database of the brand.

welcome even more cordial and personal. It is much more challenging in a store. Good vendors may remember the names of a hundred or maybe two hundred of their best customers. For the others who get the information only at the checkout counter, a good database would highlight some details that they could comment on while the customer is being escorted to the door. These parting words should not be the same for each visit, and would serve to show the customers that they will always be welcome and appreciated.

Using the Customer Database

Evidently, these customer identification practices are unique to physical stores. On the e-commerce sites, customers are led to identify themselves with their address (for shipping) and e-mail (to create the account), but the use of specific external software allows to qualify the base even better.

Once the database has been created – note that it takes more than two years to collect reliable data – one has to ensure that everyone in the company adopts it. If not, those concerned will lose interest and will not take pains to update it. Also, one should demonstrate to managers and staff how the database could benefit them in their day-to-day work.

Finalising and Verification

A database is only useful if it is accurate and if it is regularly updated. One can assume that vendors will make every effort to get correct and complete addresses. In fact, they are often encouraged by the 'capture rate' target mentioned above. However, they might sometimes be tempted to enter wrong phone numbers to prevent other vendors of the same or other stores of the brand from 'poaching' their best customers and convincing them to switch over to them instead. Therefore, random verification of the data provided should be carried out to evaluate the accuracy of data obtained from one store or another.

However, as one knows, updating data is the biggest hurdle. For vendors to make the effort to update the database, one should impress on them how useful it is in their regular work.

Setting Up the Database   The simplest and most obvious use of this database is by the marketing team. It can analyse the purchases of different types of customers and answer questions such as:

- Are the important buyers more 'trendy' or 'classic'?
- What makes some customers buy fashion products rather than accessories? What do we know about them and where do they come from? The same question would apply to those who mainly purchase accessories.
- How do we create around ten customer profiles to whom special editions of catalogues should be sent?
- How does one approach a customer who has this or that purchasing behaviour?
- How does one approach customers who are apparently buying products far from their home base?

To motivate the sales staff of the store, they should also have access to a terminal with all the available data: the percentage of buyers (or turnover) who come from the vicinity of the boutique; the percentage of buyers from another city; the percentage of foreigners; a list of customers expected in the month, their visiting frequencies, and dates of previous visits; average invoice by store and by vendor; the number of products purchased per invoice, etc.

Improving Customer Experience According to Their Potential

The customer database provides important information. It describes the buying habits of each group of customers. As an example, for a luxury brand with a turnover of €700 million and a customer database of 1.2 million, one finds the figures as shown in Table 6.2 (based on confidential data gathered by the authors).

What is striking here is that 5,000 customers generate 10% of the brand's turnover. These deserve special attention and should be treated with care and consideration. However, what can be quite obvious at the level of a group is more complicated when applied to a single sales point. Let us assume the brand we are describing has 250 stores around the world. Some stores will have around twenty customers of this category whom they know well and they recognise. Other stores may have

Table 6.2 Example of Consumer Groups for a Brand with a Turnover of €700 Million per Year

	Percentage of total sales (%)	Percentage cumulated (%)	Average yearly purchases
First 1,000 clients	4	4	€28,000
From 1,000 to 5,000	6	10	€10,500
From 5,001 to 10,000	4	14	€5,600
From 10,001 to 50,000	10	24	€1,750
From 50,001 to 100,000	6	30	€700
More than 100,000	70	100	*

*This figure is not available because it includes many customers whose addresses are not known.

only three or four, and it would be difficult to organise special campaigns for them. Each shop manager could, of course, send a bouquet of flowers with a handwritten card to each customer on their birthday, but appreciation can be shown in other ways too.

Some luxury brands invite their best clients to their fashion shows. However, the programme should be well organised and the rules well established from the outset, because if they are invited once, they might expect an invitation every season.

As for the top 100,000 customers, as indicated in Table 6.3, they could be invited to the boutiques nearest to them for cocktails and a preview of the collection, and if they have a 'sales' profile, to special discounts prior to the sales season.

It is essential to organise a comprehensive follow-up programme for the principal customers, firstly at the level of the brand, then in each country. Each sales outlet should organise events that will help to strengthen ties with its main customers. When store managers organise these events correctly, they would have to rely less on facial recognition at the entrance of the store because they will know their main clients and would have to use facial recognition only as a form of 'catching-up' session.

Table 6.3 Concentration of the Main Customers

First 100 customers	4% of turnover
First 10,000 customers	14% of turnover
First 100,000 customers	30% of turnover

To conclude, we could describe what one calls the 'paradox of efficiency'. One might think that non-customers are the best targets to increase sales. This would be true if half of them could be persuaded to make a purchase once a year. The turnover would multiply by two or three. Occasional customers could also be persuaded to purchase more often, but what is really easier and more effective in the short term is to persuade regular customers to come back once more the following year.

However, as we said at the beginning of this chapter and in the introduction to this book, the behaviour of luxury consumers is changing and loyalty to a brand is less and less assured. Brands are therefore faced with the need to renew their customer base – and therefore to put in place communication strategies making the *drive to store* a key objective.

To recap:

- *It was observed* that clients were generally more willing to share their contact information if they felt they were part of a respected and privileged group.
- *What is certain* is that the quality of data collected depends largely on the motivation of the sales teams. But the availability and empathy of the team responsible for ensuring the quality of this database and 'selling' it internally is also crucial.
- *Once the database is created*, it should serve its purpose and prove its effectiveness. Else, little by little, the data becomes outdated and unreliable, quickly turning useless. The 'capture' rate reminds sales staff that it is essential to update data regularly. This capture rate, which is lower, of course, in boutiques visited mainly by tourists, should be regularly analysed and verified by the teams.
- *Once the system is set in motion*, it obliges sales staff and marketing managers to be creative with regard to the 'gifts' that one should know how to offer, and in the 'personalising' proposed. Customers will then feel that they are important for the brand and that they are being treated with high regard and consideration.

Chapter 7

The Challenges of Offline and Online Integration

I believe that online sales and offline sales will continue to complement and reinforce each other to give our customers a better comprehensive approach.

−François-Henri Pinault[1]

E xane BNP Paribas, in one of their studies (Exane BNP Paribas and ContactLab 2015a), introduced the notion of the 'digital playground' of luxury brands. This breaks with the silo vision

---

[1] *Vogue France*, 25 November 2017.

of compartmentalised sales channels based on single points of sale (in a boutique or e-commerce site) and adopts a client-centred vision – more precisely on the customer experience. This is the perspective adopted in this book and one we introduced in Chapter 4. This 'digital playground' (see Figure 5.5) is only expanding, and the forecasts for 2020 made by Exane BNP Paribas are significant:

- Sales from the 'digital playground' (the total of online and offline sales resulting from online searches – 'Research Online Purchase Offline' of ROPO) will increase up to 51% (compared to 27% in 2014). This is a radical change for luxury brands.
- O2O customers spend 60% more over the year than shop-only customers (and this number is increasing year after year) *and* they are buying more and more online: the O2O circuit therefore develops global sales.
- Luxury brands are able to identify 90% of their boutique customers either in digital form (e-mail) or in the form of a comprehensive data file (registered customers). In 2014 they already represented 73% of the customer base.

An extensive study done in Great Britain and Spain (Frasquet and Miquel 2017) also shows that omnichannel integration (or O2O) increases customer satisfaction, which in turn has an effect on loyalty – both in the online circuits and offline circuits. The authors also point out that there is no direct connection between online loyalty and offline loyalty – which means one has to double one's efforts to build customer loyalty.

Also, a recent McKinsey study (see Figure 7.1) shows that during the customer journey leading to a purchase, the increase of contact points is as much online as offline (McKinsey 2018). Whatever the country studied, there is a balance between online and offline contact points – which invalidates apocalyptic predictions proclaiming the disappearance of the brick-and-mortar stores and shows that the two channels complement each other. We also note that the customer journeys tend to grow longer: between 2014 and 2016 they increase by two units. The final purchase decision is even further away.

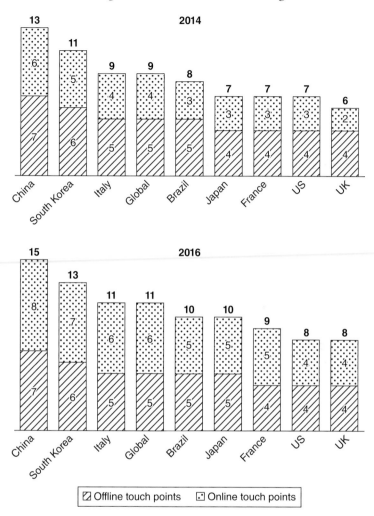

Figure 7.1 Average of the Number of Contacts Online and Offline Before Purchase
Source: Adapted from McKinsey (2018).

Similarly, when we look at Chinese consumers who, we are often told, only buy online, we not only find a perfect balance in the number of contact points between offline and online, but their customer journeys are about twice as long as Western customers. Another study

(WalktheChat 2018) shows that 64% of Chinese 20/30-year-olds prefer to buy luxury goods in boutiques.

These projections lay the groundwork for luxury brands but have to be 'operationalised'. We see two major operational challenges for brands:

- Challenge 1: Integrating the digital and the physical. Organisations are traditionally structured with a distinction between three separate divisions: retail (boutiques), e-commerce (both integrated into the sales department), and social media (integrated into the marketing department). At least two of these walls will have to be demolished: the one separating sales and marketing and the one separating boutiques and e-commerce.
- Challenge 2: Making global customer databases available. In fact, being able to identify 90% of its customers says nothing about the ability of a brand to track them and having tools to analyse their sales at its disposal. Most brands have regional databases but they are not interconnected.

To better understand how to respond to these challenges we will consider two key subjects: criteria for integration between offline and online, and global customer tracking.

What Are the Criteria for Offline/Online Integration?

As Exane BNP Paribas states:

Few brands have achieved the holy grail of physical and digital integration. (2018a, p. 155)

This conclusion is based on an analysis that is currently the most detailed and exhaustive available[2] on the digital practices of luxury brands. We synthetise the essential elements here (see Table 7.1):

Eighty-five criteria grouped into seven categories shed light on both the e-commerce strategy and the digital experience of the customers of

---

[2] Just like all the remarkable studies that this team carried out on the luxury industry for several years.

Table 7.1   O2O Integration Criteria

AXES	CATEGORIES	CRITERIA
STRATEGIC REACH (22 parameters)	1. E-commerce strategic reach	1. Online geographic coverage 2. Online product range
	2. 'Made in' explained 3. Customer engagement strategy	3. 'Made in' explained 4. Number of languages
		5. Email reach
	4. Website experience	6. Visualisation of products 7. Product presentation 8. Product selection support 9. Basic customer service 10. Personal services
DIGITAL CUSTOMER EXPERIENCE (63 parameters)	5. E-commerce experience	11. Online shopping 12. Delivery
	6. Cross-channel experience	13. Store locator 14. Cross-channel services
	7. Customer engagement experience	15. Email proficiency 16. Share 17. Apps

Source: Based on data from Exane BNP Paribas and ContactLab (2016b).

34 luxury brands.[3] The potential of each criterion is rated on a scale of 100, and the brands are attributed scores on the basis of their achievements. They may thus achieve only 60% or 50% of their total attainable potential.

Overall, e-commerce sites are efficient when it comes to their visuals, sales, supply, languages available and basic services (potential achieved is above 65%). In presentation of products, selection of products,

---

[3] For some criteria, the analyses are global; for others they only pertain to the US market.

identification of boutiques and sales assistance the scores are average (50% to 65% of potential).

It is of interest to identify the criteria in which brands show the widest margins for progress in 2018 – that is, where they globally attain less than 50% of their full potential.[4]

- The two criteria that show the poorest results (below 45% of potential) are, as one might expect, 'personal services' and 'omnichannel services'. Brands have a poor grasp of online services (the various kinds of assistance: chats, telephone, e-mail, making appointments, personalisation of the offers) such as O2O services (customer location, maps, opening hours of boutiques), e-mailing a boutique, contact in the boutique. Delivery services are also wanting with only 46% of potential attained (although it is one of the key elements in customer expectations today).

Example

One brand that has integrated this O2O dimension is Audemars Piguet with its 'Click to Try' feature: when customers are on the brand's website[5] and find a product that interests them, they can click on it and make a direct appointment with the nearest outlet to try on the watch.

- Brand offers are mediocre (57%) when it comes to e-mail relationship strategy: a separate study (Exane BNP Paribas 2016a) shows that luxury brands do not really know how to use this indispensable tool in a customer relationship. Much progress has to be made (the authors call them 'primitive practices') in terms of e-mail structuring, customer acquisition, editorial planning and sharing (on social media, with friends).

---

[4] It should be noted, however, that significant progress has been made since 2016, the date of the first study.

[5] Audemarspiguet.com

- Only 51% indicate where their products are made – there is no mention of 'Made in … ': they lose a real competitive advantage unless this 'forgetfulness' is proof that many luxury products are not manufactured in the country of origin of the brand (which would be surprising for brands like Hermès, Chanel or Cartier who never mention it either).
- Only 37% have their own apps that help to increase the customer experience when they are away from the website (and some do not always have apps that can be used on both iPhone and Android!).

The comparison of the results of all 34 brands shows, however, that a new dynamic has been rolled out by some brands:

- Six brands dominate the ranking with honourable results in most criteria: Burberry, Gucci, Valentino, Louis Vuitton, Fendi and Cartier.
- Eight brands have succeeded in improving their O2O customer experience and their strategic scope ratings (customer relationship development, highlighting of 'Made in … ', building an e-commerce strategy) over the period 2016–2018: Fendi, Michael Kors, Bulgari, Prada, Ferragamo, Celine, Bottega Veneta and Cartier.

So, we still have the remaining 22 brands whose competitive position in terms of O2O integration leave much to be desired.

Global Tracking of Customers (Especially Chinese)

Example

Imagine it is 2014, we are in a boutique on the Avenue Montaigne in Paris. A group of Chinese managers and executives (students of a renowned Executive MBA) was offered a visit to the brand's couture salons and boutique and once the tour was over they rushed to buy its products. To our surprise, no one was collecting customer information. A floor manager answers our question with: 'They are tourists … ', and pressed

(continued)

(*Continued*)

to answer, he admits, 'We do not share a common customer database with China'.

Fast forward to 2016. We are speaking in front of all the management teams of a luxury beauty brand on the question of Chinese customers – all the countries are represented. The audience is extremely attentive but someone blurts out: 'Do you know that we have 21 subsidiaries and therefore 21 different databases that are not interconnected and probably not interconnectible?'

These are just two examples amongst several that point to the blind-spot of many global brands: the lack of a single customer information system to track all their purchases and all their relationships with them.

The case of Chinese luxury customers is revealing in this respect. In 2017, they accounted for 32% of 'personal luxury goods' (D'Arpizio and Levato 2018) sales, but only 8% of these goods were bought in China! Where do they buy them? In Europe, Hong Kong or Macau (even if these destinations are losing steam), Japan and Korea (destinations developing strongly). The Chinese customer therefore travels a great deal.

But we must go well beyond the traditional sense of a 'geographical' trip: the customer (Chinese) is also an O2O voyager, travelling from the physical to the digital, constantly searching for the best prices or products not available locally. In Russia in 2014, the sharp fall of the rouble (it lost 20% of its value on 16 December) was not followed by luxury brands, which did not immediately readjust their prices in Russia. From the very next day planeloads of Chinese – travellers and 'daigu'[6] – landed in Moscow and Saint Petersburg and cleaned out the luxury brand boutiques. Chinese customers are masters in the use of the Internet to track price changes and take advantage of the best deals. This 'voyager' therefore travels from one country to another,

---

[6] Organised luxury buyers who buy products in countries where the high price difference allows them to resell them with a large profit margin on the parallel market (also the Internet).

from one point of sale to another, from the physical to the digital. No luxury brand can ignore this trend and all of them should track it.

Let us follow these travellers on their 'travels':

Geographical Journey

The most recent figures indicate that only 120 million Chinese have a passport – which represents 8.7% of the total population – but according to the CEO of Ctrip this number should reach 240 million by 2020.[7]

Their mode of travelling is changing and these changes will structure their way of buying luxury goods in the coming years. The first factor is the emergence of young travellers (under 35), more educated, with significant means and who travel alone. These travellers, like the young Chinese generation, have made their mobile phone the nerve centre of their lives. They communicate with their friends, they buy the basics, they find all the information they need. The role of their networks (friends and family) should not be underestimated. Their choices are dictated by the recommendations they receive through their networks, whether in the form of evaluations found on sites like Ctrip or Meituan-Dianping or in the form of referrals from their WeChat Moments.

This has an immediate effect on luxury brands. It is crucial to build a long-term relationship with these new travellers since they control significant referral networks. To be able to do so, it is essential to have a global database to follow them in their travels and track their domestic and international purchases.

The same travellers seek experiences above all: purchasing choices have shifted from personal items (clothing, jewellery, watches, cosmetics, etc.) to holiday resorts, spas, cruises, gastronomy. In this aspect, they follow in the footsteps of those luxury consumers who have shifted their preferences to experiences and experience products as shown in Figure 7.2 (D'Arpizio and Levato 2018): travel, food, wine and spirits or cars.

---

[7] https://jingtravel.com/number-of-potetial-chinese-outbound-tourists-double-by-2020/

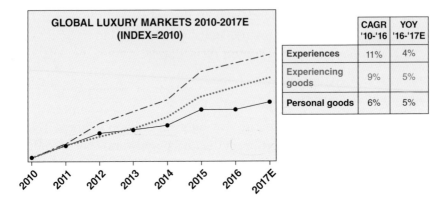

	CAGR '10-'16	YOY '16-'17E
Experiences	11%	4%
Experiencing goods	9%	5%
Personal goods	6%	5%

Figure 7.2 Progression of 'Experiences', 'Experiencing Goods' and 'Personal Goods' Between 2010 and 2017
Source: Adapted from D'Arpizio and Levato (2018).
Note: 'Experiences' include hotel stays, cruises and restaurants. 'Experience products' include cars, wines and spirits, private planes and art objects. 'Personal items' include all other luxury goods.

Virtual Journeys and Customer Journeys

Chinese luxury consumers today have the most complex consumer profiles imaginable. They will buy at boutique prices and, at the same time, look for bargains by flitting from one sales point to another, both offline and online. This complexity in customer journeys will only increase as time goes on, and will progressively include all luxury customers.

In order to better understand this radically new paradigm that luxury brands have to deal with, we propose to start by categorising likely points of sale – i.e., wherever a customer (Chinese or not) of luxury goods is able to access luxury products. We rapidly see that the proliferation of offers (and we are not considering here new offers where a customer can buy second-hand products or rent luxury goods) is a problem for the brand. In reality, many of these sales outlets are not under its control. We therefore have to try and categorise them to understand them better. For this, two dimensions should be recognised, both of which have to do with the notion of control:

- A first distinction concerns the level of control exercised by the brand: some sales points are owned by the brand, others are controlled by the brand, others are fully controlled by third parties.

- The second distinction relates to prices: sales at 'full' price, sales with discounts on certain products, sales with systematic rebates. The brand's desire to control price levels cannot be satisfied everywhere – particularly on the e-commerce sites where the entire parallel market operates. The lack of discipline of their wholesale partners is accentuated by the digital medium *and* the brands themselves, which seem to be sawing off the branch on which they sit. As Exane's analysts say: 'A brand that sells at higher prices in China than in Europe or the USA, but then gives Chinese consumers the opportunity to buy at European or American prices from its websites in Europe or the USA is obviously going to have to deal with several problems' (Exane BNP Paribas 2016b).

Figure 7.3 shows the distribution of these sales points. One notes, *de facto*, the proliferation of sales channels that are available to all luxury consumers, Chinese or not – for instance, Yoox, NET-A-PORTER and Farfetch, which we mentioned earlier.

We can see that the rise of digital sales is accompanied by a multiplication of offers that benefit customers and a complexifying of the landscape that brands find difficult to control. The control of

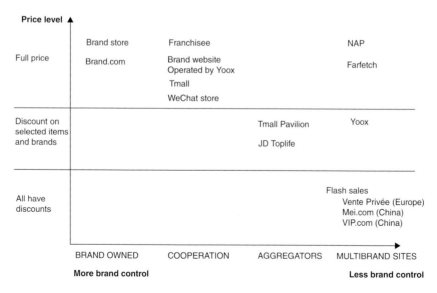

Figure 7.3 Mapping of Luxury Distribution Channels
Source: Adapted from Bain & Co. (2017).

distribution – which is essential for luxury brands in order to achieve their 'business model' and their profitability – is therefore undermined by the many new operators who only benefit customers. Some brands may thus fear a form of trivialisation.

Given these facts, brands have to solve a seemingly insoluble quandary: How does one 'track' a customer who moves from a point of sale controlled by the brand to a point of sale of a third-party partner to an 'uncontrolled' point of sale? The answer lies maybe in the forming of concrete partnerships with the new big players in the sector: YNAP and Farfetch in the West, Alibaba and JD in China. (With regard to China, the reluctance of luxury brands to sell through Alibaba or JD was partly lifted when they created their 'upscale/luxury' Tmall Luxury Pavilion[8] and JD Toplife.[9]) All of a sudden, Alibaba and JD, long ostracised by luxury brands (especially Alibaba for not having wanted to strongly combat counterfeiting), are set to play a crucial role in the Chinese market.

The complexifying of the retail landscape is therefore evident. To the traditional brick-and-mortar sales outlets mentioned in Part I (shops, department stores, travel retail, etc.) have been added a multitude of online sales points. This being so, we believe that luxury brands will have to respond to three new imperatives:

- *Imperative 1: having a single information system* enabling it to track a customer. All global companies are currently faced with this challenge. It is interesting to note that Alibaba (a pure player, if ever there was one) only realised this in 2017. It has set in place the Uni-ID, a unique identification system covering all their customers, whether they are from Tmall or Taobao (e-commerce), Alipay (mobile payment), Didi (taxis) or any other planet in the Alibaba galaxy (such as insurance). All data on the purchasing behaviour of all their customers is now therefore available – and analysed.
- *Imperative 2: Move from a CAPEX ('capital expenditure') logic to an OPEX ('operating expenses') logic.* The slowing down in opening

---

[8] Where one finds about fifty brands, including Burberry, Maserati, Zenith, Guerlain, Hennessy, La Perla, La Mer, Rimowa and Tag Heuer.
[9] Where one finds Fendi, Rimowa, Saint Laurent, Emporio Armani, Tod's, Mulberry, Oscar de la Renta, Alexander McQueen, among others.

directly operated boutiques that one noted among all brands – and hence for a lower CAPEX – has made way for new (operational) investments:

- Brands should invest in the renovation of all existing stores (and therefore avail of new approaches to store maintenance). In fact, maintenance costs could represent 5% of sales under normal circumstances and attain 15% of sales during renovation.
- Set up global information systems, recruit the required talent in digital marketing and global brand management,[10] the elaboration of customer experiences – all of this will increase a brand's operational costs.

- *Imperative 3: Find solutions for price discrepancies that are incompatible with the positioning of the brand.* When one analyses the status of luxury brands according to two aspects – the average discount at which the products are sold and the percentage of products found on the Internet in the 'systematic discounts' channel – we see that many brands are in bad shape (Exane BNP Paribas 2018b):

  - Michael Kors, Stella McCartney, Christopher Kane, Marc Jacobs, Hogan and Brunello Cuccinelli, and Armani are selling at discount prices (applying both criteria). Their situation is therefore critical – at the risk of trivialisation and loss of status.
  - Many brands manage to control their discount sales but not their availability in the 'off price' circuits: Versace, Dolce & Gabbana, Emilio Pucci, Emporio Armani, Valentino. One can justifiably ask questions about the sourcing of the products of these brands that one extensively finds in the parallel market.
  - Ralph Lauren is pretty much the only brand that organises its own discount sales, but this is part of its business model where the (many) factory outlets are part of the channels controlled by the brand.

Controlling the prices in a global market where the number of online distribution channels is growing becomes the proof of the know-how of a luxury brand.

---

[10] Without taking into account other creative talents – in supply-chain management, sales, etc. – as the analysis of Exane BNP Paribas (2017) shows.

To recap:

- *Omnichannel integration* enhances customer satisfaction and increases brand loyalty, something that one finds both in stores and on the Web.
- *Online and offline customer data need to be connected*, but one also needs to know how to interconnect the data of all the brand's international subsidiaries.
- *Control of distribution* is becoming increasingly difficult because certain services of the company, usually external services providers and unfamiliar *stakeholders* or integrators, have to be federated.
- *This need to integrate all that is online and offline* is not limited to personal luxury products; it also extends to customer experiences and products experience.

Chapter 8

Logistics Adapted to a Digital Culture

The limit between order and disorder lies in coordination.

—Sun Tzu[1]

W hat strikes one the most about digital innovations are the new services they offer to customers. When Nordstrom opened its first East Coast store in New York in September 2018, it provided its customers with two new services:

- If a customer in New York wished to buy a tie, or a suitcase, in the middle of the night, for example at 3 a.m., all they had to do was choose it and pay for it online, then go to the new department

---

[1] *Thirty Six Stratagems of War,* Chapter 5, Verse 4.

store on 57th Street, where a Nordstrom employee would be waiting outside the door with the item they had just bought.

- If another customer bought a pair of shoes the previous day and they were not happy with them, the customer could also bring the shoes back at any time of the day or night, scan them at the digital kiosk and place them in the locker or bin. The amount paid for the product would be credited to the customer's bank account the same day.

From an omnichannel perspective, these services are just a normal outcome of the smooth interaction between physical sales and digital commerce: everything should be possible at any time, and physical and digital services have to complement each other to offer customers services that are the most comprehensive possible. However, this seamless interaction requires comprehensive and positive flexibility on the part of employees and partners of the brand, and logistics that are flawless and efficient.

The video clip regarding Amazon's warehouse system on YouTube is worth watching. When we imagine an employee working in the dispatching department, we picture him going from shelf to shelf, searching for the products ordered. But here, it is the racks themselves that move when the computer scans an order bringing all the articles ordered to the employee responsible for packing it. Small motors attached under the racks can lift and slide them to the employee who has to pack it, positioning them according to the sequence of the order. The rack then moves to a new location chosen by the computer according to the probability of a new order for the products it carries.

We sometimes marvel at the size of these warehouses which are as large as 59 football fields, and the automation that fills the packages, but in fact it is the entire system that is impressive, designed to provide automatic, faultless and economical service. The only word of caution is that with such a system, every operation has to be monitored, to keep costs as low as possible, but more especially to reduce errors.

The Traditional System

The Little Boutique Around the Corner

In a neighbourhood grocery store, all the products available are placed on the shelves. For example, the salt, which people do not buy very frequently, is placed next to the milk, which people buy several times an hour.

It becomes apparent that it would make sense to have a back room for storing a part of the stocks of fast-moving products so that they do not take up too much space in the store, and slow-moving products where one needs to display only a single article. In a women's fashion store, it may be practical, for example, to display a 'bestseller' dress in all sizes (36 to 48) in the boutique, and only size 38 and 40 of a slow-moving model, keeping the other sizes in the back room. It would indeed be a shame to dedicate too much floor space to dresses that are slow-selling and which might make the whole boutique look dismal and unappealing. *Shelf-space management.*

When fashion stores receive their stock of clothes for each season in one batch (the spring-summer collection in March and the fall-winter collection in September) the store director may be tempted to display all the models at the same time, but then, customers who visit the boutique four or five times a season, in April and May, and October and November, for example, may have the impression that there is nothing new to see. So, it would make good sales sense to reserve some models and bring them out progressively to give the impression of novelty. The back room can sometimes serve this purpose as well.

Buffer Stocks or Dispatching?   Some retailers have storage facilities or warehouses located in proximity to their points of sale. This allows them to select products for display in the stores and keep others in reserve.

Let us take the example of a brand that has several stores in the same city, like a leather goods brand with 12 or 15 stores in the Paris area. Every evening, one of its employees is entrusted with the task of computing the stocks that were sold out and stocks that were likely to be sold out within the following days. The employee then has to identify the boutiques where there were extra stocks of these various items and organise transfers during the night or the early hours of the morning. Today, however, one does not require an employee to do this work. A computer optimises these transfers as soon as the last store in the Ile de France region closes and also recommends transfers or deliveries to all its stores in France over the following 48 hours. This digital system therefore already exists. All that remains is to be done organising of the physical transportation of the products and making the process as seamless as possible.

There exists another system used by pharmacies, opticians' shops and garages as well. The stocks kept in the stores are limited, but dispatchers, less than 45 minutes away by truck from each outlet in the region, make a first trip in the morning, then a second one in the early afternoon, to all the outlets, to deliver the articles they require. A mechanic, for example, who has to repair the clutch of a car that was brought to him at 8:30 a.m. will receive the necessary spares around 11:00 a.m. and the car would be ready for the customer to pick up in the afternoon. The dispatcher system reduces physical stocks and increases service efficiency at each point of sale.

However, the dispatcher system requires a very precise analysis of available stocks, uses forecasts and warehouses that are as automated as possible. It also requires a well-organised and faultless transport system that would include regular deliveries and collection of insured merchandise, and also high frequencies.

With the digital revolution, the customer often goes to collect an item ordered online from the store, but not always. Often, too, for the sake of convenience, the customer would like the order to be delivered, so brands have to ensure that the logistics for last-mile coverage are seamless and precise, a major challenge for all operators.

We are so accustomed to 'going shopping' that we do not really appreciate the convenience of home delivery, even though it is really quite straightforward. But one always prevaricates:

- 'The parcel will arrive while I am not at home, my order will get lost and I will have to start the purchase process all over again'. This is a risk, of course, but it can easily be averted. One has only to specify a time that is convenient and delivery will be made accordingly. (But is it truly? The last mile challenge is being tackled by Amazon and Alibaba simultaneously by integrating their own delivery systems in their eco-systems. But what about the others?)
- 'I am buying a very expensive piece of jewellery and I would really like a "Purchase ceremony"'. In fact, having your order delivered by a professional and uniformed employee, who will bring it to your

home, sit at a table with you and show you the item, and maybe even other similar items, is in the realm of the possible. There is a rumour that the NET-A-PORTER.com drivers in London use a Rolls Royce when delivering jewellery. Maybe it's true. In any case, in Paris, one can have a gift purchased from Hermès delivered by a uniformed deliveryman.

What is sure is that home delivery to clients has become quite common, so companies have to take steps to organise it, ensure its security, and make it a completely natural process.

Number of Stores in Each City

Customarily, a brand first opens a store in every major city, then in each second-tier city. It may decide to open a second or a third store in very large cities. But often, all the stores in the same city do not serve the same purpose. The largest store would stock the entire range of products and act as a reference. It is generally located in a prestigious and commercial part of the city centre. The other stores, usually smaller, contribute towards strengthening the brand's presence. These are stores for 'convenience', meant to make purchasing easier, saving customers a trip to the city centre.

Usually, major brands classify their store networks into A, B and C categories.

The A stores are the flagship stores. They stock the entire collection and, in big cities, also act as the brand museum by offering what the specialists call 'Retail-tainment'. Their mission is to convince the public of the strength of the brand, its diversity and its appeal.

The B-category stores are smaller. They do not stock the entire collection. One may stock the women's fashion collection, for example, but not have enough space for the men's collection. Certain B stores of some brands stock the formal collections, but do not stock leisure-wear or outdoor collections.

The C-category stores stock a limited range with only the bestselling references.

An Example of a Logistics Tool: The RFID

The radio frequency identification device (RFID) was developed in the United States in the 1970s. It was meant to equip the various items with a chip for identification and tracking purposes.

RFID chips can be read at a distance of several metres. In addition, unlike barcodes, supplementary information can be added to the chip when it is in the proximity of a reader/transmitter.

This system was used in retail sales for the first time in 2005 by Freedom Shopping, Inc. in North Carolina. An RFID chip, fixed on the label of a product (it cost 5 cents per item) is able to record, for example, the date on which the product passed quality control, when it was sent to the warehouse, when it was placed on the shelf (identification of the store, display of the price), the date it was sold, and the date it was returned (if applicable).

Using this system, a brand is able to track each item from the point of manufacture to the point of sale, and know the exact number of days it remains in the store. It is also possible to locate the product and thus organise transfers from one store to another.

This type of analysis is not new, and any efficient electronic system is able to identify the number of stock-keeping units (SKUs) that were delivered to a particular store, how many were sold, and how many are still in stock. However, with the RFID, the difference is that the electronic information can be cross-checked against the physical presence of each item in the store. For example, one is able to determine whether the SKUs that arrived first in the store were sold first.

In 2005, Walmart asked 100 of its major suppliers to fix RFID chips on items that were intended for their stores. The distributor also uses the system to track the progress of promotional campaigns. One can track how many products tagged at a special price (valid for a limited period) left the factory, how many items were sold at the reduced price during this period, how many items were sold at a reduced price outside this period and how many articles intended for a promotional offer were finally sold at full price.

For luxury goods, the RFID system can locate each individual item over time, identify the store where the merchandise was last seen. If it vanishes from the inventory, the system can pinpoint a possible theft.

Additionally, it allows the company to identify the origin of a product found in the 'grey' market, thus making it much more difficult for operators in this market who have to keep the identities of their precious suppliers a secret. Note, however, RFID tags can be deleted by microwaves.

Although RFID is not the only system for managing information, it is the only way to track articles individually.

Details Are Important in a Logistics System: An Example

One of the authors worked in a company where a preliminary diagnosis of its logistics, as established by sales point operators, revealed the following information:

American outlets opened all the packages they received because:

- The information on the packages was incomplete or incorrect (for 30% of shipments) or delivery slips were missing.
- There were no labels at all on products that came from one of the factories (representing 20% of the total volume), which obliged the US subsidiary to invest in its own labelling equipment.
- In 10% of the cases, the delivered goods did not conform to the order.

The Tokyo and Hong Kong branches opened all the parcels because:

- The quality control criteria for Asian, and in particular Japanese customers, are different and more stringent than those applied by European factories, and corresponded to the company's standard procedure.
- The labels on the products did not meet Asian market requirements either, and all products had to be relabelled.

Reading this today, one may think that the story is exaggerated and that the situation could not have been quite so bad, but it was actually the case. And the reasons were the following:

- The European factories had failed to take into account the specific needs of Japanese and US distributors and end customers.

- The logistics systems had never been clearly and completely set up for systematic processing.
- The various stages of the processes, from production, shipping and delivery to reception had never been clearly identified or carefully organised.
- The different factories used different codifications and the synchronising of these systems had not always been done.

The system was not transparent enough, not robust enough and not really reliable. It left too much room for possible loopholes. It was unacceptable at the end of the chain, that is, when goods finally reached the shops.

A committee was formed comprising information systems specialists, logistics experts, product development managers, quality control teams and factories, as well as representatives of distribution subsidiaries from different parts of the world. It drew up a list of recommendations and advised a complete revamping of procedures. A precise timetable was drawn up, procedures laid out, new manufacturing and quality control processes set up, investments made in new labelling and logistics information systems, and two years later it was able to implement a plan that was infallible.

When this company wished to analyse supply chain processes, the levels of control that its various competitors ostensibly had were studied. The results can be seen in Table 8.1.

We have taken the liberty to publish its evaluation sheet as the situation and therefore the observations have definitely changed over the past years. However, the point we are trying to make is that a streamlined and efficient distribution process is only possible if:

- All the actors involved, suppliers, subcontractors and in-house factories, are fully coordinated, working towards the same set of objectives and using the same procedures.
- The system is user-friendly and has been developed with a thorough understanding of the requirements of sales outlets and full back office staff support.
- The procedures are smooth and foolproof and have been tested and retested over time.

Table 8.1 Different Logistics Models[2]

	Raw material supplies	Manu-facture	Distri-bution	Remarks
Bally	Average control	Weak control	Total control	Needs to be improved
Ferragamo	Average to high control	Weak control	Total control	Leverage too strong on suppliers
Gucci	Average control	Average control	Total control	Open but efficient system
Prada	Average control	Total control	Total control	Strong control over suppliers
Sergio Rossi	Average control	Average control	Average control	Improvements underway
Valentino	Average control	Very weak control	Total control	Priority given to growth

It is only then that one can conceive of an organisation that takes full advantage of the brand's strengths to focus on its main task: providing each customer with a memorable experience.

The New Logistics Systems

If estimates show that a very large number of orders will have to be delivered, logistics systems will have to be completely revamped.

Should Stocks Be Kept in the Store?

If the existing system shows that 40 to 50% of products purchased are to be home delivered, the goods in the store are there not only to be delivered, but also to be displayed. This changes everything. For a dress,

---

[2] *Source:* Confidential document.

NB: Most of this data is probably outdated today, many of these companies having focused on improving their logistic systems in order to align them with their business excellence objectives.

for example, there is no need to stock all the sizes. It is enough to have one or two reference sizes for each model and a sample model or two in all the sizes to reassure the customers.

If a fashion brand has a dozen stores in Paris, it will only need a centralised, well-stocked warehouse from which deliveries for the same day or for the next day can be organised. Each time a product is sold, the central storehouse is consulted and the article is identified, reserved and immediately earmarked for delivery at a specified time.

With this system, the size of a typical fashion store could be smaller as it does not have to keep large quantities of stock. It would be, in a way, both a showroom and a fitting room. Each product could be displayed in one or more sizes to allow the customer to touch it, examine it in the light of day and form an opinion on the quality of the finish. That would be all that is required.

The positioning of sales outlets in a city can then vary. One could contemplate, for example, a central store which will stock the entire collection in all sizes, and subsidiary stores, relatively smaller and located in high-traffic areas, with limited and customer-adapted stocks. Any deliveries could be made the same day or the next day.

In this scenario, dividing stores into A, B and C categories is not relevant. At first glance it would appear that having a single and very large store, which would play the role of both showroom and sales point, would be sufficient.

Does this mean that all the other stores in a very large city will become redundant? One often hears this remark, but it is not true. For if the goal of a roll-out of six to ten outlets in a big city was to ensure the proximity of the brand, these are still needed in the digital era. Some customers wish to be able to touch the products, get help from vendors or advice from specialists.

The only difference is that the distinction between B and C category stores will no longer exist. Besides store A, all that the company would need is a few stores with limited stocks, but which have the capacity to present the full range, thus reassuring its customers. Therefore, the B stores become superfluous except, of course, in second-tier cities where there was never an A category store to begin with, and which these B stores will continue to serve.

The new configuration is therefore simple: A and C stores in the big cities, B stores in the others.

Operating Criteria for Warehouses

What is of prime importance is to ensure that the logistics model is centralised, economical and precise. It should aim to achieve 'zero defects'. In France, for example, one could conceive of a warehouse in Paris, and several others strategically located around France (Lyon, Bordeaux, Rennes and Reims, for instance).

Should these warehouses belong to the brand? Though this question may be pertinent when considering the very large brands, it does not arise for the small ones. For a small brand in France, the management of five decentralised dispatch centres even with the ambition of providing impeccable service, seems excessive, and the results are unsure. The easiest solution would be to subcontract an outside service provider who would have to adhere to specific and well-synchronised procedures. But the scope of the system should not end there. The 'network' should extend outside France. It has to be internationalised, and one has to select logisticians who will be capable of providing identical services whether it is, for example, in the United States, China or Japan.

One may think that it is not necessary to have rapid and premium delivery services everywhere, and that setting up collection points in proximity to customers, like those that exist for mass-market online businesses, would be enough, but in such a case, companies would alienate themselves from the specificities and unique ambience of the luxury industry.

Speed of Execution

But the technical performances of the warehouses are not the only criteria that should be considered. The robustness and flexibility of the IT system should bring additional efficiency to the organisation.

In France, for example, La Redoute's system enables it to clock an average of 2.15 hours between the online customer's final click and the placing of a package in a truck headed for the hub of the transporter assigned to the customer. This presupposes a highly efficient computer network, rapid locating of the product in the warehouse, suitable and clear packaging and, of course, a very fast last-mile transport system when it leaves the warehouse.

The 'Battle' of the Platforms

As one can surmise from the preceding explanation, developing online sales includes the creation of error free, efficient and economical platforms, and a brand that does not have access to these platforms, and whose volume of business is not high enough to build its own, will not be able to fast-track its digital revolution and exercise full control over it. However, simple alternatives exist:

- Either it outsources all its online sales to specialists, such as YNAP or Farfetch (in which case it will not be able to fully control its distribution), and the coordination between its online business (an exterior online retailer) and its offline business (its own stores) may not be seamless, or
- It handles the management of online sales in-house and settles for outsourcing its warehousing and delivery to a third party. This would presuppose, of course, that the two digital systems (the one for sales, and the one for warehousing and delivery) are perfectly coordinated.

Furthermore, a small or medium-sized brand within a large group (for instance, Kenzo at LVMH), will have an additional advantage. It can outsource all its online business to a fellow brand of its group (Louis Vuitton or Dior in this case), who will then act as a subcontractor.

We realise that today brands are advancing in all directions:

- The very big brands are building their own systems (online sales, warehouses, delivery).
- The independent operators (YNAP, which belongs to the Richemont group, and Farfetch) and the big online groups (like Amazon) offer comprehensive services and manage everything that is digital and everything not sold in the store – although, as we saw previously, they now offer the possibility to manage the complete operations, both online and offline, by integrating all channels for a brand.

- Brands are trying to conclude specific agreements with online companies. For example, the Chanel group signed an agreement with Farfetch in 2018 and also acquired a stake in its capital.

Everything is changing, everything is possible, but time is of the essence.

Stores Without Sales Staff

We should open a parenthesis here to describe the new supermarkets being tested in China. When customers enter the door, they hold their mobile phone in front of a sensor which scans it. They are then identified and traced by the cameras that record their name, bank details, silhouette, face and clothes. The customer walks around the store and picks up the items required from the shelves. Each item has an electronic code and is identified by its location in the store. The shelf on which the item is displayed is not your run-of-the-mill shelf. It is in fact placed on a weighing scale invisible to the customer and enables the system to detect whether one or several products have been taken off the shelf. All the purchases are systematically registered, and while leaving the store, the customers receive a message alert on their smartphone confirming that all their purchases were recorded, the invoice calculated, and the amount deducted from their bank account (through Alipay or WeChat pay). This is not science fiction: visiting the Alibaba Hema supermarkets and visiting the Li & Fung Explodium in Shanghai shows how all this is almost at our door.

Of course, this system is not on the agenda for the majority of luxury product brands, but it will surely interest a boutique like Sephora. Not only is it an original and remarkable system, but it reinforces the customer's impression that the shop is really at the cutting edge of technology and that it is more innovative than ever.

The Challenges of Logistics

In the very rapid development of comprehensive and seamless logistics systems, there lies a paradox: the cost. Setting up such a system is expensive and it can only work and become profitable if it is inclusive, integrated, and all its pieces have been verified and are working smoothly. The system then becomes a tool that offers a huge competitive advantage in business and financial terms.

If several operators installed identical automatic warehouses and equally prestigious delivery services in the same country, manufacturers would have a choice amongst several systems and the competition between them would grow stronger. It is quite certain that fully automated storage and dispatching platforms will develop and will one day have to fight to maintain a large volume of business in order to stay competitive.

Also, a few other questions would still need to be addressed, including: Should the structure be global, regional or national?

Traditionally, luxury firms had a national structure. They adhered to rules relating to customs duties and tax regulations in each country (e.g. VAT and local taxes). They also granted market exclusivity for territories, either through store franchise agreements or exclusive distribution agreements. In these agreements, customs duties and other local taxes were evaluated and taken into account. When logistics platforms become international and tens of thousands of packages are sent, for example, from Ireland to Germany or Russia, these platforms are liable to pay these various local taxes and respect all territorial exclusivities. Are they able to do so? When a bag from a major Italian luxury brand is sent from Dublin to Russia or China, are all the exclusivity rights of the Russian and Chinese distributors fully respected? The answer is not that easy.

This gives rise to another paradox where the aforesaid Russian distributor has to comply with all requirements in its country, including the payment of customs duties, while the extraterritorial platform is not always obliged to do so. Customs duties thus work to the disadvantage of those who scrupulously follow the rules, and benefit global platforms that are not bound by them, what one could call a distortion of competition. In other words, in global competition, these customs duties penalise domestic firms. Countries themselves are not consistent and allow these non-symmetrical competition situations: China for instance strictly regulates the importation of perfume (they have to be registered with the China Food and Drug Administration (CFDA) and taxes are to be paid) but nothing is imposed on cross-border e-commerce. The system should definitely change. In any case, as it stands today competition is non-symmetrical and favours the most powerful players and those least rooted in a particular country.

But that is not all. Some luxury goods distributors such as Imaginex, a Hong Kong-based company and distributor of brands like Tory Burch and Isabel Marant for mainland China, also offer special services such as store supply management, recruitment and monitoring of shop personnel, or offline administrative management without the constraints of a distribution agreement. With the multiplication of limited or comprehensive logistics service providers, offline and online partners, powerful and small companies, all services and all forms of partnerships are possible and every variation can materialise.

In passing, one should also mention HAVR, a small French company that has developed digital locks connected to a smartphone, where the owner of a flat can remotely open the front door to a delivery person when they arrive, to allow them to leave a package inside the flat and also ensure that the door has been closed when leaving. This is an innovation that may seem minor, but which may offer a solution for one of the last questions of the puzzle: What does one do when the customer is not at home?

To recap:

- *The comprehensive and natural continuity between purchasing methods and customer relations* will become an integral part of our daily lives, and though it appears difficult to organise today, it will soon become a normal part of a routine.
- *The last-mile service for the delivery of a product should be impeccable*, but the entire purchasing ritual should be revamped and fostered, both at a point of sale and in a customer's home.
- *Developing an online logistics platform* obliges companies to rethink their systems of international offline and online development completely.
- *It looks like the game is not yet over* and that in ten years' time, other players will no doubt exist in the digital and logistical fields, and the current configuration will have, of course, changed enormously.
- *The function of sales outlets* is going to change and the concept of flagship stores that offer a comprehensive experience will grow.
- *In five or ten years*, the stores that are best adapted and the most profitable for a brand will not necessarily be the same as today.

Part III

Making Client Relationships More Meaningful

Chapter 9

Customer Behaviour in the Store or Online

The thing is, I do not want to be sold to when I walk into a store. I want to be welcomed.

—Angela Ahrendts[1]

Selling is essentially a matter of direct experience. Nothing will ever replace observing customers, their relationship with the products, the way vendors behave, and the interaction between these customers and the brand. Luxury brands know that customers are not passive spectators in awe of a brand and a product. They are key

---

[1] Glaser (2012).

stakeholders in the relationship (which we will examine in Chapter 10). Therefore, observing how customers behave in a store is a crucial element for any vendor. This is true for all industry sectors, but especially in the luxury domain.

Unfortunately, not many studies have been published on the behaviour of customers in luxury stores. The vast majority of these studies are a collection of confidential information zealously guarded by each major luxury group for internal analysis and assessment.

However, if one looks at analyses of the mass market, and in particular of the fashion sector, one can draw some general conclusions about how consumers behave in a store. What one needs to look at in a sales point is not just the decor, products or customers, it is the way the experience unfolds: a customer experience that probably rouses all the client's senses and is part of what observers call the purchase ceremony. Is the client seated? Is the client comfortable? Does it seem like the client has plenty of time?

Some years ago, some external observers proclaimed that online shopping would never develop in the luxury goods industry because, they said, 'The purchase ceremony will never be replaced', and it is true that there was never any question of discontinuing it. But the practice has now been slightly modified. A client enters a store and looks at the products, then goes home and consults the website of the brand. They also explore the sites of other brands and if they come back to the store, they will already have gone through a complete experience. Then, once they have made their purchase, they will continue to visit the company's website for information: their relationship with the brand then becomes permanent and continuous.

Also, vendors have to adapt to a new role and connect with clients who have already learnt about the brand and its products and who may sometimes buy in the store and sometimes elsewhere, but still consider the store their point of reference. If these customers had a product delivered and it does not suit them, or it is the wrong size, they would go to the store to return it, exchange it or ask for assistance, but it would never occur to them that the store could tell them that it was not equipped to take it back, exchange it, or give them advice. The experience and the purchase ceremony, partly online, partly offline, should therefore be integrated in a continuous process that is smooth and seamless.

That is what Manuel Diaz (2016) explains very well:

The luxury boutique should refocus on two essential missions: the cere-monial and the buying experience, as well as the initiation of a shared experience, as the upstream phase now takes place online.

At the same time, still according to Manuel Diaz (2016):

Customers should be able to choose the product that interests them online, and if necessary, depending on their size, or even the colours they wish to try out, the shop should be able to make an appointment for them the day it receives the product in question.

Store Behaviour Patterns

One of the pioneers in analysing customer behaviour in stores is undoubtedly Paco Underhill (2008), who formalised the first customer follow-up studies. Today more systematic means have emerged.

The Origin: Tracking Studies

Paco Underhill's company, Envirosell Inc., developed a study system using *tracking*. The principle was to use a team of two or three *track-ers*, armed with a floor plan of the store or shopping centre, who had the task of recording the way customers entered and walked around in a store: Which itinerary are they actually following? What are they touch-ing? How do they behave? What are they looking at? What are they buying? How are they paying? What do they do after paying? All this, in addition to identifying the places they went to.

Such a study could contain information regarding the itinerary of each client observed, for example:

3:25 – Client enters the store.

3:27 – Approaches the brand X perfume counter, looks at the perfume Y, takes a tester, sprays and smells the perfume, puts it back; looks at another perfume from brand X.

3:31 – A shop assistant approaches to start a conversation: the client walks away.

3:33 – Looks at ladies' shoes, checks the prices of three models.

3:36 – Goes to the belt display rack; examines five items, chooses one, tries it on.

3:40 – Goes to the checkout counter; pays by credit card.

3:45 – Leaves the store.

How Mobile Phones May Also Be Used Now

A French start-up, RETENCY, has developed a receiver that is able to track customers in a store using geolocation, and follow all their movements through their mobile phones. It considers that the data thus collected can be distributed or used without permission because the anonymity of the client is fully respected. It is therefore possible to capture the movements of a large sample of customers in a store, their hesitations, their pauses, and most importantly, as with the tracking studies described above, the areas of the store that are the least visited or the least attractive. This information also traces a client's route through the store and the time spent in each department, much like a 'paper' version. An apparently similar application, NEOMA, has also been developed in Hong Kong.

Follow-up and Outcome of These Studies

The results of this tracking, obtained either by conventional methods or using more modern ones, help when making decisions about changing the interior decoration or layout of a store to alter the predictable itinerary of the customer in a store.

When people come to a store, the first thing they do is to enter, quickly. So, the entry point of a store is certainly not the most effective, commercially speaking. People also tend to use the entrance as a meeting point, which does not make it quite so pleasant for the others. Also, when customers enter a store, they are moving from one environment (the street, the gallery) to another (the store), and this requires a few seconds of sensory adjustment before they can absorb what they now see around them. This place of transition is not a good spot for selling, contrary to popular belief. It is only after having passed this transition point that customers will relax and be ready to look at what the store has to offer them.

When entering a store, customers have a tendency of not heading in a straight line but angling slightly towards the right. That is why, in most supermarkets, the main entrance is not in the centre, but located on the right side. People angling towards the right will quickly come up against a wall and change direction, finally covering a larger area on an average than they would have done if the door had been located in the centre or on the left.

While browsing in a store, people tend to touch products most often with the right hand. Even in countries where people drive on the left, people push their shopping carts on the right side of the aisles, so that it is easier to reach the products. Will they stop to read a complicated-looking signboard? Probably not, since they tend to look straight ahead and not pay attention to details.

Do they like to be seen from the street? It depends on the type of products that the store sells. For fashion or luxury, people generally prefer not to be seen by passers-by in the street when they are trying on an expensive dress or watch. That is one reason why traditional luxury stores have no see-through windows and fashion stores have discreet corners and recessed spaces; fitting rooms are usually hidden deep inside the store (and usually on the left, the least visited area).

What can help increase the conversion rate of a particular store? By conversion rate, remember that we mean the percentage of people coming out of the store with a purchase, compared to the number who entered the store. Surprisingly, the longer customers linger, the higher the conversion rate. It is therefore in the interests of the store team to ensure that people feel welcome and comfortable, encouraging them to stay a little longer than they would in a competitor's store.

Paco Underhill measured the average time spent at a home decor store in the United States. The results are shown Table 9.1.

Bring another friend perk.
Lady + Lady discount.

Table 9.1   Average Time Spent in a Home Decor Store

A woman with a woman	8 minutes 15 seconds
A woman with a child	7 minutes 19 seconds
A woman alone	5 minutes 20 seconds
A woman with a man	4 minutes 41 seconds

Expectations and Perceptions in a Store

Table 9.2 summarises what people expect when they enter a store, and what they do not want. For example, customers like to look at and touch the products, but some brands, such as Louis Vuitton and Hermès, make sure that customers do not have direct contact with them. It is their way of creating an impression of scarcity or at least the feeling that every product is very special.

People also like to be able to look at themselves in a mirror, but they do not want to be surrounded by mirrors like those found in US supermarkets and drugstores, which are hung at a 45° angle so the employee at the cash counter can see what the customers are doing in the aisles. They do not want to be spied on, but like to see their reflection here or there while walking through the store.

A similar situation arises with regard to interaction with sales staff. Customers say they like to chat but they do not want to feel intimidated by the vendors. They are looking for a pleasant and reassuring environment in which they will not feel compelled to do this or that.

Customers also say they wish to find a good deal (see last line in Table 9.2). This does not necessarily mean that they are only looking for promotions or big discounts. They simply do not want to be misled, and need to feel that they have made a purchase at the right price, in a pleasant and positive environment.

Paco Underhill identifies many other behaviour traits. He found, for example, that when planning a visit to a supermarket, 90% of women prepare a shopping list, compared to 25% of men. And yet, in 60% of cases, both buy items that were not on their list.

Table 9.2   Customer Expectations and Perceptions in Stores

They want	They do not want
To touch the products	To queue up
To see themselves in the mirrors	Too many mirrors
To find things for themselves	Being forced to ask stupid questions
To chat	To find illegible labels or obscure codes
To be respected	To hear that the article they want is out of stock
Find a good deal	To come face to face with intimidating vendors

How do consumers react to having to wait? To evaluate this, one can measure the exact time that people actually spend waiting and then ask them how long they think they have waited. It is interesting to note that there are no differences between actual time and perceived time for a 90-second wait. On the other hand, two minutes is perceived as too long.

This is an important point because we know that waiting time is the number-one criterion in assessing service quality. Anyone waiting for more than three minutes in line is likely to be annoyed.

How does one resolve this problem? By showing customers that one cares about them. Clients feel better as soon as they have the opportunity to interact with someone. In the store of one of the leading luxury brands in Hong Kong, the management was worried about the long lines of Chinese and Japanese customers waiting to enter the store, so they rented a flat in the building next door, and asked the security guards to distribute cards to everyone waiting, which said: 'We are sorry for the wait at the entrance of our store, it is too small to welcome so many customers simultaneously. To make sure that you are served as quickly as possible, we have rented a flat on the 21st floor of the tower next door where you can go if you wish to be served immediately by one of our vendors.'[2] Most people read the card, nodded and stayed in the queue. They appreciated the courtesy, but preferred to stand in line and be received in the 'real' store.[3]

In addition to interaction and attempting to reduce frustration related to waiting, other techniques can be employed to make it more pleasant. In a bank or post office, well-organised queues or other systems to ensure the principle of 'first come, first served', reassure people. In these situations, separate queues with four or five counters are appreciated while a single queue that leads even to twenty counters (as seen in train stations or today at Fnac and food stores) is not. When there are too many people in the queue, people tend to get restless, even if the line is moving very fast. For example, three lines of six or seven people each can be managed much more efficiently and

---

[2] As told by a vendor to one of the authors.
[3] The Chinese restaurant chain, Haidilao, is famous for its 'waiting' experience where the clients can play, get a drink, have a manicure, etc.

customers have a choice of waiting at any counter they please. The lines will probably advance more or less at the same pace, but most customers will be satisfied with the choice they made.

Another simple way of easing the tension of waiting is to create a diversion: some banks have television screens showing news channels continuously to make sure people have something to occupy them while they wait. The Champs-Elysées Louis Vuitton flagship store when it opened had reserved a space for men accompanying women to sit, relax and watch TV. This seems to be a very effective way of dealing with the problem.

The Basic Rules of Supermarket Merchandising

As we shift our attention from specialty stores to supermarkets, you might think that we are straying quite far from the specificities of the luxury business. But in the aisles and the middle of vertiginous display stands, there are countless simple responses to customer behaviour, precisely identified, and professionals from all business sectors often draw inspiration from them.

A first area of study is that of *facings* and their extensions. The 'facing', for a customer, is the visible side of a product that is on the shelf. A facing does not refer to the items placed behind the first one: they are the rows of products that are visible to the client while moving around the store. And, depending on the size of the store, the reputation of the brand and the loyalty of its customers, if a facing is doubled, its sales increase by about 30%. Therefore, in a given product category, with limited dedicated shelf space, one could optimise the sales, ergo the profits, of the category by increasing the facings of items that sell fast or are very profitable and decreasing those of items that do not sell so well or that are less profitable. One calls this practice 'product category management' in marketing jargon and it is an important element in supermarket merchandising. This is not an easy task, however, as it changes according to variations in the price of one product or the other and also promotional and advertising campaigns.

Does this apply to the luxury sector? Naturally. Not as much as to supermarkets, but the concept of 'category management' certainly applies when determining which spot should be allotted to which category of product and to which article. In a perfume and cosmetics boutique, every product is not allotted the same shelf space. Some brands should have more space, and others less, in order to achieve a more efficient commercial layout.

The *height* at which the product is placed on the shelf is another important factor. The lower shelf, close to the floor, has less success than the one at eye level. In supermarkets, merchandisers representing the various brands do battle to ensure that their products are not placed at floor level and try to persuade store managers to place their products on the higher shelves.

A study called *Colonial* was conducted a long time ago and has apparently never been replicated. It concerned the sales figures of 400 different products, moved from the upper shelves (at eye level) to the intermediate shelves (within reach) and then to ground level. The results are shown in Table 9.3.

The important lesson to be learnt is that when a product moves up from hand level to eye level, its sales increase by about 50% and when it moves down from hand level to ground level it decreases by 30%, which is quite significant. And between the ground level and eye level, we see that the figures are more than double. The question of position is therefore very important in managing product placing in a store.

Given its importance, 'product categories management' constantly provides rules for optimisation.

How effective are promotional campaigns? In fact, several studies have shown that, regardless of its market share, a product displayed on the end of the aisle sells four to five times more than when it is on a shelf. These presentations are therefore more effective for fast-selling shelf products than for others. However, products that are slow selling will attract more new customers than if they are on the shelves and

Table 9.3 Variations in Sales Volumes According to Position on the Shelves

	Increase when going up	Increase when going down	Index
Eye level	211	100	148
Hand level	141	65	100
Ground level	100	47	70

thus help to increase their market share. The fact that in its larger stores Sephora uses promotional spaces where products are piled up to attract the attention of new customers seems to indicate that what happens in supermarkets could also happen in a perfumery store, and probably with the same impact (many say that Sephora transposes all the techniques of mass distribution to the beauty industry).

An important conclusion to be drawn from supermarket merchandising studies is that new products tend to be less successful when placed in gondola heads than older products. If we stretch this deduction to include the perfumery sector, this probably means that promotions for new fragrances in Sephora stores would be less effective than promotions for older products, except when, in addition to the presentation, a special promotional campaign or in-store demonstration of the new product is organised.

All these tools from sectors other than luxury offer very interesting ideas about what can happen in a luxury store and how the managers of such stores could respond to make their store more efficient and more profitable. The products are no doubt very different, but, in the end, customers are customers, and will have similar reactions whether it is a sophisticated boutique, a regular textile store, or a supermarket.

The moral of the story is that, like any other store, luxury stores should understand the expectations of its customers and ensure that nothing is left to chance. Everything should be thought through, planned and implemented in the most efficient manner possible. This becomes obvious to anyone involved in business operations in the luxury sector.

To recap:

- *In-store behaviour analysis tools* are also evolving, and geolocation and facial recognition can revitalise a very important activity by understanding purchasing behaviour in a store.
- *Category management* is not limited to supermarket merchandising policies. It is also useful whether it is for presenting the accessories of a fashion brand or watches in a jewellery store.
- *Considering the cost of renting floor space* in the most prestigious locations in the world, any means that could improve understanding of individual behaviour patterns and use of available space should be implemented.

Chapter 10

The Importance of Stores for Building Customer Relationships

So many designers forget that the customers are, in the end, the VIPs.

–Paul Smith

L uxury brands have a challenging task: retaining customers in a highly competitive sector. Most available studies show that about 20% of customers generate 65% of a brand's revenue (see Table 6.1 in Chapter 6). This means that a brand has to find ways and means to build a loyal customer base. Retaining customers and converting new customers into loyal clients are crucial for a brand. We have also seen (in Chapter 5) that customers' baskets are fuller when online customers subsequently buy offline. The store is therefore the stage on which everything plays out. That is where the brand encounters its customers. That is where relationships are born. That is where the customer journey, as complex as it is, materialises.

Two aspects, which we will analyse one by one, are essential here:

- Managing a store is a profession in itself and requires specialised skills and tools. We describe most of them and provide exhaustive tools regarding job descriptions, recruitment, salaries and career development in Part IV.
- Long-term customer relationships should be established by focusing on the development of personalised service (a subject we will cover in Chapter 12).

Why Sales Staff Need to Know Everything About the Brand

Example

September 2008, at the Paul Smith boutique in Paris. It is an extraordinary place, reflecting the philosophy of its creator: 'classic with a twist'. The walls are covered with framed objects, paintings and books. It is really quite uncommon in the very polished universe of luxury brands.

One of the authors was looking for a wallet for a gift to a friend. The saleswoman showed him several models and among all those that featured the emblematic multi-coloured stripes of the brand, one of them caught his eye: on one side was printed a reproduction of a letter addressed to Mr Paul Smith. The writing was feminine, or perhaps that of a child. On the clasp side, there were five enigmatic letters in the same writing: S.W.A.L.K.

He asked the salesgirl why this model was so different from the others. Pointing to the wall near her, she explained that Paul Smith collected the letters sent to him and that the most beautiful amongst them were displayed in the stores. He then asked her what the five mysterious letters stood for. A silence. She did not know.

On returning home, he tried to solve the mystery. Those letters certainly meant something! They were not there by chance! And of course, they did have a meaning, and even a story behind them. During the war, British soldiers and their wives were unable to write about their feelings and desires freely in their letters because of censorship, so they used acronyms to circumvent the problem:

B.U.R.M.A.: Be Upstairs Ready My Angel.
M.A.L.A.Y.A.: My Ardent Lips Await Your Arrival.
B.O.L.T.O.P.: Better On Lips Than On Paper.
H.O.L.L.A.N.D.: Hope Our Love Lasts And Never Dies.

And S.W.A.L.K.? Well, it meant *Sealed With A Loving Kiss*. What an excellent and poignant symbol! On this wallet, an item intimately feminine, in which women keep innumerable precious and futile things, this acronym, this message of love, acquires a genuine authenticity. Paul Smith, in creating this object, charged it with a whole world of emotions, referring not only to his own letters (who is the woman or girl who writes to him in this way?), but also to the immortality of love letters. For the woman who owns this wallet, it will become more precious than all the others.

Paul Smith said one day,

So many designers forget that the customers are, in the end, the VIPs.

He is absolutely right, but the experience of one of the authors shows that this message is unfortunately not applied in his own stores. This example is only an illustration of the fact that luxury brands are still far from realising the importance of making their sales staff the living repositories of the history of their brands and the stories they narrate. The very special, very emotional, relationship that develops between a customer and a brand has to be constantly nurtured: its history and its telling is an essential part of it. When he was Director of Human Resources at Bally, one of the authors made training and development of the sales staff's skills one of the main focuses of his action. One should never forget that sales staff play a key role in the relationship that exists between the brand and its clients. Vendors are the vectors of the uniqueness of the brand and its communication; they are its front-line ambassadors – well, before the 'happy few'.[1] They should therefore be better paid, better trained and better managed: this is an investment that luxury brands should be willing to make.

The Problem of Retail: Retaining One's Clients

If you have recently visited luxury brand stores, as the authors did during the preparation of this book, you might have had similar and distressing experiences. These negative experiences ranged from not being greeted by vendors who seemed to be bored to death, to arrogant attitudes that made us feel that our place was not in the store. We saw vendors ignore us completely as people. Their only goal seemed to be to make a sale, giving us the feeling of being little more than walking credit cards. We once witnessed a surprising incident. A salesman had just spent 20 minutes with an older gentleman, and after he left, told us that he was a very good customer of the brand, and that he was looking for a particular item that he had not found in his usual store. He had therefore come to find it at the flagship store and 'would come back'. When we asked the vendor whether he had noted down the name and address of the

---

[1] We can only recommend reading the book written by the CEO of Zappos, an American shoe sales site (now bought by Amazon) where he describes the importance to them of the call centre – because it's the only one when they 'meet' with their customers: unlimited talk time, no scripts, services that go far beyond just the product – everything is designed to make the customer happy (Hsieh 2010).

gentleman in question to be able to keep in touch with him, he seemed nonplussed. Had he missed something? Yes.

We have taken entire groups of students and professionals to visit luxury brand stores, and they always came back with the same comments:

- The stores are dirty, sometimes in disorder, and do not correspond at all to the idea of luxury they have.
- The staff are arrogant or not very dedicated.

Whenever they came back with a positive experience, they kept raving about it. Similar expeditions to the stores of the same brands in Paris and Shanghai, for example, make one ask oneself: Is it really the same brand? Why is the vendor's approach so belligerent? Putting your students in the most difficult situation – adopting a mystery shopper attitude and then buying nothing – is an excellent way to gauge the type of service a brand is willing to offer potential customers.

A somewhat dated but very revealing 2001 study by Euromap, a French marketing company, is even more telling.[2] The survey related to 600 European women (called 'leaders'), connoisseurs of luxury and luxury brands. In fact, they were real experts. Even so, 20% of them found the luxury stores in which they did their shopping intimidating, 22% found they were unwelcoming, 20% felt like they were disturbing the sales staff, and 20% thought the sales staff did not listen to what was being said to them! Have things changed at all?

Luxury brands are like spoiled children. They are so used to seeing customers lining up to buy their products (Chinese customers today; previously Japanese) that they rarely pay them any attention. Two noteworthy cases deserve mention here:

A few years ago, a French brand, inundated by hordes of Japanese customers, attempted to offer its European customers preferential treatment. Stores were organised in such a way that Japanese customers queued up on one side and were treated like cattle while non-Japanese customers were entitled to the red-carpet treatment. Fortunately, it did not last very long.

---

[2] Study carried out in France, Germany and Italy. The figures were the same as those of the preceding study, in 1977. Although dated, these findings are illuminating.

Asked whether they had a customer base, the executive director of an Italian fashion brand said:

> Of course not. That gentleman you see there, buying a dress for the woman with him? She could be his mistress. It would be totally inappropriate to ask him who he is, or even send brochures to his home address that could cause him trouble!

There are many excuses for not treating customers as individuals. Companies like Tiffany (but it is an American brand, for which such approaches are normal, while the approaches of European luxury brands are much more 'elitist') have developed *clienteling* techniques over more than 40 years, mainly with the purpose of tracking each customer's purchases.[3] This is a first approach to customer relationships. A purchase is really the culmination of a complex interaction between the customer's desires, the attitude of the sales staff, the customer's current situation and the range of products being offered by the brand. All this can and should be recorded.

Managing a Store: A Very Special Job

Most of the time, when the heads of a luxury brand visit one of their stores, they concentrate on visible things: the merchandise ('Was it delivered on time?'), presentation ('It should not be done that way'), and turnover ('What are the sales figures for last Saturday?'). Their only interaction with the sales staff, if there is one at all, is through the store manager. The best managed luxury brands view their stores as financial entities in their own right, which have to be headed by real

---

[3] Before anyone even invented the term CRM, American companies like Tiffany & Co. collected individual data on the products sold and carried out targeted marketing to the topmost segment of the market. This technique is called *clienteling* and Tiffany even has client data on microfilm and microfiches dating back to 1956. In 2000, they brought out an application to match stores to purchase plans for the clients. But, it is not an exact science, admits Bill Haines, Director of the Systems Development Centre at Tiffany, in Parsippany, New Jersey. 'It is a challenge to match, in a precise and continuous manner, specific purchases with individual clients', he says, 'and even if you succeed, what people buy and what they say they like are often two different things' (Wilder 2001).

professionals, managing and leading teams of motivated and well-trained salespeople. Louis Vuitton has transformed this into a real competitive advantage. They hire store managers, graduates of MBA or major engineering schools, organise extensive training programmes for the sales staff and have a corresponding wage policy.

To look at a store as a full-fledged financial entity requires an excellent understanding of the main obligations that are assumed (we will come back to this in detail in Part IV). For luxury brands, everything related to merchandising and its image is centralised (similar to clothing standards – see Chapter 14). The only domain left under the direct responsibility of the store team is sales itself: managing the customers, managing the store team and managing relationships within the ecosystem of the store. This is where one can make a significant difference.

Store managers and their sales teams should be considered as professionals and, therefore, receive special nurturing. This includes making sure that employees' results are in line with the company's financial objectives and encourage investments – which brings up four fundamental points:

- *Recruitment*: Luxury brands should realise that their traditional recruitment pool (most often, other luxury brands) is only one of possible recruitment sources. It is *talent* they have to look for, and talent is found in services-critical sectors such as luxury hotels or even private banking. Store managers should be considered directors of financial entities whose capabilities in the domain should be established. Traditionally, the best vendors were promoted. In the current environment, this could be catastrophic because their leadership abilities may be very poor and their financial skills nonexistent. Recruiting MBA graduates directly as store managers is an innovative idea and can prove successful if they are given long-term career development incentives (see Chapter 14, Tool 2: Managing the Recruitment of Sales Teams).
- *Compensation*: Usually, the remuneration of sales staff has two main characteristics. It is low, and pay structures vary from one region to another. In Europe, the fixed component is the more important element and the variable, individualised component is much smaller. In the United States, almost the entire remuneration is linked to the

vendor's sales performance. In Japan, the fixed component is essential.

- *Two issues need to be addressed*: Remuneration levels need to be increased across-the-board[4] and a specific compensation system[5] needs to be introduced, which would include a fixed component (for vendors to feel protected), a personalised variable component (which would recompense individual merit) and a collective component that is variable (to reward teamwork). (See Case Study: Comparison of Sales Staff Salaries in Europe; and see Chapter 14, Tool 7: Defining a Fair Retail Compensation System.)

- *Encouraging skill development*: To be an effective vendor or store manager, specific skills are required, and the brand should continually seek to improve them. Brand training, product knowledge, techniques for building up the customer base, store management techniques and team leadership techniques are essential. Training is indispensable for setting standards and sharing know-how. However, this can only begin to change behaviour if it includes hands-on experience and feedback that employees can learn from (rather than just lectures and presentations), and if it is accompanied by continuous monitoring in the field. Sales directors should pilot the performance of their employees, rather than simply sending them for training and waiting for miracles. They should also be aware of the factors that weigh on these performances and be able to influence them. They should become trainers themselves.

  Management has a key role to play here. It should support training initiatives by being present during their implementation and by monitoring them in order to send a clear message. The role of brand trainers is, in reality, the training of store managers, by providing them with the skills, tools and support they need to guide the performance of their employees. Trainers are performance consultants and should form a truly functional partnership with brand

---

[4] The Marketing Director of an Italian luxury brand, when asked how he was going to implement a cost reduction programme, recently said, 'Of course, on the store staff. Who could ever imagine reducing costs of products or on advertising and communication?'

[5] Each region would then adapt the system to local practices and restrictions while remaining within the limits set by the brand.

managers so that they can assess the attitude necessary to obtain good performances, and also instil that attitude. (See Chapter 14, Tool 1: A Typical Sales Organisation, and Tool 4: Job Descriptions.)

- *Career development*: Usually, sales staff do not leave their 'sales' profession. The best performers become assistant managers or store managers, or are poached by the competition. There is an extraordinary ballet going on around the Place Vendôme and Avenue Montaigne in Paris, on Via Montenapoleone in Milan, from Plaza 66 to IAPM in Shanghai – like in all the arteries of the luxury world: employees move from one brand to another, with a salary increase each time, to finally come 'home'. The salary increase they would never have obtained by staying in the same store is thus obtained by rotating. Clear career development incentives should be offered to sales and management staff. There are at least four possible career paths, and each should be taken into consideration (see Chapter 14, Tool 5: Career Advancement):
  - A change of store or category to improve the employee's skills.
  - Promotion to Assistant Store Manager or Store Manager.
  - Becoming a buyer for the brand, locally or at headquarters (depending on the organisational structure of the brand). Their expertise in local sales is an asset here.
  - Becoming a trainer.

Case Study: Comparison of Sales Staff Salaries in Europe

One of the authors – then HRD of a luxury brand – commissioned a study on a European scale in order to understand why there were differences in the salaries of sales staff among various luxury brands. Two staff categories were examined: store managers and vendors. The results were enlightening, and led the author to completely redefine the remuneration system of the brand's sales staff.

(continued)

(*Continued*)

The results of this study are out of date, but the main lessons are still valid, especially the following three:

1. Remuneration levels vary from city to city due to differences in purchasing power; this is the case everywhere.
2. Remuneration levels vary greatly from one brand to another. For example, at the time of the survey, in a certain city, vendors at Gucci or Chanel were earning around 50% more than those at Bally or Hermès.
3. Compensation systems vary widely between brands and *within* the same brand. Take the example of brand X. Store managers were paid:
   - In Paris / Milan / London / Munich: fixed salary + individualised variable part.
   - In Geneva / Brussels / Madrid: fixed salary + collective variable part.

For brand Y, it was another story:

- In London / Geneva / Brussels / Madrid / Milan: fixed salary.
- In Munich: fixed salary + individualised variable part.
- In Paris: fixed salary + collective variable part.

This means that the pay structures were not determined by local practices (since they varied from one brand to another in the same city) but by the local history of the brand, and the unfortunate fact that no European remuneration strategy system was set up at the time. This was confirmed by the pay structure in the company where the author worked. As we know, the remuneration system has a significant impact on the way in which a customer relationship develops. *This implies that luxury brands, if they consider this relationship as strategic, should first and foremost review the remuneration system of sales staff.*

Building a Customer Relationship: The Challenge of Individualised Service

The challenge that luxury brands increasingly face is the building of customer loyalty, which can only be achieved at the store level through its quality of service.

Twenty-first-century consumers wish to be seen as individuals, not as anonymous credit card holders who, in the best of cases, will receive an offer based on their last purchase, say for example, from Carrefour, because Carrefour has set up a system for analysing purchasing data. Or when connecting to Amazon, where the customer receives a message on the screen, 'Hello Mr X, here are some suggestions for you'. These companies use a technology that recommends products based on previous purchases, and they ask the customer to fine-tune these suggestions by giving them more information, such as their opinion on the products purchased.

Carrefour and Amazon consider people who buy from home as customers and not just anonymous consumers, which is at least a step in the right direction.

However, the consumers of the twenty-first century wish to be considered as individuals. They want to be recognised, pampered and reassured and their singularity taken into consideration. And they quickly spot the difference between an automatic computer-generated offer and a truly personal offer.

The task for luxury brands is to build on one of their constitutive myths: their customers matter to them. They should learn to develop individualised relationships with all their customers, to satisfy and motivate them to return to any of the brand's stores. They should in fact become luxury service providers.

To this end, five objectives are crucial:

- *Developing clienteling*: Each individual client should be recognised as such, and their personal information should be treasured. *Clienteling* means establishing an interpersonal relationship between a vendor and a customer. This can only be done through special behavioural approaches and with the help of specific tools.

- *Sales staff that focuses on customers*: Every person entering the store should be considered a future customer, either today or in a year, whether in that particular store or in any of the other stores of the brand. Each client should be assessed and profiled, their motivations and expectations should be noted and each piece of information saved. Customers are always revealing information about themselves to those who are attentive – during a conversation, when sending or receiving packages (business, holiday, or other addresses), when choosing gifts (names, tastes, addresses and important events in the life of their parents, friends, partners), from conversations between customers, their business cards. The goal of every vendor is to gain the trust of their customers; only then would they consider the vendor an able advisor.
- Tools can range from the most basic to the most sophisticated. A *client book* is a basic tool that every vendor should have. It allows them to acquire an intimate knowledge of the customer, to become an advisor and to prepare the following season.[6] An IT solution with CRM software and a database can be an alternative, provided that all the qualitative data that vendors collect about their customers, not only the figures, is entered, to the extent, evidently, that the legal framework within which the store operates permits the collection of such data.
- *Making service quality the cornerstone of a customer relationship*: Shopping by appointment, private presentations, help in putting together a wardrobe, delivery of purchases (or centralisation in a department store), handwritten thank-you notes, providing tourists with information on the nearest store manager in their home country, those are just a few of the services that can be offered to a customer in a luxury brand store (Gutsatz and Auguste 2013, p. 106). One could also offer special benefits, like those that Neiman Marcus (InCircle

---

[6] Thanks to an intimate knowledge of the clientele and a good visualisation of the store's collection and budget, a dynamic salesperson can predict the sales for the season. By listing what to sell to a specific group of key customers, they enhance the management's ability to predict volumes and manage flows. The vendor identifies important customers, analyses their purchasing preferences and compares them against the store's collection. Based on the specificities of the collection, the vendor foresees which items to sell, and when and how to present them to the customer. This requires a regular and sincere dialogue with customers, and an in-depth knowledge of the whole collection.

program) and Saks Fifth Avenue (Saks First) have been offering successfully since the 1980s. Service benchmarks should be fixed at the brand's headquarters, and its subsequent implementation at the store level is crucial.

- *Recognising the key role of sales staff*: Every vendor has a vital role to play in identifying customers, caring about their needs and providing them with the best service possible. As Russell Reynolds Associates stated in one of their brochures, 'It's not information that creates a company; it is not science; it is not intuition; it's not promises; it's not the volumes; it's not borders; it's people'. This brings us back to recruitment, compensation, training and career development. This also reminds us of the respective roles of staff and customers in these relationships. Far too often, these roles are asymmetrical. The vendor either regards the customer as a parasite (arrogant attitude), or a sort of superior being who is able to spend in five minutes what he earns in a month (attitude of inferiority). A balanced relationship should be built on the premise that the vendor and the customer are on an equal footing, and are engaging in a business transaction. The Ritz-Carlton has forged a motto on which all luxury brands should meditate: 'We are Ladies and Gentlemen Serving Ladies and Gentlemen.' We can also take inspiration from the model of Grands Vendeurs developed by the high jewellery brands (Gutsatz and Auguste 2013, p. 106).

Case Study: The Four Vendor Profiles[7]

Wharton's annual report on customer dissatisfaction found that it stemmed primarily from issues at the personnel level, rather than from the store or the brand. This led the authors of the study to identify the main traits that an ideal vendor should have. Among them there are four that are important:

- The most important: Taking the first step. The vendor should know how to take the first step, smile and stop

(continued)

---

[7] Knowledge@wharton (2007).

(*Continued*)

whatever it is they are doing to assist a customer. It is this quality that one finds lacking generally, and in all categories of stores.

– The second most important: The vendor should be an 'educator'. They should be able to explain the products, offer advice, tell customers where an item can be found. They should be able to help the customer find what they are looking for, give them information, teach them something.

– The third trait of the ideal vendor: Attentiveness. They should be alert to the customer's time constraints, and help the customer to save time instead of standing in a queue. They should know that, thanks to their assistance, things will move forward quickly. For the customer, someone noticed the problem and came to fix it.

– The fourth trait: Sincerity. The study shows that customers want 'sincere' vendors who let them browse at will and are genuinely interested in helping them, whether they buy something or not.

The combination of these four traits makes a good vendor.

To recap:

- *Whatever the customer's experience is* (online and/or offline), in the end it is the quality of the relationship created in the store that will tip the scales.
- *Brands should recognise the vital role of the sales staff;* they are the only people who are in direct contact with customers. Multiple techniques for recognition and empowerment should be applied.
- *The performance of vendors* should be linked to the compensation model: brands should streamline it to include both the individual and variable collective factors.
- *Individualised and personalised service* will be the next challenge for luxury brands.

Chapter 11

Customer Experience and Building Loyalty

When people enter a Louis Vuitton store, they should find the best level of service in the world.

–Bernard Arnault[1]

O ffering unparalleled service and personalising relationships with every customer is the main challenge facing luxury brands today. How does one achieve it?

---

[1] In Socha, Conti and Diderich (2010).

We recommend subdividing it into six important steps:

- Focusing on the customer, by placing the customer at the centre.
- Turning regular customers into brand advocates.
- Offering a unique experience – and delivering it.
- Defining the contract between the brand and the customers and adopting specific tools for the optimisation of the business (customer segmentation, CRM, etc.).
- Defining customer journeys.
- Rethinking the concept of the experience lived by the customer.

The luxury industry is now faced with four major customer concerns, concerns that will shape its future:

- All over the world, luxury customers are looking for more than just a product: they are seeking an experience and a personalisation of the relationship. They are looking for a level of service that is far beyond what luxury brands offer today. Bain's studies on luxury attest to this year after year. In its 2017 report (d'Arpizio 2017), it highlights that luxury is 'changing skin', it is becoming 'millennialised', all its customers now look for a new relationship with luxury, inspired by the much more informal, driven by the millennial generation (born after 1980). Bain identifies, among others, two essential elements around which luxury brands should build their strategies: the search for luxury experiences (travel, gastronomy, beverages, art, home, etc.) and the feeling of belonging to a community while expressing its own style. Traditional luxury brands are therefore facing competition from new services or products such as new streetwear brands. They have to learn how to transform their sales spaces into areas of experience between online and offline. This will involve new skills – particularly in sales and marketing – and a new way of building customer relationships.
- The luxury industry is entering new markets (such as China and India), which will be levers for future growth but at the same time it will have to find sources of growth in mature markets. Brands will therefore have to adapt to different cultures in their customer base and deal with the transformation of customer expectations in mature markets. This will require striking the right balance between new

markets and new customers, and boosting short-term revenues in these regions while maximising long-term revenue through existing customers in mature markets. Alas, the very strong increase in foreign tourists (Chinese, Russian, Brazilian, etc.) in their European and American boutiques does not encourage them to do so.

- Selling is a profession that luxury brands have traditionally not mastered. The most important brands (often those belonging to large groups) have grasped it since the development period of their own stores, that is, the mid-1990s. As we saw in the previous chapter, the stakes are high for the brands in each of their stores because that is where the brand meets its customers. They must therefore recruit managers, train sales experts and review compensation grids. A senior luxury manager from the large department store sector told one of the authors of his surprise when he was recruited as Managing Director, France, of a famous Italian brand: 'Everything is organised around creation and the creative calendar! They have absolutely no real retail structure.' That was precisely why he had been recruited: to transmit the know-how of department store retail to the brand.
- Building lasting relationships with customers requires luxury brands to define real customer relationship strategies.

This means that, finally, for luxury brands, the customer will be king. Brands that have built their growth on a strictly pyramidal model to attract new customers (more products in more stores in more countries) should instead study how they can increase their business by having faithful customers who come back often (and thus help to boost income and profitability). They have to ensure that the customer is effectively at the core of all their activities and have to become truly 'customer-centric' in their approach. Unfortunately, many brands have trouble accepting this type of power transfer to the customer, because they believe that they have to exercise full control.

Step 1: Focus on the Customer

Luxury brands spend enormous sums of money to launch new products, open new stores and send messages to their customers via traditional communication channels. Marketing expenses can represent up to 25%

of annual sales. But not a penny of that money is worth more than actually meeting its customers. When customers throng to the boutique, why care about who the customer is or what their expectations are? We can therefore understand the rush to China (where luxury brands, after the excitement of the early years, found that they had opened too many stores and were forced to close down) and to emerging markets (Louis Vuitton and Zegna opened stores in the Mongolian capital, and Gucci opened stores in Azerbaijan and Yekaterinburg in central Russia). Many brands will therefore prefer to open new stores in new markets.

None of us sell basic necessities; luxury is a matter of desires that one creates and one satisfies.
–Belinda Earl, CEO of Jaeger (cited in Bain 2012)

Let's face it: luxury brands run the risk of trivialisation.[2] Having too many stores kills the sense of exclusivity necessary for a luxury brand to establish its image. There was only one Hermès boutique in Paris until 2010. Now there are three, and there are seven in Hong Kong! Luxury brands seem to be quite unaware of this. Besides, they face another problem: the decline in turnover per square metre in existing stores.

Four main factors contributed to this decline:

- The economic crisis.
- The emergence of the Internet, which contributes to the transfer of power to the consumer.
- New consumer mega-trends, among them the growing importance of the 'eco-attitude' and sustainable development.
- The situation in Asia. Luxury brands have recently made the same mistakes in China as they did a few years ago in Japan. We said in our first edition that Japan is a very important market for luxury, where, convinced that the appetite of consumers for their products

---

[2] The year 2012 thus saw a sudden halt in the development of luxury brands in China. Some of them, like Louis Vuitton and Gucci, were faced with a trivialisation, even a rejection, of their products on the part of consumers. They therefore decided to stop opening new stores, becoming aware of the risks of being over-exposed. They then bounced back in 2016.

would last forever, brands opened store after store (in 2012 during the writing of the first edition of this book, Burberry had 75 stores in Japan and only 32 in the US, Hermès had 64 as against 30, Prada 35 as against 15 and Bulgari 31 as against 17 – in other words, twice as many stores in Japan as in the United States, even though the markets are of comparable size), and even though sales had been declining since 2006. The situation in China is exactly the same – luxury brands are overexposed:

– In 2009 the 18 most important brands opened 150 stores; 160 stores in 2010, 150 stores in 2011, 160 stores in 2012; 100 stores in 2013.

– In 2015 the top 20 brands had a total of 1,125 stores. They closed 144 in 2016 and 2017, and opened 138 over the same period. The number of stores has finally stabilised (at a very high figure[3]).

As a result, luxury brands are (slowly) realising that markets are maturing faster than they thought possible. Focusing on their current customers has become a key issue and business optimisation is now at the top of their list of priorities (Socha et al. 2010). They are striving to become better traders to improve their turnover per square metre, and therefore have to gather in-depth information about their customers and their expectations.

Companies need to continuously improve their results and are under ever-increasing pressure to do so (for example, marketing outlays and their return on investment). This focus on data collection, measures and results has been around for a very long time now in the cosmetics and wine and spirits sectors, where luxury brands have always clashed with mass brands within the same distribution channels. Fashion, watches and jewellery, distributed mainly through very selective channels, now face similar challenges.

The traditional marketing strategies of luxury brands are ineffective here: above-the-line / sponsorship / endorsement by celebrities / product placement / advertising, all of this does little to build personal relationships with customers.

---

[3] See Chapter 13.

Case Study: The Question of Footfall

All luxury stores do not have to manage the same footfall volume. Some indicators are given below:

- Flagship store of a French fashion brand (in Paris): 800 customers a day (3,000 during sales).
- Flagship store of an Italian fashion brand (in Paris): 600 customers a day (1,000 on Saturdays).
- Stores of a French leather goods brand (in Paris): flagship store, 4,000 customers a day; secondary store, 500 customers a day (1,000 on a Saturday).
- Flagship store of a French jewellery brand (in Paris): 25 customers a day.
- Flagship store of a European luxury durable goods store (in Paris): 100 customers a day.
- Flagship store of a top-of-the-range perfumes and cosmetics distributor (in Paris): 9,000 customers a day (20,000 on Saturdays).

Needless to say, there is a huge difference between managing 25 clients and 30,000 clients a day. As far as we are concerned in this chapter, since the open-space distribution of perfumes and cosmetics belongs to a very different category, we will focus on the more traditional outlets of luxury brands. It seems to us that several luxury models are at work here:

- *Model 1: The Private Sales Model.* In stores with fewer than 100 customers a day, the number of vendors is typically around 7, which is about 10 customers per vendor per day. The brand organises its sales on the basis of one-to-one contact: each customer will receive the time and attention necessary to finalise a sale.
- *Model 2: Luxury Sales Model.* Stores receiving 500 to 800 customers per day will typically have 35 to 50 vendors, or

approximately 15 customers per vendor per day. The brand strives to always maintain the right balance between the perception of luxury and the strain of the number of customers.
- *Model 3: Business Process Model.* Stores with more than 1,000 customers a day will have around 200 vendors, or up to 20 customers per vendor per day. The sales process is completely professionalised, but the brand has to be very careful not to blur the perception of luxury.

Step 2: The *Loyalty* Effect – Transforming Regular Customers into Brand Ambassadors

Luxury brands, which have always focused on traditional marketing techniques, are now entering the age of customer relationships.

Benchmarks help to evaluate the positive business impact of loyalty marketing strategies. They increase the average spending of each customer by 7% and the frequency of visits by 10%. Such benchmarks also illustrate the importance of word of mouth:

- The probability of a positive result through word-of-mouth by members of a loyalty programme is 1.7 times more than that of non-members (Colloquy.com, 2009).
- Word of mouth drives sales.
- 'Over a typical week, the average American consumer participates in 121 conversations, during which brand names are cited 92 times. From another angle, Americans participate in 3.5 billion conversations every day! Brand names are mentioned 2.3 billion times a day. Brands, it can be said, are a major subject of American conversations.' (Keller 2007)

But luxury brands should be aware of the omnipresence of the terms 'loyalty' and 'customer satisfaction'. It could be interesting to refer back to a seminal article in the *Harvard Business Review* (Reichheld 2003) which said, 'One question alone can serve as an indicator of future growth ... the propensity of customers to recommend a product or service of the brand to someone else'. The exact wording of the question was, 'Would you recommend Brand X to a friend or colleague?' It was followed by a scale separating 'promoters of the brand' – that of clients with the highest purchase and referral rates, answering the question with a probability of 9 or 10 out of 10, and 'brand critics', with ratings between 0 and 6, and 'satisfied passives', with ratings of 7 or 8. Going one step further, the article recommends graphically depicting brand revenue growth according to its rate of 'net promoters', that is to say, the percentage of promoters minus that of detractors. This fascinating study (followed by many others) shows that:

- Word of mouth is crucial for a brand.
- Detractors can be damaging.
- The promoters are real advocates of the brand.
- A brand should make great efforts to convert its customers into promoters.

Other important studies confirmed that client promotion was a growth factor in all categories. Brands and companies with high net promoter rates and low negative word-of-mouth rates grow four times faster than companies with low promoter rates and high negative word-of-mouth rates (Marsden, Samson and Upton 2005).

Most commercial companies find it difficult to build strong relationships with their customers, as shown in Figure 11.1.

The all-important question is therefore: How can a luxury brand transform its customers into brand ambassadors? Our answer is simple. One should provide the customer with an experience that exceeds his expectations and his previous points of reference. Every client can remember experiences that are similar – very often outside the luxury domain – that serve as benchmarks. For example, imagine a perfect experience at Apple, where the brand offers a smooth and seamless transfer of all the content from your old computer to your new Mac with its *One-to-One* service. This will become your yardstick in terms of experience. (See also 'Case Study: Weston – Splendid Service', later in this chapter.)

This remains valid regardless of the sales model. If a brand chooses a personalised model, it should know what customers' expectations will be

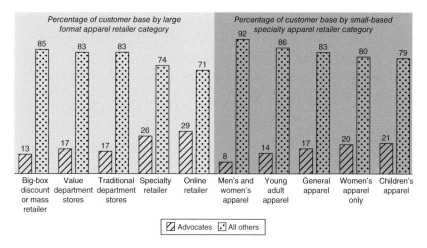

Figure 11.1   Most Apparel Retailers Find It Difficult to Build Strong
Relationships with Their Customers
Source: Adapted from IBM Institute for Business Value (2008).

even before they cross the threshold of the store, be prepared to exceed those expectations and set a new benchmark in the customers' minds.

Every consequence arising from it is a question to be addressed by luxury brands. For example, a brand with several stores having different rates of frequentation will have to apply different sales models to take into account each situation (the luxury sales model in its flagship store *A*, and the personalised model in its secondary store *C*). It will have to resolve a tricky dilemma: Does it offer the same level of experience in every store, or does it offer different experiences to customers who might be the same?

A typical example is that of Louis Vuitton, a brand which, given the footfalls in its stores, is faced with this question daily. An initial response was offered by Bernard Arnault to experts during the presentation of the results of LVMH for 2009: 'When people enter a Louis Vuitton store, they should find the best level of service in the world.' Yves Carcelle, then Chairman of Louis Vuitton, added: 'We focus our energies to offer our customers a more refined experience.' Even as, at the same time, a family of (wealthy) customers with a baby stroller was refused entrance to their flagship store on the Champs Elysees on the pretext that it was closing 'soon' (half an hour later).

This shows how large luxury brands are starting to shift their focus to the quality of service – not only for their VIPs – and still finding it hard to achieve it!

While luxury brands are just starting to look at how to build such an offer, the luxury hotel industry has a long track record in the matter because they have always had to focus on the expectations of their customers and not on the promises of the brand.

The most stressful experience that guests usually have when arriving at a hotel is waiting to check in. Standing in line after a tiring trip can be trying. The Four Seasons has organised a unique customer experience for its best clients. When guests arrive, they are taken directly to the room and the formalities of check-in are carried out there personally.

The Ritz-Carlton is another example of the same kind of service. True to its motto,[4] it has perfected the method for entering data into their CRM. If a guest asks for an extra pillow because their back is hurting, they will find one waiting for them at their next stay in another Ritz-Carlton hotel, or will find the same babysitter who took care of the children during the previous visit ('You see, they already know me … ').

Step 3: Offer a Unique Experience – and Anticipate All the Possible Consequences in Terms of Internal Organisation

An experience will truly be exceptional only if all points of contact are in sync and all staff, whether in sales, marketing, or management, are properly informed and, most importantly, convinced and motivated.

---

[4] '"We are Ladies and Gentlemen serving Ladies and Gentlemen" – the Ritz-Carlton hotel is a place where the comfort and attention provided to our visitors is our most precious mission. We are committed to offering personalised service and the most sophisticated equipment to our visitors, who will be able to enjoy an ambience that is as warm and relaxing as it is refined. The Ritz-Carlton experience awakens the senses, instils wellbeing, and responds to the wishes, even those yet unexpressed, of our guests.'

The experience is built at all levels of the company, and the consequences are important and fivefold for luxury brands:

- The organisation of the brand should be restructured in a manner that places the focus on the customer. Particular attention should be given to information systems and cross-functional elements of projects. This implies that this customer-oriented culture should be part and parcel of future recruitments of all staff (not only those of commercial staff) *and* that information systems be rebuilt as customer-centric – that is a huge task for some brands that have built their information system by layering different software. Nevertheless, their information system should be their number-one investment in the future.
- Training should also include brand culture, values and guidelines for service quality, not only rules and procedures.
- It will be necessary to recruit new talent for the positions of Retail Performance Managers, CRM Managers, Loyalty Programme Managers and Customer Service Managers.
- The skills assessment grid of sales staff will have to include new criteria: priority given to service, knowledge of the culture of the brand, and ability to act like ambassadors of the brand.
- Compensation grids will reward performance based on brand values, in order to reinforce the focus on customers and the capacity to offer them a unique experience (see Case Study: The Compensation System Question).

Case Study: The Compensation System Question

As we saw at the beginning of this chapter, compensation systems vary from one brand to another and from one country to another. Starting from real examples, let's look

(continued)

(*Continued*)

at some situations where pay systems have a very definite impact:

- Case A: Vendors receive either a variable monthly commission on sales, or compete in an internal system indexed on a 'basket' variable where the vendor who sells the highest number of 'baskets' over a given period receives a bonus. An annoyed customer enters the store with a question to ask, after the sale – this visit will clearly not result in another sale. Most of the time, since the after-sale process is long (for administrative reasons: do you have your bill, where did you buy this item, can you show us what is wrong?), the seller will have no motivation to make sure the customer leaves satisfied.
- Case B: Many luxury brands have developed appreciation programmes (employee of the month, for example) leading to competitive behaviour among the vendors rather than encouraging cooperation. But serving a customer, especially an unhappy customer, often requires the cooperation of several store employees. Vendors should therefore be encouraged to cooperate. For example, innovation contests can be held to put the customer's brand experience to good use. An excellent example is the 'Make Nordstrom Special' contest, which helps strengthen the group's values and the excellence of the service provided to the customer.
- Case C: Usually, luxury brands offer commissions to their sales staff on the basis of their turnover. We have seen in Chapter 7 that luxury customers travel very often. A sale for an expensive article may be initiated in London and concluded in Dubai. In a classic setup the whole commission will be paid to the Dubai store! However, more and more brands are aware of the complex situations created by customers who travel, and have organised shared commissions – each shop involved in the sale receiving a predetermined percentage of the commission.

One finds the same scenario online. Working with influencers will, no doubt, lead the brand to realise that in the complex journey that leads to a purchase, several influencers have 'swayed' the final choice of the customer: the first one introduces the future customer to the brand's website and a second (or a third!) instigates the purchase. How does one recompense them? There are now affiliation systems offering 'split commissions' divided between the various people involved in the customer's journey to the final sale (see Figure 11.2).

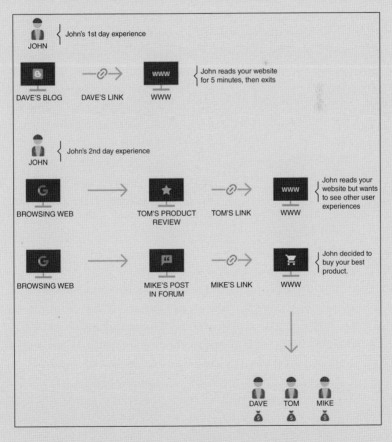

Figure 11.2 A Typical 'Split Commission' System in Affiliation

Case Study: What American Customers Expect from Luxury Brands

Many studies have focused on the expectations of luxury customers in different parts of the world. Here are the main results regarding customers in the United States, and recommendations drawn from them.

Luxury Brands in Department Stores

For a study by Alix Partners in the 13 July 2006 issue of *WWD*, customers were asked to rate, on a scale of 1 to 5, a list of their shopping expectations for five stores: Saks Fifth Avenue, Neiman Marcus, Nordstrom, Lord & Taylor and Bloomingdale's. Below are the 10 main expectations, which should indeed be at the core of the implicit contract between a luxury brand and its customers.

- Courteous and respectful employees: These qualities, as basic as they are, are considered by the customer to be at the core of a luxury experience.
- Being able to return merchandise quickly and without being embarrassed: customer services departments are often understaffed, leading to long waiting lines. This study shows that clients often feel uncomfortable or even being suspected of dishonesty when they have to answer the battery of questions asked by the staff.
- Staff who know how to respond proficiently to the expectations of customers: How can one serve the customer is the essential question. To be called when a product that was ordered has arrived, or maybe sending a birthday wish, these are gestures that luxury customers expect.
- Staff who treat customers like they value them.
- Staff who know how to wrap items up correctly and rapidly.

- A minimum wait when making a purchase. Customers buying luxury products wish to be able to complete their purchasing quickly and easily; they will not wait for more than
  just a few minutes.
- Staff who are correctly attired.
- A store that is visually pleasing.
- Vendor outfits that complement the store.
- Easy phone access to information. This emphasises human
  contact by phone.

A study from Luxury Institute, 'Leading Edge Insights into
the World of the Wealthy' (2010), concludes: 'Another finding of the report was that the mystery shoppers preferred the
customer service and aesthetics in brand's retail locations over
the experiences in department stores selling that specific brand's
products. Mystery shoppers found the company stores to be better maintained, with a more welcoming environment, than the
brand's area within a department store.'

Our Comments and Recommendations

Luxury brands organise and control both their own stores and
their counters in department stores, but it seems a lot more
attention is focused on what goes on in their own stores, which
may be a mistake. Customers go from one contact point of the
brand to another, and expect similar experiences at all contact
points. The question that luxury brands should ask themselves
is: What draws a customer to a department store counter and
what brings them to the brand's store? The answer should help
them to better serve these customers by responding to their
various expectations at each of their contact points. A typical
example of this is enlightening: customers often go to Sephora
to see the new products, but buy them at the brand's counter
in a department store, because they know they will be attended
to. Are counter salespeople trained for this? Do they know what
the brand displays at Sephora?

Case Study: Weston – Splendid Service

Attracted by one of the items in the window, I pushed open the door of the J.M. Weston shop on Boulevard des Capucines, in Paris. As soon as I entered, my instinct told me I did the right thing. My experience was a rare demonstration of service quality – half an hour of pure pleasure.

It was a Saturday morning and the (small) shop was full: a dozen people, men in their forties, well dressed but in a range of different styles (from jeans to casual chic). I strolled around nonchalantly, looking at the models. A man came up to me and I told him that a model in the window had caught my eye; he escorted me outside to identify the model in question and then led me to a free seat. Shortly thereafter, a shop assistant approached and, this was my first surprise, she already knew which model interested me. The information had been correctly relayed.

A second surprise: she offered to measure both my feet for size, because, she explained, our feet are rarely the same size, and this measurement was essential to be able to choose the best size. She then returned with two sizes, telling me that I could choose one or the other according to the comfort I was looking for. She then went on to explain that the width she showed me was adapted to the morphology of my foot and that the construction of the shoe was the contribution of Michel Perry, the designer of the brand.

Third surprise: while she was taking off my shoes, she offered to have them polished by the shoe shine installed at the entrance to the store. Wonderful! I could leave with shiny shoes even without buying a thing. She then told me about my shoe brand (Paul Smith), saying that they had very beautiful models, in good quality, and that she kept abreast of what they were doing. (Even if it was not true, it made me feel good, a few words reassuring me about the wisdom of my choice.) She then led me to a full-length mirror (many luxury brands selling shoes have no such mirrors). I made my choice, then asked to try on another model, which arrived in the right size and the right width. I decided to buy both. After asking me whether I would like to add my personal information to their database, she brought me a form to fill and a pen on a wooden tray, offered me a drink, asked me to wait a moment.

Fourth surprise – she came back with the bill (in my name) and the credit card swipe terminal on a tray. Why queue up to pay when you could just as well pay while being comfortably seated? I left the shop, absolutely delighted.

What Can We Learn from This Experience?
The attention was totally fluid, every moment was thought out and prepared, my expectations as a male client were anticipated.

The experience was totally different from a 'typical' sale, with a non-commercial aspect (shoe shine) and the 'disappearance' of the payment counter (have we not seen this already in the Apple store?).

A wish to return. A benchmark for my future experiences.

Case Study: Oprah Winfrey

In 1999, a young unshaven man in T-shirt, jeans and sneakers, entered the flagship store of a famous French jewellery brand in Paris. The saleswomen did not give him a second glance and did not even try to talk to him. He walked around and then

(continued)

(*Continued*)

left the store. One of the top executives of the brand (who told this story to one of the authors) returned to the store at that moment and asked, 'Wonderful! Did you sell something to André Agassi?' The vendors then rushed outside to try to catch the future winner of Roland Garros and number 1 tennis player in the world.

André Agassi did not follow the dress code of the luxury clients of the time but all brands today ensure that the way one dresses is no longer a criterion by which a customer who enters a store is gauged. Clothes in this case, but how can one explain the misadventure of which Oprah Winfrey was a victim in Switzerland in August 2013?

Come to attend Tina Turner's wedding, Oprah Winfrey entered a famous luxury boutique in Zurich where she asked to be shown a Tom Ford bag in crocodile costing SFr35,000. The saleswoman does not show it to her, but shows her less expensive models instead. Oprah Winfrey tells the story herself in an *Entertainment Tonight* interview, saying that she was dressed in Oprah Winfrey style, but without the diamonds[5] and that she insisted on seeing the bag. The saleswoman explained that the Tom Ford bag was too expensive and she would not be able to afford it (National Post 2013).

Once more, the (visual) profiling of luxury customers creates a problem. Anyone entering a store could turn out to be an excellent client. The old codes of the European bourgeoisie are no longer valid, less so at a time when Louis Vuitton's Artistic Director for Men is Virgil Abloh!

---

[5] 'I didn't have anything that said, "I have money": I wasn't wearing diamond studs. I didn't have a pocketbook. I didn't wear Louboutin shoes. I didn't have anything.'

Step 4: Define the Contract Between the Brand and Its Customers and Adopt Four Tools for Business Optimisation

---

In this world there are only two tragedies. One is not getting what one wants, and the other is getting it. The last is much the worst, the last is a real tragedy!

–Oscar Wilde, *Lady Windermere's Fan: A Play About a Good Woman* (1892)

Based on our experience in different sectors, we recommend that luxury distribution focus on four main tools:

- *Defining a brand contract*: as Cailleux and Mignot (2009) said:

  - The first step of a good CRM is to define the 'basic contract' of the brand. Luxury brands should stipulate their own, non-negotiable vision of quality, innovation, service and attention. Any customer (current or potential) should implicitly become a party to this basic contract as soon as he or she enters the store.

  Why? Firstly, because of the fundamental principles of the label. Secondly, no one can predict how customers' profiles or their desires and values will change as time goes by. The 'basic contract' will show customers that they are already part of the family – even before they purchase anything. A brand where such a vision is clearly defined is Hermès. Reacting to the idea that Hermès was a brand, its former Chairman, Jean-Louis Dumas-Hermès, said to one of the authors: 'We are not a brand, we are a signature … you see my name on every product we sell. It is as if every time we sell a product, we sign a contract with the customer who buys it.'

- *Segmenting clients*: All customers are not identical and more precisely, all customers do not have the same needs and desires. This is why we believe it is important for a luxury brand to carry out a careful segmentation of its customer base that will enable it to categorise customer profiles that correspond to different expectations.[6] Most often, unfortunately, customer profiles are limited to demographic data (age, sex, nationality, etc.). A proper segmentation will also identify psychographical profiles or communities of clients with common objectives. The most suitable method for doing this is to create 'buyer personas' (Heinze et al. 2016). This will allow the company to build these demographics into a real human story, to understand the motivations behind a purchase, to choose the appropriate means of communication, etc. For each profile or segment, there will be a customer profile biography, a description of their motivations, preferred channels and content, important contact points where the trust in the brand is built, and also the negative points (*pain points*) with respect to the brand, the influencers the customer follows as well as keywords recapitulating the profile.

This is a far cry from the strictly quantitative approaches, such as those adopted by American department stores, which use only a single criterion to segment their customer base: the dollar amount bought.

A customer segmentation that is tailor-made for the brand is the best place to start. There can be no ready-made solution; each brand should find its own. We strongly recommend basing the segmentation on in-depth interviews with customers in order to gain a deeper understanding of their relationships with the brand.

Case Study: Customer Segmentation in the Beauty Sector

In this context, one of the authors, in a study for a luxury beauty brand, used an exclusively qualitative method based on open-ended interviews to distinguish the different segments among the brand's customers. Twelve interviews

---

[6] The Managing Director of an excellent French luxury brand, speaking of one of its Asian markets, thought it necessary to explain to us, 'A customer segmentation? That is only for fast moving consumer goods!'

were conducted in France comprising five topics: lifestyle, relationship to beauty, experiences in beauty care, the brand and luxury.

These interviews revealed very different beauty practices and enabled him to identify three client profiles:

- The fight against ageing is a ritual centred on the products themselves and scientific research – care is not a luxury.
- The pleasure for oneself or beauty care is a way of life and a moment of pleasure.
- The brand is an indicator of social standing and success and the product is an access to the brand.

This study also identified an important distinction for beauty clients between:

- the 'salesman', focused on sales and profit; and
- the 'counsellor' (often referred to as a beautician), focused on sales, of course, but adapted to the client (focused on the relationship to the product and the individual specificity of the client).

The good counsellor is the one who says frankly (and regardless of the price): 'This cream is not for you.'

Managing the Client Database

CRM and Database Management   It is crucial to build a complete and detailed database. Take the example of Clarins: it is one of the few brands of luxury beauty products to have developed very early on a well-oiled CRM strategy. 'We collect all the feedback from our customers on all our products by postal or electronic mail, telephone, fax … We centralise the data in a single marketing system, to analyse the impact of the same product in different European countries and carry out a more efficient segmentation of our customer base,' the director of organisation and systems at Clarins explained. This unique database was also used when the men's line was launched: in June 2002, a first message was sent to the brand's female customers, asking them for information about the 'Men in their lives' and to fill out a short questionnaire. The result? Clarins was able to gather 17,000 coordinates, the strategy enabled it to build a database of 24,000 male customers in seven months and it become number 2 in the market within a year!

The compiling of a unique customer database is one of the main challenges for luxury brands today as we indicated in Part II, and it seems that many brands have not yet invested enough in the renovation of their information systems. Yet the stakes are high: identifying a customer who travels abroad and makes purchases in more than one country is the basis of a real strategy of personalisation of the customer relationship.[7]

Measure and Measure Again   The Lego[8] example also teaches us the importance of measuring. It measures loyalty and recommendation indicators, rates their promoters and detractors, and focuses on four main factors: the product experience (immediately after a purchase), the online experience, the store experience, and the customer service experience. Measure, measure, measure. Unfortunately, most luxury brands only have recourse to mystery shoppers for calculating their indicators. But that is only a first step: customer experience, commitment, interaction, reaction to messages, everything should be measured regularly, applying a multidimensional technique, as Lego illustrates.

Step 5: Define Customer Journeys and Identify Important Contact Points

To achieve this, a customer-centric approach should be established that includes the before-and-after impressions of the store experience, which is the customary reference point for luxury brands.

Luxury brands should strive to understand the journeys followed by customers. Clients search for a product or a brand and embark on

---

[7] It is true that many brands have a CRM, but established by country, and these often turn out to be incompatible between them. It is therefore imperative to coordinate them.
[8] See Chapter 5.

an odyssey through various channels and places before buying (or not). This leads them to many encounters with the various contact points of the brand, with some of them being less than pleasant. Luxury brands should be aware that their customers could have had negative experiences in the course of their itinerary before or after a purchase. By way of illustration:

- A customer in a jewellery store may be hesitant and the vendor is unable to close the sale. The customer returns the next day to their home in another country. Quite often, the vendor will have omitted to give the customer the name and contact information of their counterpart in this city, because 'I will not get the commission!' This results in a lost sale and a negative experience for the customer.
- After-sales service can be trying. The Managing Director of a very large luxury brand said to one of the authors, 'It is not normal that when you bring a watch to be repaired, you have to wait for a month to see it again.' Tiffany, to remedy this problem, set up a repair shop near La Guardia airport in the United States – the item is routed through UPS and sent back to the customer in less than 48 hours.

We know from experience that customer journeys will depend on customer segments.

The customer experience should be built and reinforced at each point of contact: in-store, online when the customer is searching for something, online when the customer comes in contact with the brand on its website, during all communication campaigns and customer events, at every opportunity for interaction, and during all contacts for service (guarantees, cleaning, repairs, etc.).

Step 6: Elaborating the Customer Experience in Luxury Brands

It is crucial for luxury brands to reconnect with their customers by redesigning integrated customer journeys, including all distribution channels and contact points between the brand and its clients. To this end, we have designed an original method that is described below.

One Method, Five Phases

- *Know your customer*: A thorough understanding of customers is the *sine qua non* for a brand that seeks to improve the customer experience. Qualitative interviews should be conducted with clients by a specialised psycho-sociologist to gather precise information and gain a comprehensive understanding of consumer motivations, expectations and behaviours. The results can be consolidated in the form of 'personas', each of which will combine and represent the various client segments. These will become the foundation for the new blueprint of customer journeys.

- *Develop internal cooperation and share knowledge*: This would require several workshops cutting across all operations and comprising participants from the business, marketing, CRM, product and country departments. It will encourage discussions and exchange of knowledge between managers and employees from the various areas of the organisational chart who often have very few opportunities to communicate directly with each other. This will form the base for building a team dedicated to the Customer Experience Project.

- *Design ideal customer journeys*: The Project Team then creates journeys for the various customer segments, using prototypical experiments: transforming abstract ideas into low-fidelity prototypes that can be tried out and evaluated by potential customers; the results will be conveyed to management.

- *Construct scenarios*: In addition to the concrete improvements made to existing touchpoints, the project team should also build various scenarios to construct a sustainable vision of the products and the brand and create original and radically improved customer experiences. These high-level scenarios are then broken down into concrete actions and individual projects that can be carried out immediately.

- *Prepare an action plan*: All the results, discussions, prototypes and scenarios should then be merged into an achievable plan, with a roadmap and actions that can be launched immediately.

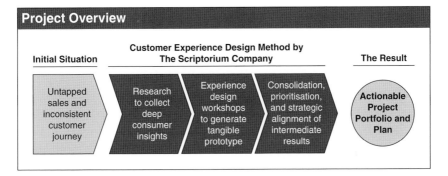

Figure 11.3 Methodology for Designing a Customer Experience

The Advantages of this Method

This unique methodology enables a brand to produce concrete ideas and prototypes for solving underlying problems thanks to the reflections and insights of customers and analyses provided by experts (see Figure 11.3). The method (Gutsatz and Schindholzer 2011) has the following advantages:

- It focuses on the experience lived by the customer.

  In-depth knowledge of the clientele: The qualitative interviews conducted by a psychologist facilitate the identification of very distinct customer segments, according to their motivations and behaviour.

  Comprehensive integration of customer journeys: the integration of the various sales channels into a single comprehensive journey makes it possible to identify real opportunities for cooperation between the different channels and to strengthen the relationship between consumers and the brand.

  Creative reframing and brand vision: questioning and putting existing assumptions into perspective shakes up the status quo of established daily routine and generates ideas and visions of the brand that are completely new.

- It is a method for designing experiences that is:

  Inclusive: the inclusion of the different departments in the inter-active process for idea-generating and workshops for prototype development allows participants to pool their ideas, and stimulates discussions between different divisions, which is not possible in the normal course of work.

  Tangible: rather than producing observations on market share figures, consumer trends or abstract ideas, the workshops engender tangible prototypes to solve real problems within the various sales channels. Using these prototypes, it becomes possible to share, experience, evaluate and communicate ideas and solutions.

Why should one concern oneself about all this? One of the authors, attending a Walpole conference in London a few years ago, overheard a fascinating conversation: a senior manager of Coach:

We have a database of over a million customers and we are developing new products using datamining techniques.

A senior executive of a British luxury brand:

If I were you, I would not boast of having a million customers in this database. I would be proud to have ten thousand.

Two worlds facing each other. Which world should one belong to?

To recap:

- *Brands should offer customers unique experiences* – while knowing that customers recall experiences drawn from various other sectors (hotels, mass market brands, communication brands, etc.).
- *As customer journeys become more complex,* brands should acquire tools to analyse them.
- *Brands need to segment their customer base* and build customer relationships tailored to each customer segment.
- *The clients of the future are the millennials and Generation Z.* One should get to know them and adapt to their expectations and their ideas of an experience.

Chapter 12

How the Internet Has Shattered the Traditional Sales Model

Victorious troups will first win and then go to battle, while defeated troops will first go to battle and then try winning.

–Sun Tzu[1]

S hattered is perhaps not the word we should use because it means 'crushed or smashed', which, of course, is not the case. But it also means 'to break (a record)', and that corresponds more closely to what we are trying to say. With online selling, or e-commerce, the

---

[1] *The Art of War*, Chapter 4.

traditional system of selling through a store is passé. It was indeed unique, but it now has to coexist with another system, which also has its own advantages and specificities, especially regarding the manner in which it communicates with customers, provides service and transacts. One can no longer talk of a one-size-fits-all model of distribution for luxury products, but of an array of complementary methods of distribution that are evolving, and most of all, reinforcing themselves and becoming more complex.

In this chapter, we will describe how online sales (or e-commerce) are part of the whole picture, and why brands do not use a single distribution system or a single operator. Also, why all the stakeholders do not limit themselves to a single operating mode or a single intermediary, but multiply the number of intermediaries or stakeholders to, over the long term, keep open as many options as possible.

Is Selling Online Sufficient in Itself?

In 2006, the PPR-Kering group sold their Le Printemps department stores. They then focused almost exclusively on the luxury sector. In 2014 they sold Redcats (La Redoute), a group specialised in 'catalogue sales'. This company – specialising in selecting articles, mail order sales logistics, particularly through the Internet – seemed to them non-strategic for a luxury group.

In 2017, the Galeries Lafayette Group picked up a majority stake in La Redoute, which it projected as the French leader in online commerce. For the Galeries Lafayette, it consisted of expanding its footprint in this famous sector that was attracting the interest of so many stakeholders. The key word was *complementarity*.

Online selling was therefore not always considered such a buoyant sector. In 2010, the Quelle la Source group, with two centres in France, one in Tourcoing (North) and the other in Saran (Loiret), went into receivership. They were acquired by Les Trois Suisses. The latter spoke of the importance of a huge database of 2.5 million customers. However, Les Trois Suisses started experiencing difficulties in its turn, and in 2017 it was bought by the small Domoti Group and was subsequently sold to Shop Invest in 2018.

One might presume (on the sole basis of these French examples) that e-commerce on its own is not really a sector of the future, but a look at what is happening in China and the United States will soon make one change one's opinion.

In October 2016, in a letter to his shareholders, Jack Ma, Founder and Chairman of the Alibaba Group, said that 'New Retail' was the future: 'Pure e-commerce will be reduced to a traditional business and replaced by the concept of New Retail – the integration of online, offline, logistics and data across a single value chain.' It came like a bolt from the blue in the business world that was largely restructured by his Internet group. In the process, one found out that Alibaba and Tencent, the two Chinese Internet giants, had begun investing heavily in brick-and-mortar stores since 2014. Below is a list of their most recent acquisitions and investments:

- Investments and acquisitions made by Alibaba:
  - June 2016: 20% of Suning Commerce (electronic products chain)
  - November 2016: 32% of Sanjiang Shopping Club (supermarkets)
  - January 2017: 73.7% of Intime Retail Group (department stores and shopping malls)
  - February 2017: Strategic partnership with the Bailian Group (department stores, shopping malls)
  - May 2017: 18% of Lianhua Supermarket (hypermarkets, supermarkets and convenience stores)
  - November 2017: 36% of Sun Art Retail (supermarkets)
- Investments made by Tencent:
  - March 2014: 15% of JD.com
  - August 2015: JD.com acquires 10% of Yonghui Supermarkets (supermarkets)
  - June 2016: Strategic agreement between JD.com and Walmart
  - December 2017: 5% of Yonghui Superstores (supermarkets)
  - January 2018: Investment in Carrefour, China

At the same time in the United States, Amazon, after opening bookstores where the offer is constantly optimised thanks to data collected on the website, bought Whole Foods. The objective was to invent the retail of the future – and this future is preparing itself, primarily in the mass market sector.

It is not because online sales are barely sufficient in themselves that it is not an extremely exceptional tool. But it is only one aspect of a whole that translates into perfect offline-online continuity, which offers customers a service that is fully adapted to the complexity of their expectations and their needs.

Is Selling in Stores (Offline) Sufficient in Itself?

If online selling is not sufficient in itself, can we presume that selling in shops is? Absolutely not. Simply because, in seeking online-offline continuity, what customers want is a comprehensive system that can be accessed at any time, whether it is online or in a store, and they can initiate an action (purchase, after-sales service, return or exchange of a product) at a sales point, or a delivery or receipt of a product of the brand at home. Zara opened its first 'click and collect' store in London in January 2018. The shop assistants are equipped with tablets to help customers order products that are delivered the same day (if ordered in the morning) or the next day (if ordered in the afternoon).

Also, it sometimes seems that offline sales specialists (traditional retailers) are so eager to display their digital prowess that they end up by minimising the physical presence of the items they are selling to appear '100% digital'. An example is Tesla, which is creating new car sales showrooms where the cars displayed are reduced to just one or two. The customers walk through the sales area[2] where they can discover the brand and the range, configure a car themselves and finally, buy it. There are screens and touchpads at their disposal and they can choose and customise their car: colour, engine type, accessories, wheels, radiator grilles, etc.

As we have seen in a previous section, since 2000, all the luxury brands are striving to 'digitalise' their businesses, but the progress is slow and often piecemeal. We will illustrate this with two very different cases – Gucci and Chanel.

---

[2] https://www.nurun.com/fr/etudes-de-cas/tesla-motors-retail-kiosks/

The Evolution of Digitalisation at Gucci

2002 We are in 2002. Gucci is very proud of having made its website more modern and user-friendly. The customer is able to access the site using a confidential code. This code is saved so that when the customer visits it the next time, they go directly to the page featuring the last fashion show and they are able to watch the show and see the latest creations and fashion trends. Based on the pages they browsed during the last visit, similar models are displayed in priority, followed by the colours and silhouettes that the user seemed particularly interested in.

The visitor can view the photos of the products in high resolution and with the zoom feature all the models can be seen from all possible or imaginable angles. The site is available in a choice of 7 different languages, and adapted to 27 different countries.

What strikes one here is that Gucci's description of 'digitalisation' offers examples of memorising the users' browsing behaviour and not of their purchasing behaviour. One notices how the concept of 'digitalisation' has evolved over the past 20 years and how the notion of systematic transition from offline to online and vice versa was not a priority at all.

2016 Fourteen years later, the same brand, Gucci, describes the evolution and strengths of its online development. It is still a question of the quality of the photos available and the attention to detail on the brand's website, and it highlights the clothes and accessories of the brand that famous people or celebrities have been seen wearing. But this serves merely as a quick transition to the next stage: the quality of the online presentation experience of the products, ease of purchase, the welcoming quality of the site, and user-friendliness. Gucci alludes, in particular, to the reputation of its site, which is a new and interesting concept.

But the main focus at that time was to ensure that the online shopping experience echoed and magnified the experience in the store. For example:

- Do the models from the last collection appear as appealing, in-store and online, as they did during the last fashion show?
- Do these models really exemplify the life of a true Gucci customer and the way she wishes to lead her life in the world?

- Do the sites, both the shop and the web, allow a client to return an item and have it reimbursed easily and at any time, offer a choice of existing options in all cases, and to receive a gift package that is luxurious and elegant?

But the questions do not stop there! It's also about whether Instagram's 'celebrity' posts are available to everyone and whether the brand's creativity is correlated to the visual culture available. Here, the question of the quality of the photos on the Gucci website is relegated to the background. The focus of the brand seemed to be ensuring the quality of the in-store or online experience, its richness and diversity.

2018   The story continues! In 2018, Gucci's management's aspirations are even more ambitious.

It endeavours to:

- Establish a completely fluid and seamless transition between the customer's online and offline experiences.
- Create a movement and facilitate the shopping experience.
- Create one comprehensive customer database.
- Allow the customer to book a product on the brand's site and collect it at the brand's nearest outlet. The purchasing experience seeks to be comprehensive and always easy.

In addition, the brand prides itself on having 8.3 million Snapchat 'followers'.

The quest for perfect fluidity between the various points of contact with the brand is very obvious here. *Gucci* also wishes to fully involve its customers in the brand and in its ecosystem.

In 2018 Chanel Upturns Department Stores' Business Model

In early November 2018, a long article in *Women's Wear Daily* described the major change taking place at Chanel in the United States (Lockwood 2018). The brand decided not to operate as a wholesaler that sold its fashion collections to independent department stores in the country, but to convert its operation strategy into that of a retailer.

As mentioned elsewhere in this book, Chanel has 23 directly oper-ated stores and 55 shops-in-shops in US department stores that sell its ready-to-wear collections and accessories. These 'shops-in-shops' are installed mainly in major retail stores such as Nieman Marcus, Bergdorf Goodman, Saks Fifth Avenue, Nordstrom and Bloomingdales. It is the status of these 'shops-in-shops' that is called into question.

The Chairman of Chanel Inc. for the USA, John Galantic, explains the difficulties he encountered:

> In these shops-in-shops, there is no 'full visibility' of the customers, and one cannot always offer them a total, comprehensive service and perfect continuity (online-offline).
>
> We are not always able to control the quality and quantity of the stocks of goods we have.
>
> We are not able to incorporate these customers into a seamless and continuous online-offline service (and without interruption). (Lockwood 2018)

In fact, one ought to be able to integrate a customer of a department store who has just bought a Chanel jacket into the Chanel customer database.

In the typical 'shop-in-shop' system, the department store receives a margin as a retailer. That is to say, if a customer purchases a Chanel bag on the Internet and wants to return it to a shop-in-shop, how does this product reintegrate the department store's inventory and what margin should the store receive for this service from Chanel? The continuity one talks about is no longer assured.

John Galantic makes it clear:

> When a customer makes contact with Chanel, whether through chanel.com, an application, or by contacting the call centre, he/she has entered the Chanel house and becomes part of Chanel. (Lockwood 2018)

Any contact with the brand is a contact with all of Chanel. There can be no question of retail margins to pay or receive from a department store.

Chanel no longer speaks of 'shops-in-shops' but of 'concessions'. It wishes to renegotiate with department stores. It no longer wants to pay a sales margin on turnover (leading to confusion when returning or selling a product which is being delivered the next day by the e-commerce site without ever being entered in the store's shop-in-shop inventory). It is therefore a question of modifying the relationship with the department store: it is enough to pay it a fixed rent, with no variable percentage calculated on turnover, and nothing else.

Chanel decided to enter into and finalise these discussions with the American department stores before the end of 2019. We realise that the model introduced by brands like Louis Vuitton (according to the brand, their 'shops-in-shops' all over the world pay rents and not margins) will become the norm. This will undoubtedly disrupt the business models of department stores – which will increasingly become simple retail space managers, much like the shopping malls. However, the most important point to remember is that – from the brand's viewpoint – it will ensure perfect online-offline continuity. We are really talking here of a strategic decision made in the name of digitalisation.

What Impact Will It Have on Wholesale Transactions?

One may assume that all the other luxury brands will be asking the same questions and improving their service continuity, and that American department stores are likely to find themselves reexamining their own model. But the issue does not end there. The same thing can be said for department stores in other countries, particularly those in Japan, Canada, South Korea, Mexico and Australia. They would also have to change their model and bring it more in line with that of shopping malls, a real estate agency, or a landlord who rents out an independent store.

In the same manner, franchised stores, of which there are a great number for premium fashion brands and where a few exist for luxury brands with relatively low volumes, do not provide perfect online-offline continuity either. These will have to change the way in which they operate very quickly, or offer a greater choice of operating systems.

The list is still to be finalised. Importers-distributors should also reflect and try to exclude anything that could slow down, or appear to be a hindrance to, this seamless continuity from their operation techniques.

Upheavals in Matters of Communication

There is a most interesting chart in the McKinsey (2018) study shown in Figure 12.1. All brand communication budgets are not at the same stage. If we look at the three most advanced brands in terms of O2O – Burberry, Louis Vuitton, Gucci – we see that their budgets are now fairly evenly divided between events (30%), print media (40%) and digital media (30%). On the other hand, many other brands still have old budget structures where print media dominates. Apparently, this is the case of watchmaking and jewellery brands, but also brands like Fendi, Prada and Miu Miu.

A Sea Change Originating in China Consumer expectations (the growing importance of 'social commerce' and the use of cell phones as the unique means of communication, shopping and payment) and changes in the retail landscape (creation of a 'luxury' portal on Tmall, Luxury Pavilion, and on JD.com, Toplife – recently merged with Farfetch China) in China have led luxury brands to change their approach entirely. For example, there are now product launches on the Internet – something that was unimaginable five years ago, or in any other part of the world. In August 2018 Tiffany opened a pop-up on

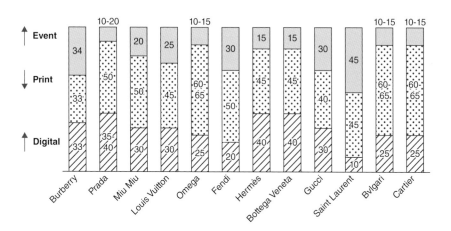

Figure 12.1 Brands Are Reallocating Budgets to Digital and Events
Source: Based on data from McKinsey (2018).

the Luxury Pavilion website to launch its new 'Tiffany Flower Papers' collection, which reached its stores only 2 weeks later. Balenciaga, for its part, joined forces with Toplife to offer a home delivery service for the brand's products purchased on the site – the delivery person arriving in a white suit and gloves. MCM proposed an offer exclusively for the Internet – 50 limited edition bags on Luxury Pavilion during the Qixi Festival in July 2018.

All luxury brands have also invested heavily in WeChat MiniApps – virtual online boutiques within WeChat – which have become real event venues of the brand.

Today China is truly the laboratory of the future for all luxury brands (see Table 12.1).

Table 12.1   Example of Activities in 2 Weeks of 2019

Brand	Details
Marni	On 24 July, the Italian luxury brand started selling its limited edition 'Caddy' bag in celebration of the Qixi (Chinese Valentine's Day) festival on the brand's WeChat Mini Program store.
Valentino	On 25 July, the Italian luxury brand launched its Chinese Valentine's Day campaign 'Be My VLTN' and offered its special collection of fashion items co-designed with Chinese actress Zhang Yixing on the brand's WeChat Mini Program store.
Montblanc	On 26 July, the German luxury brand started selling its Chinese Valentine's Day collection co-created with Chinese fashion blogger Mr Bags on the blogger's WeChat Mini Program store.
Dior	On 31 July, the French luxury brand released its 'DiorAmour' handbag for sales exclusively on its WeChat Mini Program in celebration of Qixi; prior to the new launch, the brand had already published 16 posts to promote the new handbag. When the limited edition bags sold out in seconds on its WeChat Mini Program, Dior then opened a pop-up store at Beijing's SKP shopping mall (from 5–19 August), releasing more 'DiorAmour' fashion products to further cash in on the raging demand.

Table 12.1 (*Continued*)

Brand	Details
Bottega Veneta	On 31 July, the Italian luxury brand launched its Chinese Valentine's Day campaign through its WeChat Mini Program; a number of the brand's limited special items were available on the platform, including Catena City Knot handbag and Intrecciato Maze wallet.
Michael Kors	On 1 August, the US designer brand introduced its limited edition Whitney handbag, co-designed with Chinese actress Yang Mi, on the brand's WeChat Mini Program in celebration of the Qixi festival.
Burberry	On 3 August, the British luxury brand officially launched its WeChat Mini Program, through which the brand released its two China-only limited edition bags – a red 'Belt Bag' and red 'Pin Clutch' to celebrate the Qixi festival.
Stella McCartney	On 3 August, the British designer brand's WeChat Mini Program officially went online, allowing users to place orders directly.
Givenchy	On 5 August, the French luxury brand officially launched its WeChat Mini Program store, enabling Chinese shoppers to order the brand's special GV3 handbag created for the Qixi festival.
Gucci	On 6 August, the Italian luxury brand launched its Chinese Valentine's Day campaign along with the release of its WeChat Mini Program. To celebrate the Qixi festival, the brand rolled out limited edition products, including special 'GG Marmont' handbags and 'Ace Patch' sneakers exclusively designed for Chinese consumers.
Cartier	On 7 August, the French premium jewellery brand launched its WeChat Mini Program store dedicated to selling the brand's Qixi special 'Juste un Clou' bracelet.

The Race to Organise Perfect Continuity

If Chanel started to revise its agreements with American department stores, it is because the company is well aware of the importance of offline-online continuity and wished to provide a sustainable solution as soon as possible. But other brands will have to evolve too. The system of the future is not yet as well defined as it might seem and the pieces will fall into place progressively.

The Perfect System   The perfect system should fully integrate the offline model and the online model. This is to say that customers should be able to access them at any time and be able, for instance, to buy a product in a boutique in Tokyo, return it through the Internet three days later when they return to Paris, and recover the amount paid in Tokyo.

For this system to work, the transactions in both the physical shops and the e-commerce site should be organised and controlled by the same entity. The customer should also not have to pay customs duties or local taxes anywhere. In our example above, the amount reimbursed for the product bought in Tokyo and returned in Paris should be the price paid in Tokyo, without the refunding of Japanese customs duty causing any problem. Today, we are very far from this facility, and from a practical point of view, even the perfect system will not really be able to fully incorporate customs duty costs.

From time to time, some brands commit themselves to setting 'a global pricing system'. But who pays the 100% customs duties for certain products that are imported into Brazil, for example? In fact, after a great deal of effort, as we point out in Chapter 16, price differences in retail fashion ranging from 100% to 140% are not uncommon in international fashion sales.

One can, of course, make the task easier and say that perfect continuity can be ensured for all physical stores of the brand (comprising directly owned stores and 'shops-in-shops' in department stores that have the new type of deal similar to Chanel, as we mentioned earlier) with the exception of travel retail shops. For online sales, one may sign exclusive worldwide contracts with Farfetch asking it to guarantee international coverage with perfect continuity (it is no coincidence that the company JD.com, the second digital commerce operator in China behind Alibaba, made a capital investment of US$397 million in Farfetch in May 2016. The e-commerce system is organising itself and getting stronger).

One can also imagine the contrary and build upon a fully digital structure, like YNAP, for example, and ensure continuity by connecting the brick-and-mortar boutiques of the brand in each country, and by integrating this system progressively – firstly, all the physical stores in the countries where customs duties are not applicable, then step by step, the countries with minimal customs duties, and so on. But one is still far from this ideal of perfect continuity.

A Multi-Brand Portal in a Single-Brand Site? In reality, other variances exist. A brand can choose an exclusive digital portal, as is the case for Hermès, for example. It can also be represented by a multi-brand portal such as YNAP. YNAP represents several brands: Balenciaga, Balmain, Bottega Veneta, Bruno Cuccinelli and Burberry, not forgetting jewellers such as Boucheron, Buccelati, and Bulgari. In a certain manner, YNAP acts as a sort of online department store. It has an extensive portfolio of brands and is able to outsource the entire management of online sales and deliveries, much like a department store would. And to accomplish this function for each brand, YNAP charges a percentage of 35% on products on consignment, which is less than retailers demand. In concrete terms, YNAP assumes the functions of a distributor just like a department store, except that it is online and has a global reach.

In 2012, for example, the Kering Group signed a worldwide cooperation agreement for the digital sales of its brands, Saint-Laurent, Bottega Veneta, Balenciaga, Alexander McQueen and Sergio Rossi, with Yoox (now YNAP). Kering held 51% and Yoox 49% of the new company responsible for the online sales of these brands. In addition, online boutiques managed by this entity have been launched for Bottega Veneta and Sergio Rossi.

The absence of Gucci in this plan is striking. In a manner of speaking, Kering keeps two irons in the fire:

• The first for its 'secondary' brands, for which the digital development is assured by the joint venture with YNAP, and would help accelerate the online growth of these brands.
• The second, for Gucci, which develops its own digital system.

In 2020 or 2025, the time will come to compare the results, advantages and disadvantages of the two systems, to eventually apply one system or the other across the board, or to negotiate territorial extensions or restrictions for one brand or another. The options still remain open at this time.

Chanel, which has only one brand so far, has taken a different path. It has reached an agreement with Farfetch for some of its online business, and also picked up 'a minority stake' in Farfetch's capital in February 2018. At this stage, Chanel does not wish to develop its digital sales, but intends to provide its customers with improved and comprehensive services.

It would appear that everyone is preparing for upcoming changes in one way or another, and making sure every possible and imaginable support is available to secure the future.

It seems that ultimately, two models will have to coexist with one another:

- The major brands would have to set up an ad hoc system, as integrated and comprehensive as possible, and they will do so by banking on the power of evocation and attraction of their brands.
- Less powerful brands will most likely choose to rely on multi-brand portals and this could change as they develop.

For very powerful brands, it seems that the in-house system will be more advantageous (including in terms of gross margins). For medium-sized brands, the options still remain fairly open.

Putting Together the Pieces of the Puzzle Any company seeking to establish a seamless distribution system, both in its own stores and e-commerce site, should first determine all the actions that have to be taken.

Firstly, it would have to ensure coverage of physical outlets in a certain number of countries and cities around the world. These outlets should offer homogeneous or complementary product ranges, with a coherent and harmonised retail price policy. The store or stores have to be managed, staffed, stocked and controlled in each city or country. If the company creates a subsidiary for distribution, this subsidiary may be entrusted with its day-to-day management. Else, it could appoint a manager who would assume the responsibility of the store, or perform the functions defined above, which may require payment of a fixed remuneration.

In the same way, the company could provide its own logistics service, although this is often outsourced.

The most important concern is last mile delivery. Today, delivery can be ensured easily, but what is still not certain is whether the atmosphere and manner of delivery of the object or objects comply with a purchase ceremony worthy of its name. Also, logistics platforms are increasingly prepared to collect the articles that a customer wishes to return, which means that the customer is not obliged to go to a returned-goods centre. This is what Amazon perfectly accomplishes with Amazon Prime.

Who Will Win the Race?   It seems that everyone is ready to set up a system that is integrated and coherent. Big brands are getting organised, small brands are subcontracting and joining forces, franchisees are asking how they can transform their relationships with brands, major digital management sites are setting themselves up and waiting. For many observers the dice have been cast, and companies like Farfetch or YNAP from the beginning, followed by Amazon, Alibaba and JD.com, believe that the future is theirs.

What is certain is that the Internet and digital applications have revolutionised the luxury products distribution system and everyone is striving to prepare a new structure and new rules for the game.

To recap:

- *It is clear that the complementarity between offline and online transactions* will be increasingly reinforced in the coming years. However, this result will be obtained through different paths, depending on the performance and the flexibility of the distribution systems that are being set up today.
- *Several digital models* are being developed and will compete with each other: an integrated single-brand system, with a portal reserved for a particular brand, and a multi-brand system which will act on behalf of a given brand much like a digital department store. These new operators will also try to meet the challenges of internationalisation.
- *The concerted efforts for the development of an integrated system* will have to be able to change present operating modes. Single-brand stores that do not currently belong to brands (franchisees, joint ventures or traditional shops-in-shops) will have to find simple solutions that will not hinder the elaboration of a future system of perfect continuity between offline and online businesses. One would also have to reflect on the questions of customs duties and logistical costs.

- *Also, one should not expect a 'universal' integrated offline-online system.* Each company is setting up its own system, and we can expect a wide range of solutions and innovations over the long term.
- *In this domain,* the future of retail in general and luxury brands in particular is being prepared in China.
- *The overall cost of building such a seamless omnichannel experience for customers is very high:* warehouse picking, putting in a parcel, transportation, individual 'luxury' delivery have a cost and at this point only brands with significantly high volumes can support them. High CAPEX (capital expenditure necessary to open stores) will now be replaced with high OPEX (operational expenditure) and high CAPEX (for the implementation of automated systems).

Part IV

Management Tools for Luxury Stores

Chapter 13

Location of Sales Points

In a real estate context where every square metre counts, the
ultimate luxury is empty space. A space that is not 'productive',
that is not commercial, one that encourages contemplation,
discretion, movement and luxury.

−Rem Koolhaas[1]

I n the past, the response to the question of the location of retail stores
for luxury brands seemed very simple: one only had to install them
in the immediate vicinity of their main competitors. The industry
thus seemed to have perpetuated the old medieval system, when every
member of a particular trade strove to find a place on the same street as
its main competitors.

---

[1] In Böck (2015).

But what type of sales outlet should one open near competitors? What size? And what would be its function? An in-depth analysis of each catchment area, though it might be more useful for the management of a supermarket chain or specialised chain stores, is not without interest for a luxury brand. Lastly, one should also address the question of rental costs for stores in various countries, which could explain, to a certain extent, the strategies for setting up new stores at one place rather than another.

The Classification of Stores in the Mass-Product Market

In the case of mass products, there are three types of commercial configurations: destination sales outlets, convenience stores and incidental outlets.

- *Destination outlets* correspond to situations where consumers purchase items following a complex planning process, and for which they are willing to deviate from their usual shopping itineraries. Buying a car, or a cradle, are perfect examples of this type of situation. A car purchaser or soon-to-be parents are willing to travel several kilometres to find the perfect car or cradle to suit them. There is no need to open stores on every street corner for this type of destination purchase. Customers are willing to go out of their way and take the time necessary in such cases.
- *Proximity or convenience outlets* are those where one can make a last-minute purchase, where the sales outlet is as close to home as possible, or on the way home from work. A typical example would be buying salt or butter, that is, products that one may suddenly run short of. For this type of purchase, the price is not too important to the customer. They just want it rapidly and wish to spend as little time as possible buying it, unlike destination purchasing where customers pay close attention to prices. Destination shoppers plan their shopping in advance, and are prepared to travel 10 or 20 kilometres more if they are sure to find the same product, in a similar commercial environment, at a significantly lower price.

- *Incidental outlets* are for products that are not urgently needed, and where customers do not want to spend a lot of time searching for a particular sales point. This may be, for example, getting a duplicate key made, fixing new shoe soles or buying a box of cigars. These are, of course, useful items, but no one would consider going out in the middle of the night to buy them. They are things that one generally keeps in the back of one's mind with a mental note to get it done when the occasion presents itself. These stores are not destinations in themselves, but they may be found on the way to work, in a major shopping centre, near a train station or similar places.

In fact, these three types of sales outlets end up creating two different types of buying situations:

Routine Purchases

This is a particular form of destination shopping where customers plan their shopping for groceries, for example, on a certain day of the week, or major dry food purchases on a certain day of the month. Once a routine is established for these purchases, customers no longer pay much attention to price differences, at least not in the short term, although they expect the prices to be within their budget. People are willing to travel up to 50 kilometres by car for weekly basic purchases, like dry groceries. In some special cases, such as back-to-school shopping, they may even be willing to drive as far as 100 kilometres, or even more.

Commodity Purchases

These can be purchased in a neighbourhood store, but some of them may be purchases that supplement routine purchases that are part of a destination purchase.

The location chosen and the ambience should be different in proximity outlets and destination outlets. In the case of proximities, ease of access is probably the most important criterion. The catchment area is quite limited and the sophistication or originality of the decor is not crucial. One cannot conceive of a 'Purchase Ceremony' here, and the only thing that matters is finding vendors who are efficient, discreet and nonconfrontational. In the case of destination outlets, however, customers have to be rewarded for their efforts, either by offering exceptional prices or exceptional service. For these clients, driving several kilometres for a particular purchase should be worth their while.

That is why, in the USA, major shopping centres try to anchor themselves around one or more department stores. The principal goal is simply to attract customers to the centre who are likely to walk around and visit the surrounding stores after finishing their destination shopping. They will probably end up buying things they did not plan on buying and use the occasion to do some intermediary shopping.

The same concept applies to luxury brands, but depends on the appeal of each brand. The stronger it is, the more the circumstances resemble those of excursion shopping. If the brand is relatively small, it should plan to also offer the possibility of what one would call incidental purchases or even convenience purchases that would become part of the destination shopping habit.

For luxury brands, as we will also see later, this notion of destination is fundamental. The more powerful and appealing a brand is, the more it has a 'destination' clientele, and the more it will draw to its side weaker brands that will benefit from its momentum.

In China, for example, there is a tendency for real estate developers who plan to open new shopping centres to approach the management of the most important brands and offer them commercial space at rates that are very moderate, sometimes even zero. They know that if they can attract three or four major brands with particularly strong appeal, they will have little trouble renting out the remaining space to other brands, this time at a much higher rent, by promising them a more-or-less captive clientele. This system is financially very astute, but it is nonetheless unfair, because in the end, it is the weaker brands that offset the rent of the stronger brands.

The Case of Luxury: Different Types of Sales Outlets

As mentioned above, the main criterion in luxury is the power of attraction that each brand exerts, but different types of outlets may correspond to different marketing goals.

Flagship Stores

The name is easy to understand. Their goal is not only high turnover, but to project the strength and vitality of the brand and build its reputation and image.

Besides being stores in which to sell their products, they are also showrooms where journalists, foreign distributors or licensees can view the entire collection and also get an idea of how its products should be showcased and sold.

Flagship stores are created in the city of origin of the brand. The Hermès department store on rue du Faubourg Saint Honoré in Paris is a good example. In Paris, these stores are usually the oldest stores of the brand, if not the original, and they present its full range of products. Their turnover is high, but more than that, they are real institutions. For example, Chanel, on rue Cambon in Paris, is a store of this type. It is in fact the original Chanel boutique (which has become larger over time, of course) where the whole Chanel concept and products are displayed. Another boutique of this type is the Dior boutique on avenue Montaigne, also in Paris, which is the original location of the brand.

However, over the past decade, brands have become globalised and their managements have somewhat stretched the 'flagship' concept. Leading brands have decided to open flagship stores not only in their home cities but also in all the capital cities of the countries that the brands consider as priorities: for example, in Tokyo, Hong Kong, New York and Shanghai. In each geographical area, this extension of the flagship model corresponds to a need to vitalise the brand, to develop its concept, and present its product offering in optimal conditions that help to amplify public relations events and marketing.

Also, an observation that one cannot miss: a real flagship store should never give the impression that it is just part of a public relations exercise. It should be filled with customers and appear profitable, vibrant, and brimming with activity.

Megastores

This is another concept that has developed since 1995 in the luxury sector. They consist of huge stores measuring at least $1,000\,\mathrm{m}^2$.

The definition of megastores overlaps that of flagship stores to a certain extent. Many of the latter are megastores, but one can also create a megastore with different objectives. Opening a megastore is not always about enhancing the origin of the brand or creating an institution. It can also be a display of power. The brand seeks to show everyone, competitors and journalists included, that it has the wherewithal to open a huge store in a city and to make it profitable. It is a show of strength and ambition. The idea is not so much having a big store, but to have one bigger than the others.

Of the 18 stores shown in Table 13.1, seven of them are located in Asia, where a display of power is important. Only Armani in Milan and Louis Vuitton in Paris can be considered flagship stores on a global scale. Many others play a role as banners of regional strength, intended to embody the priority given to a given territory. It is not surprising to discover Valentino on this list for the first time. This is a consecration, and an indication that the brand now intends to play in the big league.

Table 13.1 Examples of Megastores (and Their Sales Areas) in 2018

Brand	City	Sales area (in m^2)
Spazio Armani	Milan	6,500
Chanel	Ginza building, Tokyo	6,100
Hermès	Seoul	6,000
Gucci	New York, 5th Avenue	4,300
Dior	Seoul	4,200
Chanel	Soho, New York	4,150
Louis Vuitton	Champs-Elysées, Paris	3,600
Louis Vuitton	Place Vendôme, Paris	3,500
Louis Vuitton	Omotesando, Tokyo	3,100
Prada	Aoyama, Tokyo	2,800
Tod's	Omotesando, Tokyo	2,550
Prada	New York	2,300
Louis Vuitton	1 East 57, New York	1,900
Valentino	New York	1,850
Dior	Omotesando, Tokyo	1,550
Hugo Boss	Champs-Elysées, Paris	1,350
Hermès	Ginza, Tokyo	1,300
Dior	Avenue Montaigne, Paris	1,200

Source: Based on data from various press articles.

It is obvious that the development of megastores is rather like a battle of the titans where only the very big brands can compete and make money. Small brands, or even intermediary brands, are not able to participate in this game, and remain on the sidelines.

Another offshoot of this battle of the titans is that it is a very strong incitement to develop all categories of products. It would indeed be monotonous, if not ridiculous, to sell nothing but handbags in a 2,000 m² store. To stay in the megastore race, one has to offer a comprehensive product range, together with, of course, a luxury ready-to-wear collection. For a large brand, a megastore therefore represents a strong incentive to develop a full product range.

One would think that in creating these huge stores, brands seem to compete with each other, forgetting the customer (like the department stores in the 1880s did) while they create an ever-wider range of products always under the same banner. Will megastores continue to grow? Probably, as long as they are profitable and brands wish to display their strength in markets that are a priority for them. We must also remember that they are more than just stores. Megastores have a tendency of becoming real institutions in cities where they are located.

Institutional Stores

In a certain way, institutional stores are the opposite of megastores. When brands realise a large percentage of their indirect-distribution sales through multi-brand stores, they need to reinforce their image with small boutiques that act somewhat like showrooms open to the public, which convey a message, telling customers and multi-brand retailers that the brand is also a real institution like their big brothers. These institutional stores do not need to be big – 60–200 m² is sufficient – but they have to be situated in prestigious locations.

Many watch manufacturers open this type of sales outlet. They present the entire collection of the brand, unlike independent jewellery stores, which are only able to display a part of their collections because they sell products from a large number of brands. Having a prestigious address in a particular city also reinforces the brand's image and implies the guarantee of an after-sales service that is of the highest quality.

But such stores require locations that are really exceptional. If a watch manufacturer opens this type of institutional store in Shanghai, for example, but on the wrong side of Huai Hai Zhong Lu Street or in the basement of Plaza 66, it completely misses the mark.

Temporary (Pop-Up) Stores   This is a relatively recent development, and Comme des Garçons has been credited with inventing it. It has been replicated by many other brands. The original idea was to rent a commercial space, slightly off the beaten track (a destination out-let, for example) with a rent as low as possible, and sell products in a warehouse-like environment, organising at the same time a series of public relations events, such as a presentation of 'vintage' articles of the brand, so that the customer comes not only to buy something, but to participate in an unusual and original experience.

Of course, in principle, a temporary store would also earn money, especially if the rent is very low and if the collector's items and the chosen theme are attractive enough to draw a diverse clientele. This can also be a very effective public relations tool. For example, a temporary store could be set up a few weeks before Christmas, giving journalists the occasion to talk about the brand in a different and compelling way.

Comme des Garçons opened the first pop-up store in Berlin, then called a 'guerrilla shop' or 'propaganda shop', in February 2004. Many others followed: in Barcelona, Helsinki, Singapore, Stockholm, Ljubljana and Warsaw. They were temporary shops where products were displayed in locker rooms or on tables, without much refinement, often located in noncommercial areas, as a counter-reaction to the growing hyper-commercialisation of city centres. The manifesto of the brand proclaims: 'The location will be chosen according to its atmosphere, its links to history, its location away from established shopping areas or other interesting features.'

The Berlin store looked very much like a discount store, but the idea has since clearly evolved into that of a true concept boutique, with its own merchandising codes and its 'architecture'. Only the tempo-rary character and the choice of location of the first guerrilla shop have been retained.

Many other brands (Evian, Wrangler, Gap, Nokia, Levi, Louis Vuitton, Chanel and Target, to name but a few) have since adopted the idea of temporary shops, often without due reflection, preferring to create an event rather than using it as a means to reinforce the value of the brand. We offer a typology of temporary stores showing how a brand can use them as a powerful development tool.

- A means to accentuate rarity: this is the preferred option for many luxury brands. Over the past 10 years, these brands have lost some of their lustre by multiplying the number of boutiques and expanding their clientele base. They may have thereby lost some of this sense of rarity – which is one of the fundamentals in luxury – and believed that their pricing policies and the reinforcement of their image would be enough to justify their luxury brand status. Pop-up stores are a way of recreating rarity: a temporary point of sale that offers an ephemeral and exclusive collection. A brand that understands this aspect best is Louis Vuitton. The temporary shop shared with Comme des Garçons (yes, really!) was a perfect example of this strategy. Opened from 4 September to mid-December 2008 in Tokyo, it offered a series of six limited edition bags.
- A means for the brand to kindle desire in cities where it had been totally absent until then: this was the case with Comme des Garçons' guerrilla stores and it was still the case in 2009 with Target's temporary shops, called Bulls-Eye Bazaars. Absent from several major cities like New York and Chicago, and based on a concept of 'chic and cheap', they borrow the idea of rarity from the luxury sector with products created by famous designers in limited editions and with reduced prices.
- A means to test a new business concept: that is what Procter & Gamble attempted to do with Look Fab Studio, an itinerant temporary store in Canada. All Procter & Gamble's beauty products are grouped together (Pantene, Cover Girl, Olay, Nice and Easy, Crest and Venus, among others) in a space where professional stylists offer advice on skin care and hair colouring, and mini-treatment sessions. All the services were free, and there are no products on sale. But for the first time one finds a comprehensive beauty presentation from Procter & Gamble under one roof – a foretaste of future boutiques, perhaps?

- A method to launch a new product: this is the most common reason and, in our opinion, the least interesting. A brand organises an event, and instead of it being a press conference or a social event, it is a temporary shop where customers may discover the new range. That is what Gap did in San Francisco in April 2009 to launch its 1969 Premium Denim Jeans line. Its temporary boutique stayed open for 5 months. Glaceau did the same thing in New York for 10 days, to launch its VitaminWater10.

What makes people visit pop-up stores? Table 13.2 shows that, in the case of China, a strong impulse that drives people to enter a store is to enjoy themselves. Going shopping is probably considered entertainment. We see in the table that a Chinese woman spends an average of 9.3 hours a week visiting stores.

In China, friends often call each other up and say, 'Let's go and visit some (fashion) boutiques'. This 'entertainment' aspect of shopping exists in other countries to a lesser degree and, seen from this perspective, temporary shops seem to be an excellent idea.

Also worth mentioning is Hermès, which opened a temporary boutique in Paris, from May to December 2010, with an artisan specialising in leather working at a table set up in the window of the shop.

When they are able to offer high-quality entertainment, a compelling story released in several newspapers by way of public relations, and a high turnover, temporary shops seem to be an interesting new development. They now are so much top-of-the-mind of media and customers alike that in the weeks following the opening of the first Le Jardin Retrouvé Experience Store in Paris (a unique concept in the very standardised world of perfume stores, created by artist Clara Feder) all persons visiting were asking: 'Is this a pop-up store?'

Table 13.2 Shopping and Entertainment

	Number of hours per week spent shopping	Number of boutiques visited each week
China	9.3	4.6
United States	3.6	3.1
France	3.0	2.5

Source: Based on data from *Shanghai Daily*, November 2009. Also in Chevalier and Lu (2009).

Stores Where the Primary Goal Is to Increase Sales Volumes

When moving from one type of shop to another, it is important to remember that the main objective of a store is to be profitable. Management should painstakingly envisage an ideal store of a size that reflects the strength of the brand and a detailed and proven approach to marketing. Should accessories be presented separately or together with ready-to-wear? Do ties sell better when placed near men's suits or near shirts? Should there be a special area for shoes?

Since a store in a second-tier city probably looks different from a flagship store in Paris or Milan, people tend to forget that every brand conforms to a set of good commercial practices that are implemented anywhere.

Coach, for example, uses factory outlets to quickly assess the appeal of its new models in each size and colour before the finalised model finds its way to the shelves of its prestigious boutiques. The idea is not without interest: the use of test stores in discount centres to measure the impact of various merchandising tools and define the ideal presentation with the aim of increasing volumes and consumer satisfaction in its traditional outlets.

How Many Outlets Should There Be in a Given City?

Given the existing balance of each brand between local and destination locations, it should be possible to determine an ideal number of outlets in a particular city.

Looking at it objectively, we see that when a brand has a flagship store or a megastore in a city, it is often reluctant to open a second one. The sales teams probably seek to ensure that the flagship functions at peak capacity, and do not wish to take the risk of opening a second outlet immediately. For a very long time, Hermès had only one store in Paris (their flagship store), a small sales point in the Hilton Hotel on the Left Bank, and a store on Avenue Georges V which they shared with the Motsch hat brand, while Salvatore Ferragamo had more than ten stores in the same town. Hermès probably under-optimised its Parisian turnover figures. It has now opened a second store on the rue de Sèvres and the third one on Avenue Georges V. Louis Vuitton had only one megastore in Shanghai, and three stores in Beijing for many years, before it opened two more stores in Shanghai and three others in Beijing, making it a total of three in Shanghai plus six in Beijing in 2018. A flagship store, with its strong attraction, diminishes the relevance of a second sales point (in volume or in proximity), but most major cities have prestigious commercial districts and several neighbourhoods where being present is a matter of prestige.

Since we are passing from the idea of a single store (situated in the best possible location or in an exceptional place) to that of multiple stores, we need to analyse the potential of the various locations in a city in a more systematic way.

'A Store Should Be a Place of Worship' or an 'Institution'

Donna Karan's words say it all. She speaks of 'modernity', 'sensuality', 'theatricality' (in de Châtel and Hunt 2003). It is true that a luxury store should be much more than just a place where products are displayed and sold.

In fact, a well-managed luxury retail outlet organises product presentations and special events. On the walls, an iconography in the form of advertisements or photographs displaying known artists with the products of the brand should be displayed. Music in the store should convey the story of the brand's origins. Sometimes a particular aroma emanating from the leather used in the products and by the brand confers, in a way, a kind of 'sanctity', of 'sacredness' to the manner in which it promotes the image of the stylist or the star, or both, who created it.

To wrap up this section dedicated to retail outlets in a way that can be applied to both boutiques of exception and more traditional stores, let us take a look at the example of Sephora on the Champs-Élysées in Paris. It is a huge store with sales that reached €150 million in 2018. But it is more than a store, it is also a meeting point. On an average, 20,000 people cross its threshold on a Saturday, against 9,000 on a Monday. When people wish to see a film at the cinema next door, they usually plan to meet at Sephora. The average ticket of the store is very high:

€100. Because it serves as a meeting point, the percentage of customers leaving the store with a purchase is very low on Saturdays and Sundays (the conversion rate is 23%, which corresponds to 4,600 tickets), but it is much higher on Mondays (with around 33% of visitors making a purchase, i.e., around 3,000 tickets). Managing a store of this size is not just about selling products and handling the cash; it is about ensuring that the store remains an institution and that it is the best meeting point on the Avenue des Champs-Élysées. To do so, it is necessary to organise special events that position the store as a place of exception in the eyes of the customer.

In Which International Cities Should One Open Stores?

What is special about luxury products is that customers can buy them both in their own countries and abroad. A Japanese customer can very well buy a Hermès tie in New York, a French citizen can buy an Italian perfume in Germany, and Swedes can buy a French perfume during their holidays in the Canary Islands (Spanish). With these individual approaches it is clear that, if a luxury brand wishes to endure and be credible, it should be available in almost every country in the world.

When a luxury brand is not available in the USA, Japan or France, it loses some of its power of attraction. Spanish customers would prefer to buy a jewel from Cartier or Bulgari rather than one from Suarez because they know that even if Suarez is well known in Spain, the brand is almost unknown in New York or Germany and so will not impress their foreign friends. Thus, in a way, no major luxury brand can remain local. It has to advance to the world stage. Brands that are starting out may remain local initially, but only if they give clear signs that they have a desire to develop internationally in the future.

Where are brands situated in the world? Richard Ellis examined this issue in a study by CBRE on the presence of luxury brands in the various capitals of the world. The results are given in Table 13.3.

This table reveals several surprises. Firstly, the fact that 11 cities out of 18 with usual selling outlets are located in Asia (with only 2 in America, including, curiously, Las Vegas). Secondly, the fact that, among

Table 13.3   Percentage of Luxury Brands
Present in Different Cities in the World

1	Shanghai	87%
2	Dubai	83%
3	London	83%
4	Hong Kong	81%
5	Tokyo	79%
6	Singapore	75%
7	New York	73%
8	Taipei	73%
9	Moscow	73%
10	Beijing	71%
11	Paris	71%
12	Seoul	69%
13	Las Vegas	67%
14	Chengdu	67%
15	Taichung	67%
16	Milan	67%
17	Nagoya	67%
18	Kobe	65%

Source: Based on data from Ellis (2018).

the 11 Asian cities, only 3 are located in mainland China (including Chengdu), compared to 3 in Japan (with Nagoya and Kobe making up for the absence of Osaka), and 2 on the tiny island of Taiwan.

While these percentages are surprising, they nevertheless give a clear picture of the current situation. It would also interest brand managers, who probably have stores in many of these 18 cities, to know which of the 18 cities currently have the highest percentages. To get an even clearer picture this table should be read together with Table 13.4, which is a classification of the world's most 'attractive' cities for brand executives.

But how do companies choose to set up shop in one city rather than in another, and on what criteria do they base their choices? This depends on the origin of the brands. CBRE did a research on the origins of the brands in three of the streets made famous by the luxury trade (without having extended their analysis to Paris or Milan!). The results are given in Table 13.5.

Table 13.4   The Most 'Attractive'
Destinations for Opening a Store

1	London
2	Hong Kong
3	Paris
4	Tokyo
5	New York
6	Shanghai
7	Singapore
8	Dubai
9	Beijing
10	Osaka
11	Taipei

Source: Based on data from Jones Lang LaSalle
(2016).

Table 13.5   Percentage According to Origin of the Brands Located in Three
Major Shopping Streets

	Bond Street, London	Madison Avenue, New York	Canton Street, Hong Kong
Italy	19%	27%	15%
France	14%	20%	17%
United Kingdom	30%	12%	7%
United States	6%	28%	–
Switzerland	16%	4%	13%
China	–	–	27%
Other origins	5%	9%	21%
	100%	100%	100%

Source: Based on data from Ellis (2018).

In this table we notice the very strong presence of Italian and French brands, but in different locations depending on the capitals. In New York and London, Italian brands are slightly more present than the French, but they are more-or-less on the same level in Hong Kong. In Hong Kong, we notice, of course, the presence of Chinese brands. Another study by Jones Lang LaSalle lists the number of tourists in some Asian cities (see Table 13.6).

So, should luxury trade be global? Definitely, yes. But, as with many other questions, a word of caution would be in order.

Table 13.6   Number of Tourists Who Visited Different Asian Cities in 2017 (in Millions)

	Foreign tourists	Domestic tourists
Mumbai (Bombay)	4.4	
Hong Kong	56.7	
Macao	30.9	
Melbourne	2.6	8.8
New Delhi	2.4	
Osaka	9.4	
Beijing	4.2	171.1
Seoul	13.5	
Shanghai	8.0	139.2
Singapore	16.4	
Sydney	3.6	9.2
Taipei	10.6	
Tokyo	13.1	

Source: Based on data from Jones Lang LaSalle (2018).

In this table, we note the incredibly large number of Chinese visiting Beijing (171 million) and Shanghai (139 million), not forgetting those who visit Hong Kong (a major percentage of the 57 million) and Macao (a major percentage of the 31 million). We also notice that Singapore is a strong magnet for tourists (16 million, i.e. more than the 13 million in Tokyo and Seoul).

Among the Chinese visitors who go to Beijing, Shanghai or Hong Kong every day, there is no doubt those who are travelling for business as well. There are also bona fide tourists who come to visit and do some shopping. It is important that the stores they visit meet their expectations.

The Case of Mainland China

Mainland China plays a distinctive role in the luxury industry. This is a priority market, and as such deserves special attention. This is why we have reproduced a table by Luca Solca, which retraces the location of different luxury brands in major cities in China in early 2018 (see Table 13.7).

Table 13.7   Location of the Main Sales Points in China

	Beijing	Shanghai	Hangzhou	Shenyang	Others	Total
Versace	9	7	1	2	32	51
Moncler	5	4	1	2	15	27
Dolce & Gabbana	8	7	3	3	26	47
Zegna	13	9	3	3	53	80
Givenchy	4	4	2	2	7	19
Tod's	3	5	3	3	23	37
Ferragamo	8	8	5	4	50	75
Bulgari	6	5	1	2	20	32
Alex McQueen	2	2	1	–	3	8
Georgio Armani	4	2	2	2	14	24
Miu Miu	5	4	1	1	14	25
Burberry	6	7	2	3	39	57
Bottega Ven.	9	4	2	3	21	39
Loro Pian	5	3	1	1	7	17
Valentino	7	4	2	1	9	23
Gucci	6	7	2	2	40	57
Saint-Laurent	7	3	2	–	9	21
Prada	4	6	2	2	23	37
Louboutin	4	3	1	1	1	10
Louis Vuitton	6	3	4	3	25	41
Hermès	5	4	2	1	13	25
Total	**128**	**88**	**47**	**40**	**449**	**752**

Source: Based on data from Solca (2018).

Beijing heads the list with 17% of the companies, far ahead of Shanghai with 12%; the third and fourth cities are less known than, for example, Shenzhen or Guangzhou. The last two are understandably affected by the proximity of Hong Kong, a city without customs duties, as they have to pay both customs duties and a special luxury tax imposed in mainland China. What is certain is that a presence in China requires a comprehensive, elaborate and expensive development plan, including a large communications budget to develop brand awareness at the national level, as luxury consumers are spread out in at least a dozen cities. One should never forget that in fact in hundreds of third, fourth or even fifth tier cities in China customers are wealthy and underserved. These are the new territories luxury brands should explore.

Why Choose One City Rather than Another?

Lastly, to analyse the most rational locations, Jones Lang LaSalle (2016) drew up a transparency index to gauge the level of security in various countries, based on the risk involved when investing in a store. To do so, it defines the various risk levels and security levels of a financial investment for potential operators.

Jones Lang LaSalle's transparency index is based on five criteria:

- The availability of an investment performance index.
- The availability of key market data.
- Government regulations and obligations and communication of financial information.
- Regulatory and legal factors.
- Professional and ethical standards.

The premise here is that when a global player invests in a sales outlet in a foreign country, it should be certain of its value, it should be able to resell it later at an acceptable price, it should be able to find local and secure financing offers, and it should be assured that the legal and regulatory aspects of the operation are clear for everyone and that there will be no unpleasant surprises later on.

Table 13.8 shows a list of countries, where the nine countries with the highest transparency indexes are shown in the first column. It is interesting to note here that countries such as Germany, Italy, Switzerland and Japan are in the second column, because the commercial real estate situation that exists in these countries is not always as clear as one might hope for.

Under the 'poor' or 'opaque' transparency rating, one notices second-tier Chinese cities and also Algeria and Syria.

But Jones Lang LaSalle goes even further. Instead of pointing a finger at a particular country, it explains that the transparency index is correlated to the per-capita GDP, levels of corruption at a given time, and the

Table 13.8 Geographical Locations of Commercial Activities (Transparency Index)

Highly transparent	Transparent	Half-transparent	Transparency low or opaque
1. Canada	10. Ireland	29. Russia tier 1 cities	65. China (tier 2)
2. Australia	11. Hong Kong	34. Russia tier 1 cities	77. Vietnam
3. United States	12. Singapore	44. South Korea	79. Cambodia
4. New Zealand	13. Finland	49. China tier 1 cities	81. Algeria
5. United Kingdom	14. Germany	50. India tier 1 cities	81. Syria
6. The Netherlands	15. Denmark		
7. France	16. Spain		
8. Sweden	17. Austria		
9. Belgium	18. Norway		
	19. Italy		
	20. Switzerland		
	21. South Africa		
	22. Portugal		
	23. Malaysia		
	24. Czech Republic		
	25. Poland		
	26. Japan		

Source: Based on data from Jones Lang LaSalle (2009).

general economic outlook. The point made here is that as countries develop and improve their level of democracy and political stability, they become more transparent, making it easier for foreign companies to invest with confidence in local commercial real estate. However, what is most interesting is that it illustrates how, at comparable levels of economic and democratic development, some countries are simply less secure and less transparent than others for foreign companies who wish to invest.

So, should luxury trade be international? Without question, yes. But, as with many other aspects, a certain amount of caution should be exercised.

Trade Areas Analysis

Let us start with an economic analysis before a geographical analysis; we will conclude with the potential application of these tools to luxury stores.

Financial Analysis

Today, before choosing the location of a supermarket, managers carefully examine criteria such as purchasing power, suitability of the commercial area and potential for business growth. If they are able to survey the area from a helicopter, they will also be able to examine traffic flow, traffic lights, bottlenecks, and accesses and exits relating to a particular plot of land or a particular shopping centre. The financial stakes justify this degree of scrutiny. They then ask specialised consultant firms to carry out financial analyses on their behalf. The data available today is so precise that a General Manager of a brand told us that he was managing 80 stores in Seoul and that the head office of the group, based in Europe, was able to designate a location for the 81st one, even though the European teams had never visited the city.

The *average purchasing power* for almost every neighbourhood in the world is known today:

• Income per urban block.
• Number of mobile phones per area.
• Number of credit cards and percentage of credit cards overdue.
• Number of burglaries and houses broken into in the area.

One can thus determine the *suitability of the commercial area* based on the purchasing power index and the retail sales in the area. Using this approach one can calculate:

– The *net market trade advocacy*, taking into account the areas where stores are scarce.
– The *store saturation*, using a saturation index equal to the ratio of the number of consumers in the commercial zone multiplied by the average expenditure in the category divided by the square metres of a sales area. This gives an estimate of the sales per square metre in the area for each commercial zone in the world.

These indicators are then compared to the potential for commercial growth, taking into account the economic trends in the area, revenue forecasts and the previously established sensitivities to sales revenue increases in the category in question.

Geographical Analysis

The economic data should then be weighed against an elemental geographical analysis. Each commercial zone is unique in its own way, and its specific structure can have many different outcomes, for example, depending on whether it is a large furniture store, an outlying supermarket or a large shopping centre with a wide selection of goods. One also has to keep in mind people's behavioural tendencies when they move around in a particular city.

Firstly, one should take into account obstacles, such as rivers or highways, that people are reluctant to cross when they go shopping, even if the store or mall in question is actually easier to reach than the one on the same side they are on. In Hong Kong, for example, a person living on the island is generally reluctant to plan a shopping spree on the peninsula, that is, on the Kowloon side, even though one can use the underground to cross the channel. In Paris, people who live on the Left Bank tend to shop on the Left Bank, and those who live on the Right Bank are not more inclined to cross the Seine either. They would, of course, cross over for work or to go to the university, but they are less disposed to cross it just to go shopping. Why? No one has found a reason for this behaviour.

Railway tracks are also a psychological barrier, especially if they are not underground. But train stations, as we can see in the case of Japan, work like magnets, not only on travellers but also on people who never take the train.

Which are the best sides of a street? In the Northern Hemisphere, in a street that goes from east to west, the northern side is always the first choice, because it is sunnier and the southern side is in the shade. Of course, if the street is very narrow and the buildings are high, the distinction lessens, or even disappears. But on the Champs-Élysées in Paris, there are three times as many people strolling on the north side of the pavement as on the south side. Is the rent three times cheaper on the south side? Not really, but real estate agents say that rents are on average 30% lower on the south side than on the north side. The south side therefore would offer an interesting choice for 'destination' brand stores, but it would not be a very appropriate choice in terms of balancing the budget for convenience stores such as fast-food or ice cream outlets, which have to take advantage of the number of potential customers passing by. In streets going south to north, the east side is preferred because it is brighter in the afternoon, when people do most of their shopping.

How about cities like Madrid or Singapore, where the climate is very warm? In such cases people prefer to walk in the shade, but only to a certain extent, because the sun illuminates the shops on the north side, making them more attractive, as one sees in London or Tokyo.

Does it make a difference? On the Champs-Elysees in Paris, certainly yes. A store on the south side that does not have strong drawing power could see three times fewer customers entering the shop than if it had been on the north side. And this point has its own significance, because, as we just said, the rent on the south side of the Champs-Elysees is not three times cheaper than on the north side.

Clusters

In any given city, a trade area could be regarded as the result of the sum of clusters that will be defined as a function of the economic analysis and trade analysis. In a small town, the catchment areas of two supermarkets might be superimposed, but if there is only one jeweller, it would benefit from the customers of both supermarkets.

Whenever customers make a purchase, it is important to know where they live. If they pay by cheque, one can easily find their address. If they pay by card where no identity is needed, the information is a bit more difficult to obtain. An alternative is to conduct a survey of a sample group of customers as they are leaving the store. Regardless of how this information is obtained, it is useful to find out the percentage of the volume of customers living 5, 10, 20 or more minutes from the store. This can provide very valuable insights into how to go about promoting the store (and within which area to do so). This can also be very helpful in case one is considering the opening of a second store in the same city.

Reilly's Laws

William J. Reilly's laws date back to 1929 but are still considered the only way to measure the pulling power of two similar stores in two cities, or the impact of several competing stores in the same commercial area.

Reilly's First Law Reilly's first law helps to determine the point between two cities, A and B, where people will prefer to go shopping, and is set forth as follows:

$$Point\ of\ equal\ probability = \frac{Distance\ (in\ km)\ between\ A\ and\ B}{1 + \sqrt{Population\ of\ A\ /\ Population\ of\ B}}$$

In fact, Reilly evaluated the attractiveness of each city according to the number of inhabitants.

If one assumes that the distance between A and B is 100 km and that city A has 40,000 inhabitants as against 10,000 for B, then:

The point of equal probability = 33.3 km

This means that someone who lives 65 km from A, which is four times larger than B, will prefer to go shopping in city A. Only those living less than 33.3 km from B will go shopping in B.

This law remains valid today. It has been slightly adapted to take into account not only the distance but also the travel time and the various obstacles as explained above. It has also been modified so that, in certain cases, it is not the ratio between the number of inhabitants of each city that comes into play but the ratio of the volumes of retail sales.

Retail sales are a very good indicator of how attractive a city is, but very often people prefer to use as criteria the number of square metres dedicated to fashion or type of goods.

Reilly's Second Law Reilly's second law relates to the presence of similar stores in the same area, as is often the case for luxury goods. Are the brands helping or undermining each other? We previously mentioned the example of Chinese real estate developers who are willing to reduce their rents in order to attract famous brands. This shows that the market believes that the presence of strong brands could attract customers who will end up buying from other, less well-known brands as well.

It goes without saying that some businesses are antithetical. For example, a store selling wedding dresses cannot be located near a gas station or a seedy nightclub. The problem is not only the difference in prestige or location, but also the effect on the customer's mood when they enter a boutique or when they are looking for a boutique. In the same manner, a restaurant of a fast-food chain next to a Gucci boutique will have a negative impact on the consumer's disposition when entering the Gucci store. (Is this really the most prestigious location of the city?)

William Reilly attributes a positive or negative impact of the presence of two stores in the same neighbourhood according to three criteria.

- *The sales volumes of stores* A *and* B: this is reminiscent of the sizes of the two cities in Reilly's first law, to a certain extent. Clearly, the higher its sales volume, the more attractive the store is. In fact, rather than volume, it would be more interesting to look at the number of invoices generated by each of the two stores. A jeweller with a very high turnover, but who has very few customers each day, will not attract the number of customers that a tie or glove vendor will need to attain their daily volume, but the idea of comparing volumes becomes relevant when there are two stores selling the same type of products.
- *The concept of intentional purchase*, which brings us back to the idea of the attraction power of each brand. For each of the brands, A and B, we retain the ratio between the number of customers making a purchase and the number of customers who plan to make a purchase. If the percentage of intentional purchases is high, it clearly means that we are dealing with a 'destination' brand, and that its presence generates more business for others. If this percentage is low, we clearly have a brand that generates little volume on its own and depends on several others to attain its turnover, taking advantage, so to speak, of customers attracted by other brands.

  In the case of the Chinese luxury shopping centre developer, our advice would be to calculate the ratio of intentional purchases for each of the luxury brands with which the developer wishes to do business, and adjust the rental rates based on these figures. This will still mean a significant advantage to brands that generate a high volume, but that would be par for the course.

- *A degree of customer interchange* will show a positive coefficient if both brands are highly compatible (10–20% of customers in common), moderately compatible (5–10%) or marginally compatible (1–5%). The coefficient would be negative if the stores are not compatible, or if they hamper each other.

William J. Reilly's intention was to show that the increase in turnover due to the proximity of two competing stores is:

- directly proportional to the number of customers in common;
- inversely proportional to the ratio of their volumes;
- proportional to the sum of their intentional purchase rate.

It can therefore be written thus:

$$V = I(V_L + V_S) \times \frac{V_S}{V_L} \times (P_L + P_S)$$

where V_L and V_S are the store volumes (L for the largest, S for the smallest), I the customer-compatibility rate, and P_L and P_S the intentional purchase rate of each store.

For example, with:

$V_L = $ €5,000,000
$P_L = 90\%$
$V_S = $ €3,000,000
$P_S = 30\%$
$I = 25\%$

we get:

$$I(V_L + V_S) = 0.25(5,000,000 + 3,000,000) = €2,000,000$$

This should be multiplied by the inverse of the volume ratio:

$$I(V_L + V_S) \times \frac{V_S}{V_L} = 2,000,000 \times \frac{3,000,000}{5,000,000} = €1,200,000$$

and:

$$I(V_L + V_S) \times \frac{V_S}{V_L} \times V_S \times (P_L + P_S) = 1,200,000 \times 1.2 = €1,440,000$$

This additional business (18% of the total) would be divided between the two brands, in inverse ratio to their intentional purchase rate.

Applying It to Luxury

The concepts of the power of attraction, customer generation and additional business for brands reinforcing each other in the same area certainly reminds one of certain situations in the luxury sector, where brands like Loewe and Bottega Veneta knew how to take advantage of their proximity to Louis Vuitton and Gucci in Asia. Bringing together many competing brands in one place provides another advantage – it makes shopping a pleasant and varied experience for the customer.

Managing Customer Diversity

Two types of customers enter a store:

- *The buyers*: they are interested in the brand or a product and are looking for efficient and quality service.
- *The browsers*: they enter a shop for amusement and discovery. They do not necessarily wish to buy anything, and will probably leave empty-handed, but they may come back later for a purchase. They are looking for a sensory experience and even if they never purchase a product, can play the role of opinion leaders and spread positive or negative opinions about the brand.

The concept is that buyers and window shoppers alike expect much more when visiting a store than merely finding a tie or a silk scarf. They wish to take part in a meaningful experience, they wish to be amazed and diverted. This diversion can be provided in various ways:

- Japanese department stores usually have a floor or part of a floor dedicated to restaurants: French, Italian, Chinese and, of course, Japanese. They sometimes also organise art exhibitions within the premises. They strive to be more than just a department store and to play a role as a real cultural hub in their city. Sometimes a luxury brand has its own museum in some of its larger stores. The Louis Vuitton store on the Champs-Élysées in Paris has its own contemporary art gallery on the top floor (unfortunately with a separate entry and hardly any publicity) in which several exhibitions are organised each year. As for the Hermès flagship store in Seoul, its basement functions as an extremely well-decorated museum, with historical and traditional objects from the Hermès collection.

- Every luxury store, through its own design, should offer added aesthetic value and highly interesting features to the average window shopper.
- Temporary sales points and other 'pop-up stores' are effective tools to offer this entertainment dimension to both window buyers and window shoppers.

Some American shopping centres have well understood the concept of ambience and amusement. In the Mall of America, the West Market side has been designed to create a European atmosphere, the South Avenue side replicates Rodeo Drive, and the East Broadway side is designed in the form of a lotus. Of course, at first glance, this may sound very unremarkable and artificial, but the goal is to surprise people and offer them something new and different.

When a new commercial zone was being developed in Singapore, Lee Moch Suan, the Minister of Industry, explained it in these words:

The essence of our approach is to mark the 'product' in a way that responds to people's expectations, to allow them to experience this brand identity. We need to create an image here that gives a sense of unity.

Buyers and window shoppers alike would probably say that this is actually what they expect from a new type of store.

Adapt the Location to the Hallmarks of Luxury

When determining the specifications for defining a new store concept, sales managers should ask the following questions:

- Is the 'ambience' planned the correct one?
- Is the overall image of the store in line with its positioning in terms of pricing?

- Will the store attract only those who are already in the area, or is the brand strong enough to attract destination shoppers on its own? In either case, the response should be taken into account when considering the ambience of the store.
- How extensive is the collection and what does it entail in terms of product presentations?
- How many customers are likely to be in the store at a given time?
- How can one facilitate the dialogue between sales staff and customers in the store?
- What extra services can one offer (alterations, after-sales service)?

The answers will greatly depend on the planned location of the store, its surroundings and the customer target.

Example

The Example of London

In his book on retail, Emanuele Sacerdote (2007) gives us an example of a study conducted by Management Horizons Europe on the locations of luxury stores on various streets in London. Table 13.9 is an extract from that analysis.

Table 13.9   Position on Various Streets in London in Terms of Brand Image

	Classic	Classic/ Contem- porary	Contemporary	Trendy
Covent Garden		x	x	
King's Road		x	x	
Brick Lane				x
Regent Street	x			
Bond Street	x	x		
Carnaby Street			x	x
Sloane Street	x	x		
Knightsbridge	x	x		

Source: Based on data from Management Horizons Europe Project 2006, in Sacerdote (2007).

The idea is that besides its capacity to generate revenue for a given brand, the location of a store also transmits a message about the values of the brand and what it stands for. The location of a store is a powerful message in itself. It represents an investment in terms of image and the characteristics it conveys should be understood right from the early stages of the location search analysis.

The Various Types of Commercial Leases

We shall now look at the various shop-renting systems (commercial leases) that exist in the world, and also their financial implications. We also give you some examples of rental costs in various cities.

In order to obtain a prime location in a city that is a major luxury destination, it is usually necessary to pay some form of 'key money' in addition to rent. Three different systems exist.

The Japanese System

In Japan, leases are usually signed for a 9-year period, but the lessee has the option to terminate the lease at the end of every 3-year period. The lease amount, including any rent increases, is clearly specified in the rental agreement.

Upon signing the lease, the lessee has to pay the lessor a deposit equal to the rent for the entire term of the lease. Thus, for a 9-year lease, the lessor is paid an amount equal to 9 years' rent that is deposited in the lessor's account during the lease period. If the lease is renewed at a higher rent for the following 9 years, the lessee pays the deposit difference for the following 9 years.

At the expiry of the lease, the deposit is returned to the lessee, without interest.

This system is highly advantageous to the lessor as, in a certain way, he gets double rent during the lease term. As soon as the lessee occupies the premises, the amount equal to 9 years' rent can be credited to the lessor's account. In general, buying or building a shop would cost approximately 10 to 15 years' rent. Therefore, most of the lessor's investment is covered as soon as the property is leased out. This enables the lessor to purchase another property and repeat the process.

For the lessee, this system is extremely onerous, as renting and opening a new store means very heavy investment. Renting between 10 and 20 stores in Japan would require an investment that is almost impossible to assume, even for the biggest luxury brands. They therefore tend to rent only one or two stores and then open shops-in-shops in department stores. This is the reason why one finds luxury brands mainly in department stores in Japan.

At a second level, some luxury brands that are very successful in Japan decide to build stores 'from scratch'. They buy land in the best possible localities and construct their own stores to suit their requirements. For the most part, these are very beautiful megastores, or at the least, very impressive flagship stores.

The Japanese deposit system was probably an initial safeguard against excessive proliferation of foreign-brand stores. With time, it turned out to be a huge bonus for department stores, and subsequently, a strong motivation to create directly operated stores.

The American System

In the American system, the leases are also quite long, 9 or 10 years. There may be some kind of goodwill to be paid to the previous tenant, officially to cover the costs of redecoration, but this sum is minimal.

All increases in rent are agreed at the outset and specified in the contract. The contract comes into effect upon signature, and neither of the parties owes any sum to the other upon termination.

It is important, however, to bear in mind that there is no termination clause in lease agreements in the United States. This means that even if the lessee realises that the quality of the premises is not as good as anticipated or that after three or four months its brand and products will never attain the turnover expected in that locality, it will still have to pay the rent for the full term of the lease with no possibility of renegotiating the rent or ending the lease. For example, one cannot ask for a reduction in rent if sales are lower than projected. The lessee has to pay the rent even if it decides to shut up shop. The only solution would be to find a sub-lessee for the remaining period; but if the sublease rent is lower, the tenant will have to make up the difference.

Many companies have found themselves in this difficult situation, and some found a way around the system. A foreign luxury company would create a subsidiary for each of its stores. If the store had problems and needed to be shut down, the subsidiary would declare bankruptcy, thus sidestepping the problem of a long-term obligation to the lessor.

The lessors found a response, of course. They would ask the brand's head office in Milan or Paris to act as guarantors. If the location were excellent and in high demand, some companies would agree to such a clause. In other cases, they would probably refuse.

The US system is standard in China, Hong Kong and most of South-East Asia, but the lease periods are much shorter (usually 3 years), making the financial obligation (and the risk) quite realistic.

The French System

Unlike the Japanese and American systems that favour the lessor, the French system, which also applies in southern Europe, leans heavily in favour of the tenant.

In the French system, when leasing commercial premises, the lessor receives a monthly rent and no other payment. The agreement is signed for 9 years, and the tenant may terminate the contract at the end of any 3-year period. Rent increases are not stipulated in the agreement. They are based on the national construction cost index published every year.

At the end of the 9-year period, the lessor cannot oblige the lessee to leave if the lessee wishes to stay on. In such case, a new agreement has to be signed for another 9 years, with a minimal increase in rent.

The lessee is also free to transfer the lease to a third party (usually against a substantial goodwill payment), by simply informing the lessor by registered letter that the lease of the premises has been transferred to the said third party. The lessor cannot use this as an excuse to increase the rent. Even if the lessor believes that a substantial sum has been negotiated, they has no say in the matter.

The only case where the lessor could intervene in the lease transfer is if the original contract restricted the lessee to a specific market niche, such as ready-to-wear, or optics. If the sub-lessee wished to conduct a different business (for example, fast food or mobile phones), then the lessor could renegotiate the original lease and increase the rent.

The original idea behind the goodwill payment system was that a trader who wished to retire and sold their store, and often their equipment, stock and customer base, could do so against a comfortable sum of money. This arrangement was very practical at the time when small traders had no retirement pension. The goodwill money allowed them to organise their new life. However, things change, and nowadays some premises in Paris are leased out according to the 'American' system, i.e., for a period of 10 years with no key money or goodwill to pay.

In France, certain rent rates were regulated a long time ago and were never significantly increased. The amount of goodwill paid to the previous lessee therefore serves as an offset to market rates. The advantage for the lessee is that it can show the goodwill as an asset in its accounts, and use it as security for obtaining a bank loan.

No matter what the system, for the best locations, the ones everyone aspires to, the best offers will include either a higher rent, or a very high down payment (security deposit, key money or goodwill), or both.

Examples – Rents for Prime Locations

Specialists frequently publish tables showing rents in various cities around the world. For this data to be comparable, it should be tweaked to account for the various key money payment practices (see Table 13.10).

We see that New York and Hong Kong have the highest rents in the world. In New York, a 200 m^2 store would cost nearly €5 million a year. In Tokyo, it would be almost half that amount, but that is without taking the guarantee deposit outlay into account.

Table 13.10 Rents in Prime Locations in Europe (2017)

City	Address	€/m²/year
London	New Bond Street	16,200
Milan	Via Montenapoleone	13,500
Paris	Avenue des Champs-Élysées	13,255
Zurich	Bahnnofstrasse	8,310
Vienna	Kohlmarkt	4,620
Munich	Kaufinger	4,440
Dublin	Grafton Street	3,653
Barcelona	Portal de l'Angel	3,360
Amsterdam	Kalverstraat	3,000
Oslo	Karl Johan	2,831
Athens	Ermou	2,640
Luxembourg	Grande Rue	2,580
Copenhagen	Stroget	2,555
Prague	Na Pnkopé Street	2,520
Istanbul	Centre	2,520
Antwerp	Meir	1,950
Stockholm	Bibliotksgatan	1,609
Helsinki	City centre	1,602
Budapest	Vaci Utca	1,440
Lisbon	Chiado	1,380
Warsaw	Nowy Street	1,020

Some interesting points: Rents in Munich and Madrid are roughly two to three times lower than those in Paris or Milan. This may explain why we find several brands in these cities. Also, rent in Shanghai is three times lower than Tokyo. Specialists believe that the sales per square metre in luxury stores is three times lower in China than in Tokyo, and it would appear that rents have been adjusted accordingly.

In fact, on a global scale, all other things being equal, one might think that rental costs are more-or-less indexed to the expected average sales per square metre. The average cost of qualified sales personnel in each country would also affect store profitability.

(continued)

(*Continued*)

Another factor to consider is the number of hours a store remains open in various parts of the world. In Japan or China, luxury boutiques are generally open 7 days a week, from 10 a.m. to 10 p.m., or 84 hours a week. In Europe, shops are open six days a week from 10 a.m. to 8 p.m., i.e., 60 hours a week. This increase in cost of 40% compared to Europe must be taken into account in a store's estimated budget.

Tables 13.10, 13.11 and 13.12 show examples of rents in various prime locations around the world.

Table 13.11 Rents in Prime Locations in the Americas (2017)

City	Address	€/m²/year
New York	Upper 5th Avenue	28,262
Toronto	Bloor Street	2,180
Mexico ciudad	Massaryk	998
Sao Paolo	Oscar Freire Jardims	700
Buenos Aires	Calle Florida	651
Lima	Miraflores	288

Table 13.12 Rents in Prime Locations in Asia (2017)

City	Address	€/m²/year
Hong Kong	Causeway Bay	28,000
Tokyo	Ginza	14,000
Seoul	Myeongdong	10,000
Peking	Wangfujing	4,000
Singapore	Orchard Road	3,000
New Delhi	Khan market	2,000
Saigon	Best achieved mall	2,000
Kuala Lumpur	Pavilion KL	2,000
Taipei	Zhongkiao	2,000
Bangkok	Raprasong-Sukhumvit	1,500

Source: Estimates from the authors from diverse real estate agents.

Also, when weighing the various alternatives, the lessee can choose between stores where the entire sales area is on the ground floor, and others with a part of the sales area in the basement or upper floors. What effects will these various configurations have in terms of sales? The fact is that it is difficult to draw customers to the second or third floor of a store even if there are escalators.

A study made long ago, although outdated, offers some responses to the question of visiting frequency based on the floor level. William Davidson was able to trace an internal document of an American department store to analyse the various rental costs depending on the floor. The results are shown in Table 13.13.

We see here that between the ground floor and the first floor, the auditors of this department store located in Ohio recorded a decrease in footfalls to the order of 50%. On the second and third floors, they declined by 64% and 72% respectively. These figures probably give an indication of the percentages of customers who enter a store and then go up to the first, second or third floors.

The figures for the basement are very low (14%). In Europe and in Japan, it seems that department stores have found ways to make the basement and the goods that are sold there more interesting than in the United States, where it is usually perceived as an area reserved for stock disposal.

Table 13.13 Rent Levels in a Department Store in Ohio Depending on the Floor

	Percentage of the total	With an index of 100 for the ground floor
Basement	5.1%	14.0
1 (Ground floor)	36.1%	100.0
2	18.2%	50.4
3	10.3%	28.5
4	9.3%	25.8
5	3.5%	9.7
Offices	4.4%	12.2
	100%	

Source: Based on data from Davidson (1999).

Example

An interesting example can be analysed here – the new 'Beauté du Printemps' space in Paris. In July 2017, a 3,000 m² space was installed on three floors in the former Printemps de l'Homme store. On the first floor is the whole range of perfumes with a focus on new niche brands: *Acqua di Parma, Frédéric Malle Editions, Atelier Cologne, by Killian, Jo Malone*, and also dozens of others. This area seems like the ideal location for niche perfume brands (and even more so for the customers of these brands). Their shops-in-shops occupy almost the entire floor, while luxury brands are relegated to the rear, on shelves of the 'supermarket' type. Their presentations are beautiful, but the floor is depressingly empty of customers. Why?

Our analysis is that this space does not conform in any way to the elementary rules that we evoke in this book. The clients for beauty products are essentially women who have the habit of buying their perfumes on the ground floor of the main store (as is the case in the Galeries Lafayette department store nearby). They are therefore disconcerted:

- Firstly, at the sudden shifting of the Beauté du Printemps from the main store to the secondary store located on the street behind the Boulevard Haussmann. Male customers, whose purchasing habits are different, were not reluctant to go to this secondary store, which had been entirely dedicated to them. Women find it a problem to go there.
- Secondly, at the moving of the perfumes to the first floor of this secondary store – which resulted in losing a significant percentage of the customer base.

The failure was predictable. The question now is, how can this mistake be set right?

To conclude, it is quite clear that prime locations are expensive and that for a global brand, the overall fixed rental cost of 50 or 100 stores can have a huge impact on its results. In some cases, therefore, franchises can offer an interesting alternative.

During a first approximation, a rough indicator that could help a mid-range brand to determine a reasonable rent could be calculated as a percentage of projected turnover. In Europe, this would be in the range of 10 to 20%; in Asia it would be significantly higher, between 20 and 30%.

It is often said that in sales, the decisive factor for success is location, location and location. But opening too many stores at the same time could jeopardise a company's financial stability. Besides, the turnover of a new store may take more than two years to reach the projected threshold. During this period and before it breaks even, the store will have to be provided with cash and financial support. The strategy of directly operated stores is therefore valid only when the products sell extremely well and can easily attract local customers.

Sometimes, when a luxury brand is working to relaunch itself, there may be a tendency to open new stores before the new generation of products are ready for roll-out. But companies should not forget that the purpose of the game is to sell its products and should ask itself: What is the attractiveness level of the current products? Are they suitable, for example, for the Asian market or the American market? We could cite several cases where brands opened beautiful stores in Hong Kong, only to shut them down a year and a half or two years later, and at great expense, because the lease was still in effect and only a part of the decoration costs had been amortised. A similar thing happened in the United States. After opening boutiques in New York and Los Angeles, the American directors of certain brands insisted on opening stores in Chicago, Miami, Boston and San Francisco before the products could be fine-tuned to the tastes of the American consumer.

There is no doubt that location, location, location is very important, but the right product should also be available in that location. When these factors come together, things move forward without hindrance.

To recap:

- *We already know* that a luxury brand has to have a global reach and even if it places a high importance on its country of origin, the reputation it builds has to be as international as possible.
- *For a very long time, specialists in the industry* have been satisfied with locating their stores in proximity to their competitors. Today, optimisation tools exist and reflexes are honed through experience.
- *What one notices* is that in the same neighbourhood, or even in the same street, the difference in the number of clients entering the stores can vary from single to double. This requires an in-depth study of the location for new sales points and collecting of data on the frequencies of visits and behavioural habits of potential customers. This data exists today and it is easy to obtain.
- *Fortunately,* for each product and for each competitive domain there are stores adapted to different budgets or status levels, or to different commercial purposes, for each product and each competitive situation.
- *Last but not least, in this digital age,* the ideal store can play various roles. It could be a flagship store to showcase the richness and diversity of the brand and its products, it can be a small shop connected to its online business or a traditional shop that seeks to offer impeccable service and perfect O2O continuity to its local consumers.

Chapter 14

Managing Store Personnel: A Toolbox

I've tried to create a completely new way of organising my sales outlets.

−Tory Burch

In the luxury industry, which is based on creation, customers usually find themselves taking second place. The culture of customer experience has not been a key factor in this industry. In a sense, retailing is a newly acquired skill. The creative process, the product, the store concept and visual merchandising have always been more important than the sales experience itself.

As we have seen in the previous chapters, the new challenge luxury brands face is to increase customer loyalty, and this can only be done at the store level, by improving services and customer relationships. In other words, luxury brands have to become luxury service companies. Three objectives are crucial here:

- *The development of clienteling:* Each client should be recognised as such and all his or her personal information treasured. *Clienteling* means establishing a personal relationship between a vendor and a client. This can only be achieved through a specific behavioural approach and with the help of technology (CRM).
- *Making service the cornerstone of client relationships:* Shopping by appointment, availability of a particular vendor, delivery of purchases, sending hand-written thank-you notes, these are just a few examples of services a client can and should obtain in a luxury store. Luxury brands should strive to identify customer experiences – and consider their stores as being (just) one stage (albeit important) of a journey that often begins on the web.
- *Recognising the key role of sales staff:* Vendors have an essential role to play in identifying the client, in caring for his or her needs, in delivering the best service possible. Career paths in sales have to be built, innovative remuneration systems developed (no exceptions – all countries are concerned – fixed salaries, individual variable and collective variable proportions), specific on-the-job training programmes created.

Innovating in luxury marketing development means responding to new demands by introducing new entry-level ranges rather than reducing prices, providing a truly exceptional level of service, promoting and selling luxury products through alternative distribution channels including e-commerce, creating products together with one's customers and serving young clients who seem ready to purchase expensive luxury products online.

The luxury brands that are astute enough to rethink their retail and service operations and update their marketing approach to better understand and serve the customer will have a real competitive advantage.

Our aim in this chapter is to provide tools that emphasise the fact that vendors are vital in the luxury industry and should therefore be considered with greater regard. Luxury brands should uphold the same level of standards in sales management as those they apply to design, product marketing and communication strategies.

Tool No. 1: A Typical Sales Organisation

All companies and brands will have their own specific organisation – which very often will depend on the size of their operations. As soon as a significant number of stores are to be managed in a given region at least three levels of responsibilities are to be organised (see Figure 14.1):

- At headquarters: a retail operations director.
- If the company is structured by country: a country manager.
- If the company is structured by store clusters: a cluster manager (the cluster being a certain number of stores under their responsibility).

Then within a store, the organisation will depend on the size of the store (see Figure 14.2):

- For a small store (less than 10/15 persons): three positions are standard – store manager/assistant store manager/sales consultant (senior and junior may be distinguished)

Figure 14.1   A Three-Level *Retail* Organisation

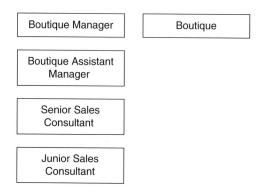

Figure 14.2   Stores with a Four-Level Organisation

- For a large store (30 persons or more): the store manager will be assisted by a certain number of assistant store managers by function (special orders/stock/administration/service/cash desk/merchandising) or by product line (men's/women's/accessories, etc.). The bigger the store the more numerous the product lines and their managers.

Tool No. 2: Managing the Recruitment of Sales Teams[1]

One should take great care not to subscribe to the common belief that a good vendor will be able to make their mark in any luxury brand store and that their experience is the sole measure of their value. We consider that this requisite experience should be coupled with an evaluation of the candidate's comportment, to enable one to better appreciate the

---

[1] To better understand the tools presented here it would be useful to read this chapter in conjunction with the book by Gutsatz and Auguste (2013), in which many of the tools have been discussed in greater detail.

additional value the candidate can bring in a sales context and in the building of customer relationships.

The Behavioural Approach

It is difficult to select and hire people who should have to adopt every day a broad range of professional attitudes such as:

- Welcoming and discovering customer needs and desires.
- Explaining to the clientele the artisanal experience.
- Dealing with client complaints and after-sales issues.
- Negotiating pricing and services, when necessary.

All these professional attitudes are about education, appropriate behaviours and personal competencies; they can be evaluated with effective interviews including a behavioural approach. The 'behavioural approach' involves 'behavioural' questions, that is to say, questions aimed at understanding what the candidate has done in a real situation, which may illustrate that they have the right competencies required for the retail job.

The behavioural approach requires significant preparation including:

- A detailed plan for each meeting with the candidates, specifying each competency to be investigated as well as the questions intended to measure them.
- Questions that should be focused on behaviours, and should be followed up with significant probing to understand what was the candidate's exact role, and what were the consequences of their actions.

Example of Behavioural Questions

We have listed some key questions that are pertinent to a large range of sales positions, and a list of technical qualifications. Figure 14.3 gives examples of these questions, centred on behaviour rather than on opinions or generalities.

Skill-set	Interviewer's questions
Retail knowledge and experience	Describe a situation in which you have invested your time to become better acquainted with a new collection or products created. How did you proceed? What did you learn?
	How do you keep yourself well informed about the main competitors?
	What did you learn from this information?
Skills and performance	Describe the best 'deal' you negotiated. How did you succeed in doing so?
	When has your network of contacts really been an asset to you?
	What have you learnt thanks to this network?
	Describe a situation in which you were personally involved in finding a solution to a customer's complaints. What action did you take? What did you learn?
Personal skills	Describe a situation where it took you considerable effort to finish something in time. What were the results?
	How do you 'recharge' your batteries?
Management skills	Describe how you succeeded in making a team more effective; what did you do?
	How did the team and the group benefit from your actions?

Figure 14.3   Examples of Behavioural Questions

Case Study: Recruiting a Store Manager

Elements provided: Job specifications and selected candidates (see Figure 14.4).

Input from the headhunter: *Evaluation and Recommendations* (see Figure 14.5).

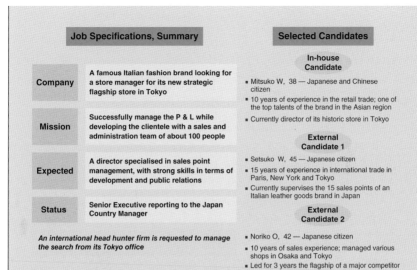

Figure 14.4 Job Specifications and Selected Candidates

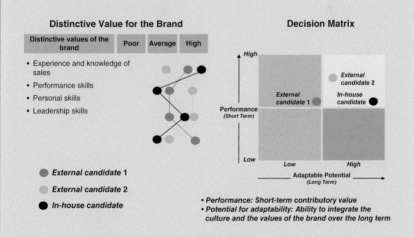

Figure 14.5 Evaluation and Recommendations

(continued)

(*Continued*)

Analysis and Comments

The key point of this recruitment concerns behaviours that should be checked, using two major criteria:

- Short-term candidate performance: delivering significant added value on commercial performances, team management and daily operations.
- The potential adaptability of the candidate, on a long-term basis, to cope with the routine and procedures, corporate culture and informal management systems of this Italian company.

In this case study the material provided by the headhunter leads us to the following comments:

- In-house candidate: despite the fact that she has less experience, her 'High Potential' status within the Italian company and a positive evaluation regarding the key recruitment criteria enable her to be a serious contender for the job.
- External candidate 1: both her performance and personal competencies seem lower against other candidates; these attributes could be a risk to integrate/fit within an Italian company.
- External candidate 2: her retail operational and management experience are an asset to lead the flagship; her current position at an Italian direct competitor gives her a definite advantage.

Tool No. 3: Defining the Responsibilities of Store Personnel

To ensure maximum efficiency and productivity in the store, all internal responsibilities should be assigned to clearly identified staff members.

When allocating these responsibilities, it is important to respect the following steps:

- Introduce the habit of assigning tasks to employees during staff meetings, if possible, to build awareness of how each individual's contribution is part of a joint team effort.
- Involve staff members in the decision-making process. They will feel more committed to a task that they have chosen.
- Delegate tasks wisely, according to the abilities and expertise of each staff member. Help them to adapt by spending time with them individually to demonstrate and explain their duties.
- Use Table 14.1 to update staff responsibilities.

Table 14.1   Responsibilities of the Staff

Department	Title	Description of responsibilities
Category A		Classify/arrange products.
		Carry out quality checking.
		Prepare products for the sales area.
		Check labels.
		Make sure all products are displayed in the store.
Category B		Stay informed of the stock situation (bestsellers, etc.).
		Prepare returns and transfers.
		Prepare sales and events.
		Follow guidelines for visual merchandising/sales/showcases.
Inventory management		Check the stock regularly.
		Prepare orders.
		Organise storage.
After-sales and repairs		Send the product to the repairer.
		Receive the repaired product/call the customer.
Visual merchandising		Follow the guidelines.
		Take personal interest in the appearance of the store.
		Implement changes in store windows.
		Train the team.
Stock movements		Check and record stock movements.
		Prepare inventories.
		Ensure the application of stock storage procedures.
Cash management		Verify banking operations.
		Send documents to the accounts department.

- Ensure regular monitoring to verify their work and provide feedback.
- Rotate responsibilities regularly to maintain the level of individual commitment.

Tool No. 4: Job Descriptions

It is imperative for a brand to have a very clear-cut and detailed job description for each job category.

The job description should be based on six basic factors:

- Purpose of the position.
- Duties and responsibilities.
- Performance evaluation criteria.
- Job profile required in terms of experience and skills.
- Functional links and positioning within the organisational chart.
- Career development perspectives.

A job description should always be supplemented by:

- A list of the *qualifications* required for the post (see Table 14.2 for a store manager example and Table 14.4 for a sales consultant example).
- A *candidate evaluation grid* to be used during the recruitment process (see Table 14.3 for the store manager and Table 14.6 for a sales consultant).
- An evaluation grid to use for the employee's *annual assessment*.

We outline below four significant retail job descriptions, two of which are detailed:

- Cluster manager
- Store manager (detailed below)
- Assistant store manager
- Sales consultant (detailed below)

Table 14.2   Store Manager Competencies

	Experience	Skills
Prerequisites	• Sales or Executive	• Charisma and leadership. • Coaching skills. • Teaching skills. • Meticulousness and organisational abilities. • Attention to detail. • Mastery over service skills. • Available when needed, ready to help. • Listening skills. • High integrity. • Discretion. • Presentation quality projects an image of luxury. • Good vocabulary and articulation. • Fluency in English.
Desirable	• Luxury sector • Store Manager	• Advanced communication skills. • Versatile, equally skilled in sales or administration. • Loyalty towards the hierarchy. • Performs well under pressure. • Dynamic. • Takes initiatives that exceed expectations. • Knowledge of the market and the luxury world. • Business skills. • Flair for marketing. • Management abilities. • Basic computer skills.
Unacceptable		• Strongly individualistic. • Lacking in leadership skills. • Impatient to obtain a higher position.

We also provide explanations concerning the job descriptions of the store manager and sales consultant. One of the functions of a store manager is that of a *coach*. We explain how the store manager can excel in the art of supervising and coaching the team. For a sales consultant, we have provided a detailed evaluation grid (see Table 14.5), which can be used by the store manager during the annual assessment process.

Table 14.3   Example of an Evaluation Grid for a Candidate for the Post of Store Manager

Competency	Rating
Provides customer service consistent with what is expected by the luxury brand	
Knows how to build customer relationships	
Knows the products	
Pays attention to detail	
Fluency in English	
Fluency in other foreign languages	
Manages the store like a business unit	
Promotes the brand locally	
Is organised and knows how to coordinate	
Listens proactively	
Is dynamic and takes initiatives	
A good leader	
Trains and coaches staff	
Excellent knowledge of fashion and trends	
Overall presentation	

Cluster Manager

Reports to: Retail Operations Director

Purpose of the Position   Ensures the implementation of the sales strategy and merchandising policy in all stores in their area. Is an ambassador for the brand.

Duties and Responsibilities

- Commercial sales monitoring and operational steering of stores within their region (five maximum).
- Ascending and descending communications relay.
- Supervision and management of teams within their region.
- Overseeing of application of the retail strategy.
- Provide authority delegation for retail management.
- Occasional sales and administrative support.

Table 14.4   Requirements for the Position of Sales Consultant

	Experience	Skills
Prerequisites	Sales If a beginner: Average level of education, minimum Bac+2	• Sales capabilities • Open-minded and curious • Pays attention to detail • Resilient • Appearance and communication • Relational and listening skills • Attention to service • Patience / availability when needed • Integrity/discretion • Versatility • Team spirit and teamwork
Preferable	Sales experience in luxury/fashion Experience Sales If a beginner: 'average' level of education, minimum Bac + 2	• English (fluent) • Adaptability beyond expectations • Enthusiasm • Dynamism • Interest in the products • Brand identification and loyalty • Masters one or more foreign languages • Takes initiatives beyond expectations • Knowledge of the market and the fashion world • Wants a career in the network (geographical and organisation chart)
Unacceptable		• Inability to communicate or relationship difficulties • Defiant, rebellious or individualistic • Unstable

Evaluation Criteria
- Commercial sales results.
- Commercial sales dynamic.
- Behaviour and quality of management.
- Team management (turnover, motivation, training etc.).
- Respect for the brand strategy and policies.

Table 14.5   Sales Consultant Evaluation Form

Job functions	Sales consultant					
Professional skills	Explanations	1 = Outstanding 2 = Above expectations 3 = Good – compliant 4 = Below expectations 5 = Undesirable				
Providing customer service consistent with that expected of a luxury brand.	Successfully applies brand guidelines in terms of customer experience	1	2	3	4	5
Building client relationships	Built a customer base – shows interest in and successfully develops repeat business relationships with customers – turns buyers into customers	1	2	3	4	5
Providing information about the products	Provides extensive information about the collection; is able to persuade clients to buy products from all categories.	1	2	3	4	5
Attention to detail	Pays attention to details that contribute to the feeling of luxury in the store, and in customer relationships	1	2	3	4	5
Able to speak to customers in English	For employees who are not native English speakers	1	2	3	4	5
Able to speak to customers in another foreign language		1	2	3	4	5

Store Manager

Reports to: Cluster Manager

Purpose of the Position   To develop total satisfaction for the clientele and optimum profitability for their store by implementing the brand strategy.

Table 14.6 Sales Consultant – Personal Skills

Listens proactively		1	2	3	4	5
Works in a proactive way and takes initiatives		1	2	3	4	5
Plays the team game	Contributes to the achievement of team goals	1	2	3	4	5
Knows fashion and trends	Interested in fashion, reads fashion magazines, etc.	1	2	3	4	5
Appearance	Personifies and applies the dress codes and behaviour guidelines	1	2	3	4	5
Communication skills	Communication, attitude when addressing clients	1	2	3	4	5
Self-confidence	Is relaxed in their relationship with others	1	2	3	4	5

Duties and Responsibilities

- Development of customer satisfaction and representation of the brand inside and outside the store.
  - Responsible for the quality of customer service (in the store, on the telephone or by letter).
  - Responsible for the upkeep and maintenance of the store.
  - Ambassador for the brand within their close environment, responsible for the store's external relations:
    in its competitive environment;
    with traditional partners (hotels, restaurants etc.);
    with local officials (local authorities, journalists).
  - Responsible for developing the clientele and local prospecting.
- Development of the store's turnover while respecting the retail strategy
  - Involvement in the design of action plans for the store along with the cluster manager
    Strengths/weaknesses, risks/opportunities reports
  - Implementation of store's action plan: steering and monitoring of results
    Determination of store objectives (quantitative and qualitative)
    Division into short-, medium- and long-term actions (3, 6 and 12 months)

Monitoring of performance indicators ('KPIs' such as: average transaction, conversion rate, units sold, number of transactions, number of after-sales service interventions, percentage of clients acquired, percentage of loyalty)

Weekly/monthly report on the period's activity and the competition, with comments and analyses

Customer campaigns: targets and resources (catalogue, mail shots, events, gifts, services, etc.)

Staff actions: training, motivation, challenge, personalised objectives, etc.

Store actions: renovation, maintenance, equipment, signs, windows, etc.

- Management of store team
  - Involvement in recruitment of sales personnel
  - On-site integration and training of new sales personnel
  - Compliance with 'grooming standards' (wearing of uniform, make-up, hair and accessories, etc.)
  - Individual objectives

    Fixing of individual annual and monthly turnover objectives linked to KPI

    Fixing of individual qualitative objectives

    Periodical individual appraisals (every 4 to 6 months)

    Proposal of end-of-season bonuses
  - Management and motivation:

    Weekly, monthly and annual team meetings

    Leadership / on the job training

    Evaluation of training requirements (linguistic, sales technologies, products, service, etc.)

    Recording of individual expectations in terms of mobility or professional promotion

    Conflict resolution
  - Administration

    Delegation of tasks and assurance of versatility among sales personnel

    Authorisation in cases where gifts or other commercial sales gestures are requested, within the policy defined by the management

Scheduling for weekly hours
Budgetary commitments
Administration

- Management of store operations
  - Stocks
    Replenishment
    Feedback with regard to theoretical stock (regular and year-end
      inventories)
    Maintenance of top sellers: request more stock if necessary
    Selling off discontinued lines
  - Till
    Compliance with legal, tax and customs regulations and proce-
      dures
    Till checks
    Bank transfers where necessary
  - Health, safety and security regulations:
    Compliance with procedures
    Permanent overseeing
  - Profitability (in areas of responsibility where they can exercise
    control): management of allowances, general expenses, third-party
    commission, gifts, bonuses and payment terms

The Store Manager as a Coach

One of the essential roles of a store manager is to be a team leader. The
store manager acts as a coach for the store team. This role calls for special
skills and talents, which we describe here.

Step 1: Ability to Listen and Observe   Far too often, store managers
are unable to give useful feedback to their employees because they do
not have enough time to observe their performances. Take the time to
observe and listen to your employees in a sales situation! It will be time
wisely spent. Note down your observations. This will uncover specific
areas in which each sales consultant needs coaching according to their
individual needs.

Step 2: Provide Fair and Accurate Feedback Once the checklist is complete, you are ready to provide your feedback. Be specific and give concrete examples of what you may have observed. It is important to be fair so as to sustain employee motivation and their desire to learn more and progress:

Stop: Play the 'Stop' card when an employee behaves in a way that is not in line with the brand's standards (e.g. 'Please stop chatting with your colleagues when a customer approaches your section of the store').

Start: Play the 'Start' card when an employee does not act according to guidelines specifically required by the brand standards (e.g. 'I would really like you to make a habit of giving your visiting card to all the customers you deal with in the store').

Continue: Play the 'Well done!' card when the behaviour of the employee abides by brand standards (e.g. 'I heard your open-ended questions to so-and-so to find out exactly what he was looking for. Thanks to that, you were able to assist him rapidly and sell him two additional items although he was in a hurry to catch a plane! Continue the good work!').

It is important to show appreciation for a job well done. If an employee does not feel appreciated, they will not be encouraged to repeat the desired behaviour. In addition to the above, all employees should receive three types of feedback regularly, regardless of their level of performance. One can always find at least one positive point and a negative point to be improved. This will boost the motivation of an employee even if they have been told that several areas need improvement, and also that of employees who have better results, and who will be encouraged to do even better.

Remember that feedback should be provided regularly; if not, it will not have any impact.

Step 3: Make Sure to Observe Your Employees While They Are Working This is the step most frequently neglected by a manager. Providing feedback is essential but not enough to change a person's behaviour. The manager should coach employees while they go through their paces. Below are three simple ways to train an employee to obtain better results:

- In a hands-on situation: Continue to observe and advise your employees as they interact with clients during the day.

- Work in tandem (in real-life situations): When time permits, spend some time selling yourself to your sales consultants. Be the example. Show them how to perform the tasks they have difficulty with and then ask them to practise it with another client. Continue to observe and offer advice while spending time with the employee. Working in tandem with your sales consultants and leading your team by example will help you earn the respect of your employees and they will be more open to your suggestions and advice.
- Role-playing: When there are only a few customers in the store, it is a good opportunity for training your employees. Role-playing can be really effective. For example, you may play the role of a customer while your employee plays the role of a sales consultant. Then swap roles to show them the behaviour to adopt. Provide advice throughout the process.

Assistant Store Manager

Reports to: Store Manager

Purpose of the Position   Helping the store manager to provide full and entire satisfaction to the customer and maximum profitability to the store.

   In case the store manager is absent, the presence of the assistant store manager is essential for this task.

Duties and Responsibilities   Assisting the manager in:

- – Turnover.
- – Team training.
- – Managing the store.
- – Projecting the brand image.
- – Supervision, coaching.
- – Achieving sales objectives.

Evaluation Criteria   Achieving store objectives in terms of KPI:

- Volume.
- Margins.

- Conversion rate.
- Budgeting (in locally controlled accounts).
- Customer portfolios:
  - General status (information level, volume, etc.).
  - Percentage of customers acquired, percentage of loyalty, percentage of attrition.
  - Stock, shrink results, etc.

Attaining individual objectives for each of the Sales Consultants in the store.

- Team development:
  - Turnover.
  - Advancement, and so forth.
- Respecting the brand image.

Sales Consultant

Reports to: Store Manager or Assistant Store Manager

Purpose of the Position To provide customers with unique and memorable experiences in line with the brand's strategy so as to increase sales and build long-term customer relationships.

Duties and Responsibilities Achieving individual objectives and contributing towards attaining those of the store:

- Key performance indicators (KPIs).
- Customer portfolio (if a customer base exists):
  - Customer acquisition, loyalty.
  - Quality and quantity of information collected.
- Assistance provided to other sales consultants.
- Assistance provided to administrative teams, if any (inventory management, etc.).

Always complying with the service standards set by the brand, including:

- Sales and service guidelines.
- Quality of greeting and service.

- Personal appearance.
- Appearance of the store and products presented (windows and displays).
- Knowledge of the brand, its products and practices:
  - Safety guidelines.
  - Procedures, administrative rules for authorisations.
  - Information systems.

Participation in the daily operations of the store:

- Upkeep and maintenance of the store:
  - Cleanliness of the store.
  - Proper maintenance of the shop windows, displays and furniture.
  - Cleanliness of the products.
  - Versatility, can switch from cash management to inventory tasks.
- Active participation in:
  - Team meetings (offers suggestions, proposals, etc.).
  - Events, competitions and regular meetings.
  - Handling customer incidents (new products, defects noticed, etc.).
  - Routine and annual inventories.
- Any other task entrusted to them at a particular moment or for a period of time specified by the store manager, such as:
  - Decoration and maintenance of the store windows and displays.
  - Replenishing and maintaining the products presented.
  - Complying with the training programme.
  - Complying with attendance requirements.
  - Information on new products, etc.

Tool No. 5: Career Advancement

It is crucial for the successful management of a store to offer employees opportunities to advance their careers within the business entity, and minimise turnover. Career paths should include the three subdivisions of the organisational chart to permit sufficient flexibility: in-store, retail and merchandising (see Figure 14.6).

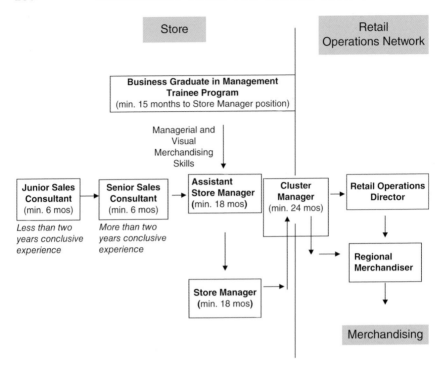

Figure 14.6 Retail Careers

Career Advancement in Sales

There are two levels of sales consultants: junior consultants and senior consultants.

Assistant store managers may be:

- Senior sales consultants with considerable sales expertise as well as management and visual merchandising skills.
- Business school graduates with good management and visual merchandising skills who wish to pursue careers in sales.

After having demonstrated their ability to lead a team and improve the performance of a store, they will be able to advance to the position of store manager.

Store managers should have the opportunity to:

- Manage one of the regular stores and subsequently a flagship store.
- Become a cluster manager once they have proved their abilities as store manager.

A cluster manager will have three possible career options:

– Retail operations director.
– A career in merchandising.
– A career in training.

Managing a Career in Sales

To render discussions on careers simpler, we have taken a model drawn from the work of Ulrich and Smallwood (2008) describing four stages in career advancement.

This model helps human resources to smooth the path for employees to climb up the group's organisational ladder, as well as to identify omissions and gaps in group-level advancement. (Figure 14.7 shows a chart representing these stages.)

The career path model allows employees to define their career aspirations and understand what is required to achieve maximum results in their current job levels. It highlights the differences between the stages and trajectories in terms of the work expected of colleagues, the types of relationships they form, and the psychological mindset in which they should place themselves.

- Learn, from others, how things work in the store.
- Master, by contributing independently, the skills and technical knowledge of the trade.

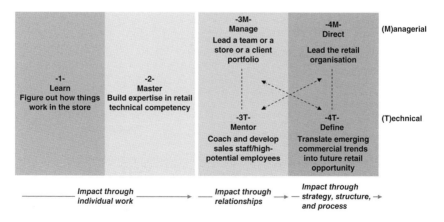

Figure 14.7   The Four Retail Stages Model of Development

- Lead, by contributing through others, a team, a store or a portfolio of clients.
- Spearhead future commercial developments among the group's senior management.

Based on this model of professional stages, we can elaborate a career development framework specific to sales at sales points:

- The categories of sales posts that currently exist in luxury groups.
- Opportunities/possible scenarios that those wishing to pursue a sales career may consider. (Figure 14.8 is a graphical representation of these steps.)

In addition to these models, and for the sake of comprehensiveness, we give examples of sales career paths that highlight the different stages to follow and opportunities to grasp if one so wishes – climbing the ladder after starting out as a sales consultant within the store team. (Figures 14.9 and 14.10 are graphical representations of these career scenarios.)

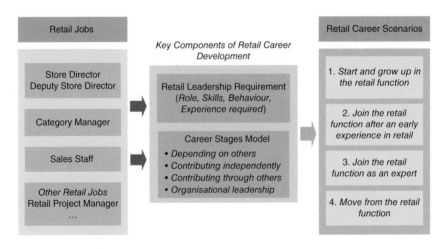

Figure 14.8   The Retail Career Development Framework

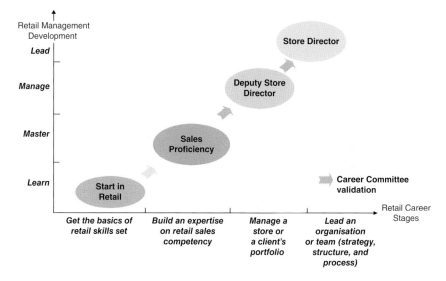

Figure 14.9   Retail Career Scenario: Start and Grow Up in the Retail Function

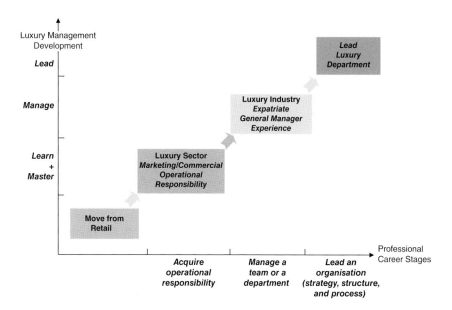

Figure 14.10   Retail Career Scenario: Move from the Retail Function

Tool 6: Setting Turnover Targets

In order to drive sales performances and ensure that they are in line with budget requirements, consistent objectives should be set across all levels of the sales organisation. This defines performance standards and improves functioning at all levels.

- Once annual budgets are set, they are cascaded down to the store management level.
- Turnover targets are set monthly for cluster managers and store managers and should be reviewed monthly (the first month's sales target should correspond to the first month's sales budget).
- The target figures for sales consultants are set monthly, weekly, and daily and should be reviewed every week. Managers should use the following forms:
  - Daily/monthly result forms for employees.
  - Daily target forms for the store.
- Sales consultants can also track their own sales and analyse their results dynamically using the forms in their client book:
  - Daily turnover tracking sheet.
  - Monthly turnover tracking sheet.
- Objectives and action plans should be reviewed on a monthly basis (weekly for sales consultants) and feedback should be provided.
- The results should be monitored and observations noted in the Sales Comments Diary.

Tool No. 7: Defining a Fair Retail Compensation System

There are three key principles to keep in mind:

- Redefining total incentives.

   The purpose is to enable the brand's commercial organisation to recognise the importance of incentive programmes for attaining financial objectives and to understand that these programmes include a significant part of the employer's overall offer to the employee. This total package should include:

- – Compensation, i.e., basic salary and short-term and long-term incentives.
- – Benefits, including health insurance and pension benefits.
- – Opportunities for career advancement, including training and promotions, changes in career trajectories, rewarding responsibilities, career prospects; in short, added value in the long run by staying in the company.
- • The overall incentive package is a key element for influencing the behaviour and attitudes of employees, especially if a change of financial strategy calls for a change in behavioural approaches (see Table 14.7).
- • Harmonising the three perspectives. Such harmonising requires attention to three distinct and yet related perspectives: that of the employer, the employee and the cost (see Figure 14.11).

Table 14.7 KPIs for Evaluating Suitable Remunerations

Important questions	KPI suggestions
Which characteristics, experience, behaviours are actually rewarded?	Technical business skills: 'critical behaviour' for customers; 'Use of the customer base', sales performance: 'high invoices' negotiating skill
What career paths and which tasks clearly lead to the employee's success?	'Quick' advancement steps, training
What are the consequences of these employee performance improvements for the company?	Lower talent attrition rate, improves employee commitment conditions, employee perceptions, customer satisfaction
What components of the total compensation package do employees value most, as reflected in their actions rather than in their words?	Importance of having a good knowledge of the brand, experience in selling the know-how to new customers, incentives for team results
Which segments of the staff contribute the most to monetary value, and how?	Store manager, sales experts, etc.

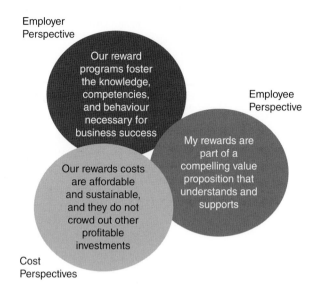

Figure 14.11   Balancing Employer, Employee and Cost Perspectives

- Measuring the return on investment.

   A business organisation should find solutions to crucial questions and thereby help to channel its investments in manpower to maximise value.

When conceiving an efficient incentive system for commercial activities, the Human Resources Department and the Executive Committee should focus on four key principles.

- *Key principle 1:* Aligning all components of the compensation system with the group's priority objectives (see Figure 14.12).

Increase basic salaries and stop individual monetary incentives (sometimes defined as 'everyone eats what he kills') that tend to push sales consultants to make a sale at any cost and treat other team members and one-time customers in a negative way (this is to be adapted according to regional practices).

Figure 14.12 Five Components of the Retail Compensation Package

Handle short-term incentives in a differentiated way by linking them to
the main drivers of business activity: employee performance, proper
behaviour, collection of customer data, use of the data.

Promote team incentives linked to the store's business, so as to encourage each member to cooperate rather than compete with each other,
and use collective performance indicators.

Plan recognition and reward solutions such as participation in high-
profile projects, tutoring programmes, or prestigious events.

- *Key principle No. 2:* Find the right balance when rewarding performance according to market and business timing (see Figures 14.13
and 14.14).
- *Key principle No. 3:* Conduct quarterly, half-yearly and annual assess-
ments in a constructive manner to keep them aligned with the company's activity. This is generally practised in all businesses, but not
necessarily applied to sales consultants. We strongly believe that they
should be included as well (see Sales Consultant Assessment Form in
Table 14.5).
- *Key principle No. 4:* Compare the incentive system to those of the best
companies serving the same types of clientele (for example, competitors in the luxury sector, or private banks).

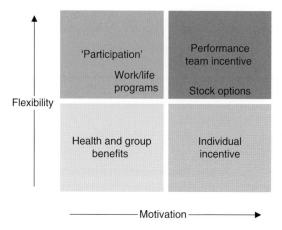

Figure 14.13   Mapping of Some Components: Flexibility × Motivation

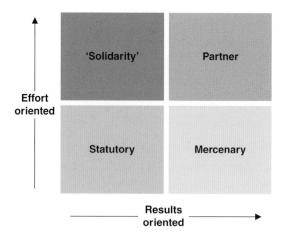

Figure 14.14   Four Ways to Reward Performance

Example

This example of engineering a global package in rapport with a sales career illustrates how to integrate the four key principles mentioned above and find the right balance between each of these elements.

- The *risk of divergence* between the candidate and the brand with respect to compensation and incentives over the course of their career. A misunderstanding on this issue could pose a serious problem for the group and result in significant loss in revenue.
- *Business goals* are those defined during the stages of career advancement. It is important to verify and validate each stage with the help of a career committee.
- *Career prospects* relating to advancement, specific training, and other relevant incentives to maintain employee motivation, ensuring that they keep pace with the group and help them to prepare for the future in a proactive way.
- *Compensation system components* represent career progression, and strike a balance between the amount of basic salary, individual and collective performance, and contribution of the management role.

Tool No. 8: Grooming Guidelines for Employees

The appearance and grooming of each employee contribute to a brand's distinctive style. Applicable codes and rules, and also uniforms, are created so that customers can easily recognise this style.

Each brand should have its own 'Grooming Guidelines'. These are defined in keeping with the values of the brand. The adherence of sales staff to these guidelines and standards reflects their attitude towards both customers and products.

Example

This is a possible example of Grooming Standards for female employees:

Hair
Haircut classic and neat.

(continued)

(*Continued*)

No hair extensions or wigs.

Hair accessories limited to hair clips or bands in neutral colours.

No bright-coloured hair clips, scrunchies, banana clips or headbands.

Neutral colours only.

Make-up
Make-up foundation:

- Minimal, natural shade.

  Eyes:

- Eyeshadow in neutral and discreet shades.
- Minimal eye liner and mascara.
- No overemphasised pencilled eyebrows.

  Lips:

- Discreet shades of lipstick.
- No contrasting lip-liner.

  Nails:

- Clear or skin-coloured varnish, single shade.
- Nails not longer than 5 mm.
- No false nails or nail jewels.

Accessories
Earrings:

- Small and simple.
- No drop earrings or loops.

  Chains:

- Fine, single-strand chain with a simple and single pendant.
- One strand of pearls.
- No showy pendants or shapes.

- A single piercing for each earlobe.
- No brooches or pins.
- Rings and bracelets should not distract from the product being presented.
- No visible tattoos.
- No piercings other than pierced ears should be visible.

Note:
- Daily personal hygiene is essential for every employee.
- Any shortcomings, and solutions, regarding appearance, clothes or hygiene should be discussed between the employee and her superior during a private meeting, not in public.
- Employees should be reminded that their appearance and the dress guidelines are not meant for the individual personally but are intended to maintain the quality of the company's visual standards.

Tool No. 9: Global Business Ethics

The Relevance of a Global Professional Code of Ethics

The present development of corporate social responsibility standards has been anticipated by many luxury brands. They developed professional codes of ethics to ensure that all employees of the company comply with the highest ethical and legal standards, wherever they may be. These apply to all employees of a luxury brand, including sales staff.

These codes are conceived to avoid any risks that could result from unethical behaviour. Often, a Global Ethics Committee is given the task of ensuring that the codes are correctly enforced.

Example

It is the duty of all employees at all levels to ensure that business is conducted in an ethical manner, and to report any

(continued)

(Continued)

breaches to their superiors or the GBEC (Global Business Ethics Committee).

Scope of the Procedure

The following issues fall under the scope of the procedure:

- Purchase of goods or services.
- Cases of conflict of interest.
- Cases where donations, gifts or other compensations are offered by competitors or suppliers (current or potential).
- Cases where members of government agencies demand donations/gifts/money from the company.
- Illegal working conditions.
- Suspicious financial transactions.
- Hostile attempts by competitors to obtain information about another company.

Any employee who becomes aware of any type of unethical behaviour among colleagues or superiors should follow the procedure outlined below.

Procedure

- Purchase of goods and services

When purchasing goods or services from potential suppliers, any employee authorised to sign agreements (see legal authorisations) shall work in an environment of neutrality and independence with regard to the said suppliers.

The employee shall always study at least two other offers from potential suppliers before taking a decision. Details of such offers should be recorded in a Purchase Log.

In cases where there is only one supplier, the employee shall contact a member of the ethics committee. The GBEC shall take the final decision and sign the order for goods or services from this sole supplier.

- Managing conflicts of interest

If an employee (or a member of their family or close friend) holds a significant share (i.e., more than 5% of the assets of the company in question), directly or indirectly, of a company doing (or seeking to do) business with the company, it should be immediately brought to the attention of the GBEC.

- Managing cases where donations, gifts or other compensations are offered by competitors or suppliers (current or potential)

If an employee, or a relative or close friend of the employee, is offered donations, gifts or other considerations by any company or person doing or seeking to do business with the brand, this should be reported immediately to the relevant management or regional CMG and the GBEC.

Any employee receiving gifts or benefits of a value greater than (*to be defined by the company*) from any person or company doing or seeking to do business with the company, or who is in competition with the company, should immediately refer it to the relevant management or regional director and the GBEC.

The definition of a 'gift' will depend on customary practices in various parts of the world (for example, the norms in Japan and the United States are different). If a doubt arises, members of the ethics committee should take a decision together.

Employees invited for business reasons by suppliers/customers or shareholders of the company may accept to be accommodated in a hotel with 'reasonable' rates to ensure the neutrality of these intermediaries.

Advantages in kind of a value greater than (*to be defined by the company*) shall not be accepted.

Examples

- Expenses-paid stays in a luxury hotel for a week for product presentations by suppliers as a guest partner.
- Holidays, long weekends offered by suppliers.
- Cash hidden in a gift.
- Credit card offered to the employee's partner for personal use.

(*continued*)

(*Continued*)

- Credit cards/petrol cards.
- School fees for their children.
- Annual membership to a club paid by a supplier, etc.

- Cases where members of government agencies request donations/gifts/money from the company

Any request made by a member of a government to an employee should be brought to the attention of the GBEC. The GBEC will take the appropriate decision in accordance with the policies of the brand and also regional standards.

- Awareness of illegal working conditions

Any employee discovering situations where legal working conditions are not respected, or which may be considered unethical or a form of harassment, shall inform all the members of the GBEC.

The GBEC will take the appropriate action to put a stop to such situations.

- Questionable financial transactions

Any knowledge of questionable financial transactions carried out within the company by an employee and likely to harm the interests of the company should be immediately reported to the GBEC.

- Hostile attempts by competitors to obtain information about the company

If a third party (supplier/competitor, etc.) attempts to obtain confidential information in an unethical manner from an employee at any level, the GBEC should be informed immediately so that appropriate action can be taken to prevent leakage of information.

- Action to be taken if an employee discovers this type of unethical behaviour among colleagues or a superior

If an employee, no matter what position they hold in the company, has evidence of unethical behaviour on the part of a colleague or superior, they should inform all members of GBEC, to ensure confidentiality.

The GBEC will protect the identity of the informant during its investigation and will decide on the appropriate corrective measures to be taken.

To recap:

- *When the behaviour of sales staff in a store* does not correspond to the expectations of customers or the anticipated ambience in the store of a prestigious brand, before questioning their behaviour or professionalism, one should examine whether the recruitment, verification or remuneration system is not at the origin of the problem. Before reproaching an employee, it is important to analyse the ramifications of the system in place.

- *The ambience in a sales point* could depend on the diversity of the employees who work there and their professional expectations. The more promotions there are outside the store or in the upper echelons of a sales point, the more likely it is that employees will consider a career in the business and think long term.

- *What creates the sense of welcome and appreciation in customers* is a sum total of the interest and solicitude shown by the vendors. This can be simply the fact that a vendor remembers their names when they enter the store, or recalls what they purchased during their last visit, also the manner in which they express themselves or how they show consideration for each client as an individual, or even towards casual visitors.

- *The personnel management department* should take local cultures into account. The brand has to, of course, impose its mode of operation and policies, but the management in each country should also take the customs and expectations of the local population into consideration.

Chapter 15

At What Price Should Products Be Sold?

---

*Many marketing specialists neglect their pricing strategies
and underestimate the effect they could have on the market.*

–Philip Kotler[1]

It was said in a previous chapter that pricing policies have no place in the definition of the sales point mix because it is an integral part of the product offering. In the luxury retail sector, price decisions are usually made at the head-office level and are not the responsibility of the Store Manager or even the Sales Manager. Pricing policy is therefore perceived as being of secondary importance from the viewpoint of sales

---

[1] Kotler and Keller (2016).

outlets. However, it remains a key element in the management of a store. Even for luxury products, comparing prices with competitors, decisions on reducing prices, and calculating the rate of reductions to be granted to increase sales volumes should not be taken lightly.

In a perfect offline system, there is only one possible price strategy: the same product has to be sold at the same price everywhere in the world so that the O2O process functions perfectly no matter how one looks at it: I search for the price of an article on the brand's website in Brazil. I go to the boutique in Sao Paulo to examine it, then I go to New York and decide to buy it in the brand's store on Madison Avenue. I should be able to find it at the same price. In fact, the price should be relatively cheaper because customs duty for this type of product is very high in Brazil and North American prices are almost identical to those in Europe. However, the continuity of the system is not perfect. For it to be so, one has to remove customs duties, and all brands should work towards selling under identical conditions everywhere. Local sales tax (which exists even in many states in the United States) should be eliminated as well. Perfect continuity would presuppose that tariffs and local sales taxes (not to mention luxury tax on retail sales, like those that exist in mainland China) are removed. We are very far from such a scenario, of course, but the trend should go strongly in this direction, as we explain in this chapter. Finally, one should not forget that all stores, even exclusive single-brand stores, sometimes belong to individual operators, exclusive importers or franchisees, who have to manage the brand while keeping their best long-term interests in mind.

For, even if decisions on prices are centralised for stores directly managed by the brand, franchisees could have a degree of autonomy in this area. The company's or division's management will have informed them what the luxury retail prices should be, but will not be able to enforce them legally because, in most countries, the manufacturer is forbidden to impose its prices. Similarly, department stores cannot decide the prices in shops-in-shops or corners though they have full control over their own counters. The question of prices therefore remains open and deserves to be looked into. In the first part, we shall discuss pricing policies. In the second part, we will focus on price reduction tactics with a view to increasing sales.

Pricing Policy Under Normal Conditions

Firstly, let us take a look at international pricing systems to identify the various factors on which sales depend. We shall then study sales margins.

International Pricing Policies

The traditional view of the luxury industry is that one cannot fix the same retail price everywhere in the world. In many countries, imported products are subject to customs duties sometimes of up to 100% of the export price. In some cases, there is also VAT (to be integrated into the selling price) or local taxes (generally not included in the retail price marked on the label but added at the payment counter). The costs of managing a store also vary greatly. Opening a store and salaries of the sales staff in Tokyo can be two to three times higher than in Madrid and rents are very different. All this has to be reflected in one way or another in the retail prices.

Usually, luxury brands do not fix a single universal price, but calculate it according to three zones, as shown in Table 15.1.

For Europe, and what is often the city of origin of the brand, the index of the retail price has been set at 100. For New York, one generally tries to fix a retail price slightly higher than in Europe, as shown in the table, i.e., at 105.

However, if the dollar weakens against the euro, the New York price could go down to 90 or 95, i.e., lower than prices in Paris. The first reflex may then be to increase the US prices. However, firstly, prices can be modified only twice or thrice a year (for example when a new catalogue is published). And secondly, as in our example, if US brands do not need to increase their retail prices, European brands take care not to increase theirs too quickly, so as to remain competitive. Thus, the New York price will be applied in the United States and will serve as a reference

Table 15.1 Price Levels by Country for Luxury Fashion and Accessories

	Paris/Milan	Tokyo/Shanghai	New York
Local market	100	130/120	105/95
Travel retail	80	104/96	84/76

for the American zone. For example, if customs duty in Argentina is 30%, the selling price in Argentina should theoretically be 105 × 1.3 = 136.5; this could be set at 130. In Mexico, where customs duty is 10%, the selling price could be fixed at 120.

In Asia, the reference price is based on selling prices of 145 in Tokyo and 135 in Shanghai. The higher indexes are supposedly due to customs duties or the high operating costs in many of the countries in this region.

As we said, when the dollar falls against the euro, it is not easy to increase retail prices because this can only be done at certain times and when no special promotional campaign is in progress or planned and announced (with, for example, promotional documents already printed) showing retail prices. Thus, the latency period before action can be taken is generally a few months or even a few quarters.

Reducing sales prices is not simple either. A brand that directly owns 100% of its distribution network can do this quite easily, taking into account the latency period mentioned above. But matters get complicated when some of the merchandise is sold through independent multi-brand stores, franchisees or department stores. If these stores are asked to reduce retail prices on products they already have in stock, they will still demand their full margin before the reduction in price. Thus, if a retailer bought the product at 50 to be sold at 100, and the brand makes the decision to sell it at 90, the intermediary will ask the company to reduce the purchase price to 45, so that its margin stays at 50%. Since it has already paid for the stocks, it will be either in the form of a refund or a credit note. This also means that if a brand wishes to implement a price reduction, it will have to send a representative to each point of sale to physically count the number of items left in stock to calculate the corresponding credit for the retailer. This is done sometimes, but it is, of course, complicated and expensive, which is why, when a price reduction is necessary because of a change in exchange rates, the tendency is rather to wait and put future price increases on hold so that the necessary price reduction will only take effect after a certain period.

In all the three price zones, duty-free prices are generally fixed at 20% below local prices. Table 15.1 shows that price indexes become 80, 84 – 96 and 104, and that it then generally becomes more expensive to buy duty-free fashion items, accessories or fragrances at Tokyo

Narita Airport or Shanghai Pudong airport than in boutiques in Paris. Hence, even if the market is globalised, differences in retail prices still exist.

Over time, these differences will lessen. In Japan, for example, the METI (Ministry of Economy) is attempting to force luxury brands to reduce this price gap by regularly publishing the prevailing prices in Milan, New York and Tokyo for some of the most iconic luxury products, but based on the differences in customs duties and operating costs, brands could justify a part of the differences in price.

Table 15.2 confirms this situation – by giving price differentials based on store readings – where luxury brands apply price differentials depending on the market. But these are only averages, hiding in fact very strong disparities between brands and between products.

This wonderful arrangement is exploding with the development of the Internet, under pressure from Chinese customers, who, remember, represent the largest number of luxury customers in the world (35%).

The first thing one notices is that luxury brands have been much more greedy than the figures we just gave. Twenty years ago, a systematic study of the leather goods sector by one of the authors showed a price difference between Europe and Japan of 70% (far beyond the justifications for customs duties, transport and operating costs)!

A study analysing the price differential between China and the United States in 2016 for luxury shoes by the Think Tank L2 shows the following differences (whereas according to the figures above, the gap should have been around 25%):

29% of brands apply a differential of 15%;
29% of brands apply a differential of 16–25%;
12% of brands apply a differential of 26–35%;
17% of brands apply a differential of 36–45%;

Table 15.2 Retail Sales Price of Fashion Products According to the Location of the Sales Point

Europe	USA	Hong Kong	Japan	South Korea	China
100	115	116	125	127	132

Source: Based on authors' estimates.

3% of brands apply a differential of 46–55%;

3% of brands apply a differential of 56–65%;

9% of brands apply a differential of more than 66%. (L2, 2016)

This means an average differential of 32% with very high variability. The perception of Chinese customers was that luxury brands have much higher prices in China and, therefore, for many years, they preferred to go shopping in Hong Kong or Macao where prices were 25–30% lower than in mainland China.

This took a rather extraordinary turn in December 2015 after the fall of the rouble. It took several days for luxury brands to alter their prices, as explained in Chapter 7. Planeloads of Chinese customers rushed to Russia and raided the luxury stores, taking advantage of the large price differences this delay caused. One should not forget that the Chinese represent not only the largest number of luxury customers but also the most alert. They are fully aware of the prices all over the world.

As a result, with the growth in online sales and the growing influence of Chinese customers, brands are now seeking to change their global pricing policies. In 2014, Salvatore Ferragamo was one of the first to increase European retail prices by 10% and maintain its prices in Asia in order to narrow the gap between China and Italy. The comparative price index then changed to 100 and 125 between Milan and Shanghai, while Hong Kong and travel retail platforms stood at 90.

Similarly, in April 2015, Chanel announced that it was seeking to harmonise its leather goods product prices by increasing European prices by 20% and lowering them in Asia (except in Japan). The aim was to ensure a harmonisation within a range of fluctuation of 10% compared to European prices. This policy was later extended to all the collections of the brand.

Additionally, one should never forget that Chinese tourists that come to France, for instance, and buy a €100 product will get a VAT refund so that the price they really pay is €85. They will then compare with the China price that may be €110 if we stay within that 10% band. The difference is still quite important: €25. This means that the pressure will be strong for brands to try to harmonize their retail prices.

The latest phenomenon that is changing the standpoints of brand managers is businesses run by online companies that sell from platforms in tax-free zones and dispatch large numbers of individual parcels to several countries in the world. How will such countries collect customs duties? In some of them it is neither organised nor possible, and in such cases the same product, bought in that country, and which is imported officially in a container by a local importer or distributor, will cost more than if the product was sent individually by parcel by a major online European platform. Moreover, many brands themselves have developed cross-border e-commerce systems, not declaring the products to be subject to any particular tax. This risks calling into question the imposition of customs duties, or in any case, reducing the amounts. One can probably expect radical changes in this area.

Also, some websites, called 'price comparators', such as MrIndex (for watches), publish the retail prices for all watches in every city of the world, in the Rolex stores, for example, or at multi-brand jewellers-watchmakers. Finding the details is as easy as clicking on the name of the city and the reference of the model one is interested in. This, of course, puts a curb on unrestricted pricing among boutique managers. It is in everyone's interest to have prices in every country clearly indicated and explained, and all differences clarified and justified – which would create a strong incentive for brands to evolve towards a harmonisation of their prices in the international markets (within a range of 10–15% that would be acceptable to clients).

Sell-in, Sell-out and Sell-through

Since we are on the subject of price policies and looking at the impact prices may have on an item in a given country (as far as competitors' prices are concerned, of course), we should also examine the concept of *sell-through* (i.e., the analysis of the output percentage of the products that the store has sold divided by the number of products purchased over a given period of time), which is a concrete indicator of the rationality of a price.

Let us start by assuming that a brand does not work exclusively with directly operated stores, but also with franchisees, department stores and multi-brand retailers.

Sell-in represents the number of units a brand has sold to a partner, for example, a franchisee. Let us suppose that the brand sold 100 units of a given item to a franchised store in Moscow.

Sell-out is the number of units that the Russian partner (the franchised store) sells in a given period of time. This represents the total number of units purchased by retail customers at the end of the distribution system chain. Say, for example, that the *sell-out* in Moscow, after 4 months of selling at full price, is 60. This would mean that there are 40 units at full price still in stock at the end of this sales period.

Sell-through is the percentage of units sold by the merchant during a given period. To continue with our Muscovite example, let's say that the *sell-through* was 40% during the first 2 months, 52% after 3 months, and (you guessed it!) 60% after 4 months.

In fashion, a product should have a *sell-through* of 65–85% during the full-price sales period, i.e., before the sales season starts.

The *sell-through* can, and should, be monitored each month. In the above example, the percentage was perhaps 25% the first month and 60% at the end of the 4-month period.

For individual products, take for example, a new leather handbag that has a *sell-through* of only 10% during the first month of its launch (for example, in September for the winter collection); we know that there is a problem. Either customers do not find the product attractive, or its price is too high. By 15 October, it might be judicious to lower the price by 20% and give the franchisee a credit note, allowing it to preserve its entire margin on the reduced price.

Let Us Look at Margins Again

As previously explained, a margin is the percentage of the profit (selling price minus the cost of the product) divided by the selling price. Sometimes the margins are only 4%, but they can be as high as 50%, and in such cases, journalists would certainly go to town and write articles where they assert that retailers make more money than manufacturers!

This gross margin percentage is in fact quite misleading. By definition, it is a gross margin, that is, the ratio of the difference between the retail price and the individual production costs and therefore does not take into account the store's operating costs, which could be very high. In addition to the gross margin, it is sometimes interesting to also look at operating margins, which include an approximate ratio of the store's fixed costs. If rent and salaries account for 30% of projected turnover, and if the gross margin is 50%, this operating margin goes down to 20%, which is not the same thing.

Should all products in a single-brand store be calculated using the same gross margin percentage? This would really have made things easier. To calculate the selling price, the store would only have to multiply the purchase price of each article by the same coefficient, but it is not always the case. If a brand uses the same coefficient for its key products (e.g. ready-to-wear), it may have to operate with a lower coefficient (and therefore a lower margin) for new product categories that are not produced in the same quantities (and economies of scale) as their standard lines. It is therefore likely that there will be two or three different margins applied in a single-brand store.

In fact, as William Davidson explains in his book on sales point management, for different product categories and different types of stores, the overall price and cost structures could differ greatly. He differentiated between upmarket fashion brand stores, regular department stores and supermarkets. Figure 15.1 shows one of his charts.

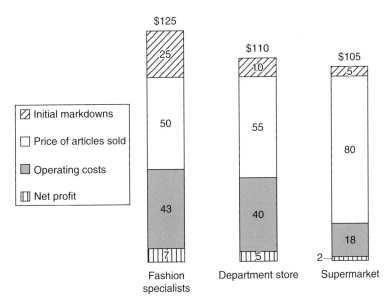

Figure 15.1 Price, Costs and Margins for Various Commercial Sectors
Source: Adapted from Davidson, Sweeney and Stampfl (1988).

Table 15.3   Margins by Category of Product
in Department Stores

Product category	Gross margin
Jewellery	70%
Women's clothing	65%
Fashion accessories	65%
Women's shoes	65%
Men's clothing	55%
Men's shoes	55%
Home decor	55%
Children's clothes	50%
Electronic goods	35%

The chart shows that fashion brands need a higher margin to counterbalance the impact of sales, something we will discuss in the following pages. Even with an average margin of 60%, fashion stores typically end up with an actual gross profit margin of 50% and a net profit margin of 5.6%. The large department stores try to limit sales, and supermarkets work with a gross margin of 20% to finally end up with a net profit of 1.9%. But even in department stores, margins can vary from one product category to another, as one can see in Table 15.3.

The Particular Case of Fashion Retailing

What would be an acceptable gross margin for a fashion store for it to be profitable? It all depends on its *sell-through*. If it is high, and only 10–20% of merchandise remains to be sold during sales, then the outlook is positive. But if a collection does not sell well, then 40 or 50% of the stock purchased (or *sell-in*) will have to be sold at reduced prices – and the greater the quantity to be sold, the more the price will have to be reduced to be able to sell more of it. In the example in Table 15.4 we have taken 30, 40 and 50% as the most likely reduction rates needed. But with a 40% margin, lowering prices by 50% means selling at a loss (although this is also permitted during sales). The gross margin generated for the whole season will therefore not be 40%, but approximately 20 or 25%. It is not easy to turn a profit under such circumstances.

Table 15.4   Impact of the Percentage of Sales at Reduced Prices and of the Level of Price Reduction on the Total Margin (Assuming a Gross Margin of 40%)

		Total margins on products sold at reduced prices				
Percentage of reduction		10%	20%	30%	40%	50%
during sales	30%	38.1%	36.2%	34.1%	31.8%	29.4%
	30%	37.5%	34.8%	31.8%	28.5%	25%
	50%	36.8%	33.3%	29.4%	25%	20%

The lesson one can learn from this table is clear: in fashion, a theoretical gross margin at full price is one thing. The average gross margin, once all the goods have been sold in one way or another, is another. In the fashion sector, one can only say it was profitable when all the goods that were purchased have been sold.

In Table 15.5, we compare three brands with different *sell-through* rates. Brand *A* sells 90% at maximum price and has to dispose of only 10% of its volume through sales. Brand *B* sells 70% at full price and has to dispose of 30% through sales. Brand *C* has a low *sell-through* (40%) and has to dispose of 60% through sales. We assume here that the initial gross margin is 60% and that the discount during sales is 40%, which brings the gross margin down to 33%.

In each of the three cases, the financial outcomes are quite different. In the first case, for brand *A*, the overall gross margin is not far from the theoretical margin, 57.3%. For brand *C*, it is only 43.8% (a difference of 13%). For a Store Manager, the financial impact of the

Table 15.5   Margins of Three Brands with Different Sales Percentages at Reduce Prices

	Brand *A*	**Brand *B***	**Brand *C***
Theoretical margin	60%	60%	60%
Percentage of sales at full price	90%	70%	40%
Margin index	54	42	24
Percentage sold at reduced prices	10%	30%	60%
Margin at reduced prices	33%	33%	33%
Margin index	3.3	9.9	19.8
Margin for the season	57.3%	51.9%	43.8%

difference between a brand with a high *sell-through* and a brand with a low *sell-through* is quite large.

Shrinkage percentages also have an impact on the gross margin. Items may be stolen by customers or the staff. In fact, it is commonly assumed that a third of pilfering is committed by customers, and two-thirds by the staff. The methods may vary. The most obvious is to pick up an item and leave the store without paying for it at the counter, but this is not always easy. Most products, especially in the ready-to-wear departments, have an anti-theft magnet or chip that has to be removed at the counter. Also, many stores have security guards at the door.

Other methods are less visible and perhaps more difficult to detect. A vendor, for example, could sell an expensive dress to a friend but enters the code of a cheaper item. Or, if a customer forgets to collect a receipt, a staff member could hold it for a few days and then cash it in, saying the article had been brought back and returned to stock. When one discovers that a product is missing during a physical inventory at the end of the season, no one would think that some of the missing items correspond to these 'returned' articles.

Shoplifting is another problem related to the pricing policy, since it has an impact on the store's gross margin. One may find that items are missing during a physical inventory while cross-checking the stocks against the items actually present in the store.

The EAS or Electronic Article Surveillance system is the most efficient method to prevent shoplifting. It consists of electronic tags linked to an alarm system. The tag in the label is deactivated at the checkout counter. If it has not been deactivated, a sensor located near the exit will trigger an alarm when the item passes through the door, alerting the staff.

A second electromagnetic system (EM) is also widely used in Europe. It can be deactivated once payment is made and reactivated if the item is returned.

However, in the luxury world, it is not easy to attach odd-looking labels to clothes, or place electronic detectors near the exit. Video surveillance and security guards would no doubt be less intrusive and may be just as effective.

As for theft by employees, controlling it is difficult, as the offender does not necessarily have to leave the store with the article. The method described above, the 'fake return', makes it impossible to trace the perpetrator during an inventory and a store manager would be unable to link a missing article to a 'theoretical' return.

In fact, the best method to reduce theft by employees is thorough screening when recruiting candidates for sales positions.

Price Reductions and Sales

What is the best way to clear unsold stock? Let us first look at typical reduction practices and special promotional events before focusing on sales.

Typical Reduction Practices

In a store, the hypothetical gross margin is very rarely attained. Even for reputed brands and collections that sell well during the season, things are not so cut and dry.

In special cases, sales staff have the authority to grant discounts to preferred clients or clients who purchase two or three products at a time. The most selective brands forbid this practice, but for the others, a reduction of 5% may be permitted, the sales staff having to conform to very strict guidelines on what they are allowed to do or not do.

The only exception that the big brands make to this rigorous no-reduction policy is for journalists and staff members, which can also, of course, have an impact on the gross margin.

Should there be a loyalty card for customers? This practice may seem unglamorous for a luxury brand, and if truth be told, such cards are not really useful. Why give a Chanel VIP card to someone who already has several privilege cards in his or her wallet? Instead, it would be far more elegant and discerning to tell a loyal customer that he or she could benefit from a 10% reduction on purchases in a particular store. This concession is to be confirmed and entered in the CRM at the payment counter. Chanel used to grant reductions of 10% to the best customers of its Hong Kong store for any purchases they made there. To tell a client that he or she is entitled to a discount will make more of an impression than to give him or her a plastic card.

Another elegant way of showing loyal and regular customers they are special is to tell them they are being given 'the same advantages as journalists', which means rebates ranging from 10 to 20%.

This is an option for VIP customers, but special treatment for a wider base of loyal customers is much more difficult to organise. Once an automatic process is put in place, it may appear systematic and commonplace, and can diminish the prestige of the brand. A common practice is to invite selected clients to attend private sales one or two weeks before the official sales begin. The reason stated on the invitation should be chosen with care because in many countries, sales periods are strictly regulated and any other type of special sale outside this period should come under a completely different heading.

In this latter case, one should also consider the question of tourists in major cities. In Paris, Hong Kong and elsewhere, it is common practice that guides bringing groups of tourists to certain tax-free outlets in the city, get paid one or two euros for each person plus a commission on any purchases they make. This is, of course, unthinkable for institutional stores or megastores as, for them, tourists pouring out of tourist coaches has nothing prestigious about it. That said, these tourists can in fact represent a large volume of business. The guides of the buses filled with Chinese that park in front of Galeries Lafayette in Paris who say they receive a commission of 10% on purchases made by these tourists are not complaining.

Does this mean that the really upscale stores do not pay commissions to tour guides? In reality, they always do, but in a more indirect way. A guide may go to a jewellery store, for example, and tell them that he would come back the next day with a princess from the Middle East and persuade her to make purchases of at least €20,000, against which he would like a 5% commission. If the answer is no, the guide will not come back, but if the answer is yes and the guide is serious, he will probably come back with the princess and encourage her to purchase expensive jewellery. The day after, the guide will come back to pick up his commission.

Special Events

In some cases, one may organise special events with reduced prices before the beginning of the sales. These events could serve several purposes:

- Stimulate the sales of regular products and give customers an occasion to visit the store.

- Offer the opportunity to sell items created especially for the occasion with full-margin prices while giving the customer the impression of getting a good deal.
- Give *a boost* to products which have weak *sell-through* at the beginning of the season and which are likely to remain unsold in a few months.
- Attract new customers to the store.

One can do so, of course, but it takes careful planning and execution. For example, products for the event should be chosen wisely: they should have high selling potential (which, of course, goes contrary to the idea of choosing slow-selling items) and they should provoke impulse buying.

This is a tricky problem. Specialists still believe that promotions outside traditional sales periods will not be successful unless they involve huge discounts.

The presentation should therefore be particularly well thought out. It could consist of:

- A 'big unpacking sale', with a large quantity of merchandise.
- An exceptional factory sale, but at extremely low prices (much lower than the usual sales).
- A collection of items that are not usually sold in the brand's store but which are sold in other stores of the brand (not in the same city) or in another country.
- A new collection, which is not yet available in the city stores and for which the brand would like to test its customers' reactions.

Even if the idea of a good deal is always present, it should never be the motivation for the event and even less its official objective.

Who should be invited? If the event is conducted on a large scale, almost all subscribers on the mailing list. If it is a more private event, invitations should be sent only to people selected through a methodical and careful process.

Sales

In the fashion world, it is necessary to dispose of the unsold goods from the previous season to free up space for the new collection and generate cash. This can be done inside or outside the store, with or without substantial discounts, with advertising or not, and for variable periods of time.

Sales on Site or Not?   The sales can be held in the store or elsewhere. Each location has its advantages.

The advantage of in-store sales is that there is no extra rent to pay and it is easier to organise. No advertising is necessary, since people know when sales begin and they stroll from boutique to boutique looking for bargains.

The disadvantages of conducting sales in the store is that the sales area gets disordered and, during sales, few or no sales at full price are recorded. It may be a satisfactory solution for normal brands, but it is a disadvantage for brands whose business depends largely on tourists, as these tourists would come to the store anyway and are prepared to buy the products on their lists at full price. If the product is on sale, they will buy it but will probably not take the opportunity to buy a second item, which means that the store will not be able to optimise its gross margins.

In Paris, for example, all major brands, such as Hermès, Louis Vuitton and Yves Saint Laurent, organise their sales away from the store. They rent a space for three or four days and hold their sales there.

The advantage of this arrangement is that sales can be concentrated into just a few days, during which the store can continue its normal business activities and give tourists the service they expect. Besides, it is easier to make these spaces look more eye-catching, and draw more people than in the store.

The disadvantage is that it is only feasible for very powerful brands that are able to attract a very large number of visitors. For example, if Courrèges decided to hold its sales 20 km from Paris, there is no guarantee that a large number of customers would be willing to make the trip.

However, for premier brands with enough pulling power to attract bargain hunters to the most remote locations, out-of-store sales help them to dispose of their old stocks within just a few days, and therefore to run their retail activities in January and July as for any normal month.

When sales are held in an exterior location, some advertising will be required (newspapers, most often) or direct mailing, but its cost should be proportionate to the volume of merchandise one expects to sell.

How About Price Levels?   The answer to this question is clear. If the goal is to dispose of surplus merchandise and improve liquidity, the markdown should be substantial and attractive.

Sales Managers are often tempted to sell at a discount of 20 or 30% during the first week, then 40 or 50% the second week and eventually at 70% the third week. However, the most experienced among those who manage sales operations say that the first markdown should be the most effective and avoid deeper price cuts at a later stage. It is better to get off to a good start with a reduction of at least 45% than to end up with a surplus of stock after three weeks to be sold at minus 70%.

Some think that starting with a small markdown of 20% helps the brand to maintain a strong identity by conveying the idea that its products are difficult to acquire. But a customer may reason differently; they may find the offer uninteresting, even misleading, and will probably not come back during the second or third week.

Who Should Be Invited?   For sales to be successful, practically everyone. When they are held in the store, this goes without saying. In an external location, entry is limited to staff and journalists during a few hours, then to the best customers, and finally to the general public on the second day.

When sales take place in the store, the most loyal customers should be invited to a preview a few days in advance, giving them the opportunity to buy their favourite products.

Invitations can be sent by mail (electronic or post). For certain types of off-site sales, newspaper advertising is necessary.

How Long Should the Sales Last?   The sooner they are over, the sooner the store can resume its normal operations. Sales in external locations generally last three or four days, and, if they are held in the store, may last up to three weeks. If most of the surplus stock is sold within a week and a half, that is best. Whatever merchandise remains can be disposed of through other channels.

Discounted Products

If the brand has its own factory outlets, it can send the remaining articles there. It can also sell them to a surplus specialist, after removing the labels, but this is rarely a good solution because the products end up in dubious outlets with large signs claiming, 'Authentic Brand X, at discount prices'. The most prestigious brands used to burn their surpluses (although it might be better to sell them at minus 80% and make at least a few customers happy!) but they now tend to avoid doing this for ecological reasons.

During this discussion on pricing policies, we have described what should be done in terms of pricing in a business environment, even though the normal selling price was a factor considered non-negotiable. The job of the Store Manager is therefore to manage the various price reductions for promotional events. In each case, a relevant differential threshold should be found, or, to put it another way, the price difference, discount or sales rebate that will motivate the customer to make a purchase should be determined. This threshold will differ from one brand to another, but the general principle is that nothing can be gained by scraping just a bit off the price. Price reductions during sales and discounts should be frank and generous. The customer should perceive it as an excellent buying opportunity: there is no better way for a brand to maintain its position, prestige and appeal.

To recap:

- *Prices and margins* should be reviewed, analysed and monitored daily. That is what drives distribution and guarantees its effectiveness.
- *International prices need to be harmonised*, taking customs duties and other accessory costs into account.
- *Sales* could offer a good opportunity to dispose of hard-to-sell merchandise. They could help to generate sales and, therefore, margins.
- *In the fashion sector*, sales that help to dispose of products that are too seasonal to remain indefinitely in the store are an integral and usual part of its management.

Chapter 16

Financial Analyses of Sales Points

Marketing Directors are being increasingly held accountable for their investments.

–Philip Kotler[1]

L
ike any other structure a luxury store needs an organisation, a budget, a management structure, and control systems. We also explained why, for a very valid reason, many stores in the United States are managed by independent subsidiaries of foreign groups, created solely to manage each point of sales autonomously. That may even be how people generally see their stores: as independent entities, with

---

[1] Kotler and Keller (2016).

their own investments, stocks, employees and day-to-day operations. That is why drawing up a budget is so important. A budget is crucial for analysing the viability of a project and to monitor its progress from the very beginning.

The control factor is also very important. When a brand owns and has to manage from 100 to 500 outlets around the world, it has to make sure that it knows exactly where the money is, where the stocks are and how sales, including the exact margins, are recorded, if possible directly with the correct margins.

To manage a group of sales points, key management criteria should be examined. In a survey initially conducted in 2010 by the consulting group A.T. Kearney, the managers of 53 US distributors were asked what information they obtained from customers and analysed to assure the day-to-day management of their stores.

Figure 16.1 shows the main results of the study. It is not surprising to see that the number of transactions per store (or number of cash register tickets) is the most common operations index, followed by the average transaction value (or average ticket). Besides the overall turnover figures, there is the obvious indicator of a store's business: How many people made a purchase yesterday (generally called: the number of tickets)?

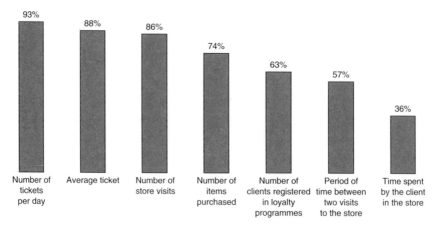

Figure 16.1 Business Information Considered as Being Very Important
Source: Adapted from Pressman et al. (2016).

The third criterion in Figure 16.1 is the number of store visits: How many people enter the store? How attractive is it to passers-by? This is an indication of the appeal of the store and the importance of its location. All shop managers undoubtedly take these three criteria into account, which is not at all surprising.

The fourth criterion in Figure 16.1, also monitored by practically every company, is the number of items purchased. This indicator reflects the efficiency of the sales staff (are they able to sell an additional article besides the article the client spontaneously chose?), and visual merchandising choices (are the socks and shoe polish tempting enough to elicit a purchase from someone buying a pair of shoes?).

None of these criteria are unusual in themselves, and we will examine them in detail in this chapter. These are the main variables in the management and control of a sales point and its presentation. However, the following facts may seem more surprising.

Sixty-three percent of sales managers closely monitor the number of customers enrolled in loyalty programmes. This means that most of these managers have set up such programmes in their stores and consider them important for their business. The message this conveys to those who do not yet have a loyalty programme for mass market products is perhaps to look at how one can be set up, even in the luxury sector, where access to products is assumed to be exceptional and discerning.

The last two criteria, perceived as the least important by US managers interviewed, pertain to consumer behaviour. The first concerns the time gap between two visits, and is considered a 'very important' indicator by 57% of these managers. What they wish to know is the visitor frequency of their stores and who these visitors are. For example, are they regular, occasional or exceptional clients? This could help them determine the most relevant periods for promotional programmes. Should the store have new products, new presentations, new showcase displays every week, every month, six times or eight times a year? The customers' visiting frequencies will help them choose the most appropriate schedule.

The last criterion in Figure 16.1 pertains to customer behaviour in the store. How much time do they spend in the store? Do they seem relaxed? Are they happy to be here? How long will they queue up at the counter without getting impatient? All of these questions will be addressed in this chapter.

Financial Analysis of a Sales Point

In this section, we explain the analysis of the breakeven point, the concept of margins and cash flow requirements depending on the various management systems. We will conclude with an example of an efficient sales outlet.

Analysing the Breakeven Point

Figure 16.2 shows an example of how a breakeven point is analysed. The breakeven point (S1) is the point at which the gross margin of the turnover is equal to the total of the fixed costs incurred to obtain the said turnover.

Figure 16.2 shows that the fixed costs (rent for the store, salaries of sales staff and other miscellaneous fixed costs, represented by a horizontal line), do not vary according to the turnover. A second line traces the turnover and a third line traces the gross margin. In the example chosen,

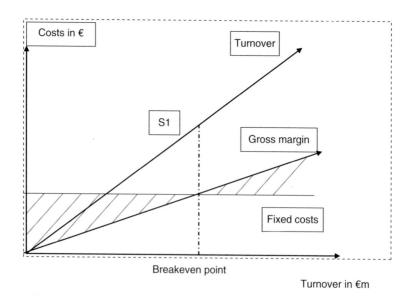

Figure 16.2   Analysis of the Breakeven Point

we have assumed that the gross margin equals 55% of turnover. The point where the line corresponding to the gross margin intersects the horizontal line (S1) is the point at which the gross margin and the fixed costs are equal. Below this point the store is losing money. The gap between the gross margin and fixed costs represents losses. Above this level of sales, the gap between the fixed costs and the gross margin, positive this time, represents profits.

One therefore sees a definite relationship between the projected turnover for a given commercial location and the fixed costs related to that particular location. The following scenarios illustrate this point very well: any brand would like to have a magnificent store in a prime location. Say, for example, $300 \, \text{m}^2$ on Avenue Montaigne in Paris. The rent would probably be €12,000 a square metre, which would correspond to €3.6 million per year. Add salaries for a team of eight people which would come to around €500,000 a year, a large proportion of which is in the form of fixed costs. The annual fixed costs of the store would therefore come to €4.1 million. If the gross margin is calculated at 50%, the store would need a turnover of €8.2 million to reach breakeven point. Can the brand attain this turnover easily? If not, can it afford to maintain an unprofitable store in this location? One could certainly argue that prime locations have a higher turnover than, for instance, a sales outlet located on a small street in a suburb of Paris, where the annual rent of a store of the same size would probably be around €100,000. The best solution may therefore be to move to smaller premises, for example, $80 \, \text{m}^2$, and still remain on Avenue Montaigne. The rent would be approximately €960,000. Another option may be to use the Avenue Montaigne store as a 'showroom' that makes no profit, and to open two shops-in-shops in the Printemps and Bon Marché department stores, where the brand would have to pay only variable costs and could generate revenue, say for example, €500,000 per year. All three sales points (the 'showroom' on Avenue Montaigne and the two shops-in-shops) together could attain the breakeven point while the brand builds a strong and profitable presence in Paris at the same time. However, let us not forget, as we explained in Chapter 1, that the brand will not be able to pocket the entire margin in Le Printemps and Le Bon Marché. It will have to share it with the department stores. The turnover in these two locations would therefore have to be relatively high to reach an overall balance.

Opening sales outlets therefore involves weighing the known rental costs against anticipated turnover. Very few brands can afford to open very large stores in prime locations. All of them have had to choose the one that is most appropriate at a given moment. For each store, besides the indispensable breakeven point analysis, three key factors may serve as performance indicators:

- The turnover per square metre;
- The number of product units sold per square metre;
- Turnover per full-time equivalent of sales staff.

With these criteria, a brand would be able to make a preliminary comparison between any one of their sales points and the average of the others.

Analysing Margins   Store managers always speak of the gross margin, which is the difference between the selling price and the cost of the product. But margins can be expressed in different ways.

It could be a *markdown*, that is to say a percentage of profit divided by the selling price, as in Table 16.1, i.e., 30%. It could also be a *markup*, that is, a percentage of the profit divided by the cost of the product, i.e., 42.8% in the same table. In retail, one uses the markdown method exclusively because it is easier to calculate and compare against sales.

The Concept of Coefficients

Sometimes the reference is not to gross margins, but rather to coefficients. In retail, the coefficient is the selling price divided by the cost of the product sold. In high-end fashion, the coefficient is generally

Table 16.1   Margin Analysis

	Markdown	Markup
Selling price	100%	100%
Cost	70%	70%
Margin	30%	42.8%

Table 16.2   Retail Coefficients and Gross Margins

	Coefficients of	
	2.4	**2.6**
Selling price	240	260
Buying price	100	100
Absolute margin	140	160
Gross margin in %	58.3%	61.5%

2.4 or 2.6. The coefficient can, of course, be translated directly as a percentage of the gross margin, as in Table 16.2.

In fact, coefficients of 2.4 and 2.6 correspond to gross margins of 58.3% and 61.5%, fairly close to the 60% we cited previously.

Stock Rotation   In our explanation of direct costs in running a store, we did not bring up one inescapable reality: the merchandise in a store has first to be purchased and financed.

The stock rotation rate is equal to the ratio of annual turnover to the average value of the stock during the year. Table 16.3 gives examples of stock rotation for the different types of stores.

- Merchandise in supermarkets enters and leaves the store rapidly, and some product categories are even delivered on a daily basis. Their stocks may rotate 12 times a year, if not more. In addition, these stores are generally granted payment facilities of 60 or 90 days, and therefore may still owe their suppliers the equivalent of 3 months' worth of stock at the end of the year.

Table 16.3   Examples of Stock Rotation

	Supermarket	Fashion boutique	Jewellers
Annual turnover	1,000,000	1,000,000	1,000,000
Average inventory at cost	83,000	250,000	1,000,000
Stock rotation	12	4	1
Invoices payable within	90 days	90 days	90 days
Inventory financial cash flow	+333,000	−187,500	−750,000

- With this system, the cost of the supermarket's stock is covered more than adequately by its suppliers, and the store will have a positive cash position of €333,000 (see Table 16.3).
- In contrast, a jewellery store has to maintain a full year's worth of stock at all times in order to be able to display a range extensive enough to trigger a sale. The suppliers, in other words, jewellery manufacturers, assist it to a certain extent, but it still needs a permanent inventory investment.
- A fashion store lies somewhere between the two. With a stock rotation four times a year, it has to finance €187,500 of stock for an annual turnover of €1 million.
- This evidently represents an additional cost for directly managed stores compared to cases where the merchandise is sold to intermediaries or a department store. The stock is then financed by them and not by the brand. When the brand works primarily through its own outlets, it has to take the funding of this outlay into account in its investment plans. The investment is particularly high for jewellery companies and it is imperative to include it in their financial forecasts when developing their commercial strategy.

What should then be the right combination between directly managed stores, shops-in-shops, store counters and wholesale? This is evidently a crucial and strategic decision, in which financial constraints play an important part.

When one talks about a combination, or mix, of systems, people sometimes have a hard time understanding what that means. The perception that all luxury brands are sold in independent stores run directly by the company is so prevalent that people tend to forget that in reality most luxury products are sold in other kinds of outlets than in directly operated stores. In Table 16.4, we illustrate the distribution mix of three brands, each with their own reputation and power of attraction: Chanel, Givenchy and Balmain.

At first glance, the three brands have more-or-less a similar number of sales outlets, between 251 and 400, but, of course, their volumes and configurations are quite different.

With 240 independent stores, mostly in Europe, Chanel has a strong presence. In two countries, the United States and Japan, it relies heavily on shops-in-shops in department stores, as we mentioned earlier. It is

Table 16.4 Combination of Distribution Systems for Three Different Brands (in Number of Sales Points) in 2019

	Single-brand boutiques	Shops-in-shops	Multi-brand boutiques	Total
Chanel	240 (E)	180 (E)	0	400 (E)
Givenchy	65	68	120 (E)	253 (E)
Balmain	19	88	179	286

Sources: Internet sites and (E) authors' estimations

much stronger in other parts of Asia than in China (in mainland China, it is the most attractive brand for customers but had only a small number of outlets: 11 in 2018).

Givenchy traditionally has had a very strong presence in department stores. It has apparently obtained the financial resources necessary to extend its policy of self-owned stores from its group. It is to be hoped that it can build a demand and an appeal sufficient enough to be profitable. It keeps a strong presence in multi-brand stores.

Balmain had only one independent store in Paris until 2014. Since its acquisition by Qatari investors, its development has accelerated and it has 19 self-owned stores in 2019, mainly in Paris, Milan and London in Europe, and in the United States, China, Korea and Japan. But a large part of its turnover it still generated through multi-brand outlets.

In each of these cases, the commercial focus is very different:

- For Chanel, the focus is on maintaining a balance between independent sales points and shops-in-shops, increasing turnover in department stores and managing the appeal of the brand.
- For Givenchy, the focus is on the development and expansion of its single-brand outlets, although its primary source of revenue is independent boutiques and department stores.
- For Balmain, the story is different. The brand's boutiques ensure its commercial presence in the large commercial centres and its reputation among customers who are passionate about fashion, but its revenue still has to be generated through multi-brand stores.

The purpose of the above explanation is to illustrate that there is no one-size-fits-all commercial strategy, but a development plan adapted to each brand's appeal and financial capacities.

Comparison of the Performance of Different Sales Outlets

Many factors explain why some stores may be profitable while others grow at a loss. Just altering two or three variables may be enough to slide from a profitable store to a store that is unsuccessful – with the end results turning out to be quite different. See our example in Table 16.5.

Store B loses 53.75% of its sales, which is truly catastrophic. What are the reasons for such a poor performance?

- The main reason is that its turnover per square metre is far too low.
- Its gross margin is 10% lower than store *A*. In fact, when sales are too low, staff often get frustrated and try everything they can to fill the coffers – including granting price reductions. Also, if the store is located in the wrong place, it may have customers who buy only the cheaper products with low margins, not those with the highest margins.
- The rent of store *B* is clearly too high compared to the sales productivity of its location.
- Compensations in store B are not controlled and not aligned with turnover.

This example is used to illustrate how difficult it can be to generate revenue when every aspect is not well optimised. The store is probably in the wrong locality and should be shut down, but its manager will no doubt find excuses for the poor results: there is some major work going on in front of the store, making access difficult for customers; the products are not adapted to the taste of the local clientele; the street

Table 16.5   Good Performance/Bad Performance

	A **Successful store**	B **Unsuccessful store**
Size of the store	200 m^2	200 m^2
Turnover	€1,600,000	€800,000
Turnover per square metre	€8,000	€4,000
Gross margin	50%	40%
Annual rent	€300,000	€400,000
Staff costs	€300,000	€350,000
Operating margin	€200,000	−€430,000

work will finish next year; the mistakes in product selection will be rectified, and we will do much better. We will then reach breakeven point.

Should one count on it? Business decisions always come back to this kind of question. Should one believe everything one says? When should one decide that the game is over? When all goes well, it is easy to open new outlets and obtain positive results, but it is quite another story when things start to slide.

Applying Key Ratios

By counting the number of people entering a store (which can be done from a car parked across the street or sitting on a bench in a mall) and multiplying the number, first by the conversion rate, then by the average invoice, one can obtain an indicator of the turnover that a given store can attain per day or per week. Is it easy to compute the conversion rate? Yes, if one works on the assumption that most clients who purchase something in the store would walk out proudly with a bag of the brand. Evaluating the average invoice is slightly more complex, but in the context of a study one could have ten evaluators note down the amounts displayed on the cash register at ten different times of the day on different days. These 100 pieces of information could be used to make a rough estimation of the average invoice of a competitor in a given location and therefore its approximate turnover. Not only will these figures enable a brand to understand a competitor's business model and predict the level of revenue they can expect from a given location, but they can also be used to compare the performances of the various stores of the same luxury brand.

Figure 16.3 is a client-performance matrix that we developed to collect data on different stores. It is based on the correlation between the number of sales and the average ticket.

When comparing the performance of various stores on an annual basis, one may see an increase in the number of tickets and the average ticket in certain stores. We call this the 'virtuous' stage. However, if the average ticket of the store decreases, it is not necessarily an indicator of poor performance if, at the same time, the number of tickets increases.

	Average ticket	
	Increasing	Decreasing
Increasing	'Virtuous' stage	'Recruitment' stage
Decreasing	Loyalty stage	Declining stage

Number of tickets (label at left, between Increasing and Decreasing rows)

Figure 16.3   Client Performance Matrix

We call this the 'recruitment' stage. And if the amounts of the average ticket increases while the number of tickets decreases, one has reached the 'loyalty' stage. The one stage to be avoided is, of course, the 'declining' stage. A store in one of the first three stages can be seen as growing, albeit for different reasons. It may be worth mentioning here that each of these different stages obviously calls for different types of promotional campaigns.

In the case of a new women's ready-to-wear range, one can immediately predict whether the sales of a new collection will be good, average or poor by tracking the conversion rate during the first two weeks of the launch and comparing it to the rates of the previous two, or maybe three, years.

Turnover Forecasts

To evaluate the potential turnover of a new location, one has to use the average values of the brand for the attraction coefficient, the conversion rate, and the average ticket. From this available information, adjusted to take into account the specific characteristics of a given location – for example, the average income level of potential customers, or the profiles of passers-by (are their purchases of the destination or convenience type?) – one could estimate the expected turnover simply by counting the number of passers-by.

In general, this turnover (and in this case both the conversion rate and the average ticket) also depends on the size of the store planned.

In fact, often, to analyse the sales figures and compare the different stores of the same brand, the managers divide the overall turnover by the size of the store. That is how the *turnover per square metre* indicator is usually calculated.

Department store groups typically use this indicator to measure the outputs of their different establishments. Taking into consideration the figures per square metre is also a means of taking into account the initial investment or the rental costs of the different stores they manage. Also, we can assume that the bigger the store, the larger the stock and the heavier the investment (in products) needed to attain a given turnover.

But the same department store can also use the indicator of the turnover per square metre to compare the success of different categories of products: women's ready-to-wear compared to men's ready-to-wear, home decoration, or perfumes and cosmetics.

This indicator has also been adapted to stores presenting their products such as perfumes and cosmetics on shelves and racks, in which case it is referred to as the turnover per linear metre, and this ratio used to compare the different stores of the same chain. A perfume chain can, for example, use it to measure the profitability of different brands or to compare the success of their perfumes as compared to make-up or care products, or the distribution of these three major categories of products among different commercial locations.

However, not all categories of products offer the same returns. That is why another indicator is also widely used: the *gross margin per square metre*. This is yet another tool for analysing sales efficiency.

Figure 16.4 shows an example of a turnover chart based on the size of the store. There is no direct relationship between the overall turnover and the number of square metres. The chart shows, for example, that

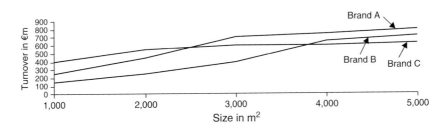

Figure 16.4 Comparison of Sales Achieved at Different Store Sizes as a Function of the Merchandising Mix Offered

brand A's sales take off slowly (when the store is too small, its products do not attract many customers, but as the size of the store increases, sales grow very fast), then reach a plateau.

Brand B, on the other hand, has products that do not sell well unless the store is bigger. Initially, its turnover per square metre is less than half of that of *brand A*; but when the store grows bigger, its overall performance almost matches that of *brand A*.

Brand C does quite well in a small store, and its results do not grow significantly with an increase in the size of the store.

The yield curve depends on the reputation of the brand. The turnover per square metre at Cartier was significantly higher than that of Bulgari in similar locations for a long time. But it seems to be evident that the smaller the product ranges, the less profitable a large store will prove. Displaying only top-of-the-line handbags and luggage in $500\,m^2$ may not be the most cost-effective way of using space.

It is not easy to predict optimal levels for turnover per square metre as this will depend on the ambience of the store, the attractiveness of the brand and the type of merchandise it offers. But, basically, in 2019, we could say that, monthly:

- For a multi-brand store in South East Asia, the target would be €1,500 per square metre.
- In the United States, a normal shopping centre has to attain €2,500 per square metre. The Mall of America earns €4,100 per square metre.
- The bookstore of the Museum of Modern Art in New York supposedly makes €18,000 per square metre.

This turnover-per-square-metre ratio is a very important indicator of sales productivity. If a luxury brand's sales managers are able to garner this information, they would be able to compare their turnover per square metre to that of their competitors. If it is lower, either the attractiveness of the brand is insufficient or the product is not adapted to the size of their stores.

Let us study the case of a brand whose revenue per square metre was always 40% lower than that of its leading competitor, a leader in the industry. The company's primary objective was to reduce this gap with a more effective advertising campaign designed to increase brand awareness and appeal.

Table 16.6 shows an analysis of Tiffany stores in the United States. We see that the number of stores in the US grew from 70 in 2007 to 114 in 2012, then declined to 94 in 2018. During the same period, turnover went down sharply, because of the economic crisis of 2008, which hit the American market, and the jewellery sector in particular, and also because Tiffany did not bounce back strongly enough. But it is only when one looks at the turnover per square metre that a clear picture of the situation emerges – it shows a 31% decline during that period.

This analysis by square metre is not always possible, as data is rarely available. In Table 16.7, for example, we show data on Coach's retail outlets in North America, but we did not find any indicator relating to variations in turnover linked to the opening, and the closing, of such a large number of stores in their annual report.

Tables 16.6 and 16.7 show the situations of store networks or performance of these same stores. The evolution of turnover by store or by square metre should be examined closely and explained:

- When a new store opens, it usually takes about two years to reach its full potential in terms of turnover.

Table 16.6 Analysis of Tiffany Stores in the United States

	2018	**2012**	**2007**
Number of stores	94	114	70
Surface area (m^2)	67,838	69,290	49,300
Average area (m^2)	722	608	704
Turnover USA	1,688,000	1,840,137	1,759,868
Annual turnover per m^2	€24.90	€26.50	€35.50

Source: Based on data from annual reports.

Table 16.7 Trends in Coach's American Sales Outlets

	2017	**2012**	**2007**
Number of boutiques	221	354	259
Surface area (m^2)	67,838	95,910	62,774
Average size	306	270	260

Source: Based on data from annual reports.

- When the number of stores of a brand increases, the new stores are rationally in secondary locations, with less potential than the original store.
- When a brand's commercial space increases, the number of items available for sale should be increased as well. It sometimes takes time for product marketing teams to realise that they should change the selection of products as well.

Inventory and Controlling Margins

We shall start this new section by reviewing purchasing budgets, followed by inventories and controlling of margins.

- Purchasing budgets

A store should only purchase what it will be able to sell during each season. The purchasing budget exercise thus begins by establishing a turnover projection that is then split by month and translated into purchases, which have to be financed.

The *Open to Buy* (OTB) idea was conceived by American department stores. Each department manager draws up a budget for each brand and then a corresponding OTB. OTB represents the amount that the manager may buy from Brand X in the course of the following year.

If the results of Brand X over the previous two or three years have been good, the OTB budget for the brand for the following year would no doubt be increased, meeting the expectations of the sales representatives of the brand. If, on the contrary, Brand X has not sold very well, its OTB for the following year would be reduced. Many luxury brand managers have had to fight against this method during their negotiations with department store buyers whose OTBs for their brands were very low.

The OTB system (under one name or another) is now used by almost every luxury store operator. The purchasing budget (OTB) by brand and by season is the basis of all purchasing systems.

Different brands use different methods, such as:

- In some cases, the store or sales manager of a given country is allowed to purchase what they believe is sufficient from a wide selection of products.

– Sometimes store managers are not the decision makers. Stocks are delivered directly to the store by the head office where the selection is automatically calculated by a centralised information system based on previous sales (colours and sizes, for example) and types of products.
– Most often, a part of the collection is automatically delivered to the store and managers are allowed to select the remaining 40 or 60% depending on what they judge is most suitable for their store.
– Sometimes, the procurement budget is divided into three parts: one part centralised at headquarters, a smaller percentage allotted to a given country, and a third part under the sole responsibility of the store manager. In this matter, each brand has to define its own policy and procedures.

In 2005, Prada had a zero-autonomy policy for its store managers and country directors where choosing the products for their stores. Delivery was automatic, with no flexibility at all. Vuitton has a policy that is also considered relatively rigid, but with data-based modifications and, in the process, a good deal of specific and intelligent autonomy. It may therefore seem that the stronger a brand, the less autonomy it allows its store managers, although that may not always be the case.

In reality, things are not so straightforward. It is well known that a Japanese store and a Chinese store distributing the same brand sell items that are completely different and therefore need collections that are adapted to their markets. Even within China, people in the north of the country prefer different colours and shapes from those in the south. If a brand is well organised and can rely on data carefully collected over the years, its head office in Paris or Milan will be able to decide which products are suitable for its store in Tianjin. If this trend data does not exist, or if the system it is integrated into is faulty, there is no choice but to ask the sales staff to make their own, subjective selections.

During the buying phase, one has to make compromises that are not always easy. Take leather items, for example. Customers usually end up buying black, brown or beige, as mentioned earlier, but for a presentation to be vibrant and eye-catching, it is necessary to have white, yellow and red on the shelves. The head office may require the stores to offer the whole range, but a manager reasoning short term may prefer to ignore these items, which would most likely end up being sold during sales.

Watches are another example in the same genre: A vendor is far more likely to make a sale if there is a complete collection to present to the client, but generally, fewer expensive gold models are sold than the more affordable and relatively cheaper ones. Store managers may therefore be tempted to stock the cheaper watches to the detriment of a comprehensive collection which would be essential to reflect the prestige of the brand. The head office will probably insist that the entire range be purchased, and subsequently assess the managers of its stores on their stock rotation capacities.

So far, we have almost exclusively focused on the two-collections-a-year system: spring-summer and autumn-winter. This calendar is in fact changing, with the introduction of 'cruise' collections that increase the number of deliveries to four per year.

In fact, retailers have realised that if they display the whole autumn-winter collection say in September, some of their loyal customers return in late October/early November asking if they have received any new models. So, they often split the collection into different themes, pre-senting some of the merchandise in October and keeping the rest in reserve for November. They in fact are transforming the system on their own initiative.

Of course, everyone in the industry has noticed that Zara has 26 collections a year and is doing very well. Some have probably wondered if they could do the same, and the answer is probably negative because Zara operates according to a different model. But luxury companies can certainly learn some lessons there. Some have already implemented a similar model, such as Tous, the Spanish mid-range luxury jewellery company, which also works on the 26-collections-a-year model.

• Stock rotation

Stock rotation is the ratio of the number of units sold as against the average stock volume in the store during a given year. In general, since product units are heterogeneous in a luxury store, the calculation is based on the sales (cost price) compared to the average value of the stock.

Table 16.8 shows an example of typical stock rotation figures in a US department store. It can be seen here that in a department store, women's

Table 16.8   Stock Rotation According to the Size of the Sales Point

$$\text{Rate of stock rotation} = \frac{\text{Number of pieces sold}}{\text{Average stock}}$$

Department store (USA) – Volume of sales/Turnover

	Small	**Medium**	**Large**
Men's clothing	2.0	2.2	2.4
Furniture and bedding	2.1	2.4	2.8
Children's clothing	2.5	2.6	3.4
Books	2.8	2.85	3.1
Household appliances	3.2	3.1	3.9
Tights and stockings	3.5	3.1	3.4
Women's ready to wear	4.3	4.5	5.4

ready-to-wear rotates 4.3 to 5.4 times a year, more than double the rotation rate of men's ready-to-wear. The seasonal sales cycle in women's ready-to-wear probably has a positive impact on the rotation rate. In contrast, men's attire, perceived as less sensitive to seasonal cycles, remains in stores longer.

• Stock shortages and transfers

There is nothing more annoying to a customer than finding out that an article they want has sold out. For example, a woman sees a product, waits two or three days before making her mind up, and returns to the store to buy it. Imagine her frustration when she finds that the product has sold out. Imagine also another scenario where a customer sees a dress in the store window and wishes to buy it. She enters and cannot find the dress in her size, or even worse, finds that all the sizes have sold out, except for the one in the shop window which is not her size. She may complain to the vendor, asking why they have displayed a product which they do not have in stock in the shop window, to no avail. She is finally told that it is the parent company that decides which items should be displayed in the window, regardless of what the store has in stock.

How does one avoid stock shortages? The simple solution would be to simply buy more of each item to ensure that the entire season's collection is available in all sizes and all colours until the last day of the full-price period, but that would be far too onerous. As for restocking, very often fashion collections for the season are manufactured in distant countries and dispatched in one consignment, and if reordered it would take 2–3 months to receive new stocks of a particular item.

Another solution is to organise transfers of merchandise between stores. Many companies schedule two or three deliveries a week to all their stores and can therefore plan returns and supplies within a time-frame of 2 days. The client can be requested to come back in a few days for the article she wants. She may not do so, but at least the service had been offered to her. We have seen in the first section of this book that this process can be fully automated if it is digitalised.

Companies with more than six stores in the same commercial zone usually make it a practice to check their inventories every night. This allows them to arrange for additional deliveries and transfers the next morning if required. Today, this procedure is computerised. All the stores are linked to a centralised information system that records sales and is able to plan the necessary transfers. One of these systems, called 'Sterling Always in Stock', is an inventory management system that is able to process such transfers. But more innovations in this domain would certainly be welcome. For example, when an item in a given size has been located in another store, it should be possible to ship it directly to the customer's home the next day: this combination of in-store and home delivery service should be developed.

Another disadvantage of having too much stock at the end of a season is that customers can often sense the situation when entering the store and hence decide to wait for the sales. It is certain that a client who enters the shop on 12 December, finds a dress that pleases her and sees that there are three or four left on the shelf, could decide to wait a few weeks until January and buy it during the sales. But if someone says to her, 'You are lucky, it is the last one left in your size', she will probably decide to buy it at full price.

After the vertiginous fall in sales in US department stores in the last quarter of 2008, the sales in January 2009 at knock-down prices were phenomenal. And so, to ensure that the customers would return in October–November 2009 and purchase the fall-winter collection at full price, Saks Fifth Avenue, Neiman Marcus and Nordstrom adopted a policy of a double-digit reduction in their purchases in these collections, to persuade consumers that they had to buy at full prices.

- Controlling margins

As explained above, a margin is the difference between the selling price and the cost, expressed as a percentage of the selling price. Since cash register terminals are linked to a centralised computer system, the margins and transactions of each store can be tracked in real time.

It is, of course, not as simple as it sounds, because different product categories have different coefficients. But the information may be displayed whenever the expected margin has not been attained.

Depending on each brand's commercial philosophy, various guidelines can be set down with regard to the discounts that sales staff are authorised to offer in order to boost sales, and in particular to increase the percentage of customers who purchase a second item. The policy of some brands is to give sales staff the freedom to grant a client up to a 5% discount and the discretion, in some exceptional cases, of up to 10%, subject to the approval of the Store Manager or the Country Director of the sales outlet. The data on these margins and the details, by vendor, have to be collected daily for each store.

Other special rates include discounts to staff (with a maximum limit per month or per season) and discounts to journalists.

An internal theft will only be identifiable if the missing article is listed during a physical inventory. Usually, stocktaking takes place three times a year, at the end of the accounting year (generally 1 January) and at the end of the two sales periods (28 February and 31 August). It may be advisable to also check inventories at the end of June, before the beginning of the summer sales, as well as in the middle of each season, say for example, at the end of October and the end of April.

Exceptional turnover verification procedures should also be put in place so that any anomaly can be easily detected.

Analysis of Returns on Investment

The question of returns on investment is common to every sector. In the domain of retail outlets, if one sets aside the cost of setting up a store and the payments corresponding to 'lease rights', the return on investment will depend on the average volume of stocks.

One can therefore speak of returns on the gross margin on investments in stock. It would be calculated using the following formula:

$$\text{GMROI} = \frac{\text{Gross margin in euros}}{\text{Total turnover}} \times \frac{\text{Total turnover}}{\text{Average investment in stock}}$$

This figure is actually the result of two well-known ratios:

Gross margin = (Gross margin in euros/Total turnover)
Stock rotation = (Total turnover/Average investment in stock)

The return on investment is therefore the outcome of these two basic ratios. Table 16.9 shows different variations with the same return on investment.

In each of the three cases, the return on investment on stock is the same and therefore their financial performances are identical, but in the first case, the store manages to rotate its stock eight times a year, meaning that the store sells the equivalent of the total of its products within a period of six weeks. In such a case, a margin of 25% would be more than acceptable while still obtaining very positive results. In the second case, priority is given to the gross margin, this time at 40%, at the expense of stock rotation. In the third case, a certain equilibrium has been found between these two indicators.

The lesson to be drawn here is that it is possible to be profitable with a small margin as long as stocks are moving fast. The important point is that if stocks rotate fast enough, the margin can be significantly reduced without affecting the overall return on investment.

Table 16.9 Commercial Strategies

	Gross margin in GMROI %	Stock rotation	ROI
Priority to turnover	20.0%	8	200%
Priority to margins	40.0%	5	200%
Priority to balanced strategies	33.3%	6	200%

Information Systems

The most important feature of an information system is that all the cash register terminals are connected to a central server, so that the turnover, the stock and the margins can be monitored in real time for each store, each sales staff member, giving details of the various categories of products.

Retail is a domain where it is necessary to react rapidly if sales increase faster than expected (stores will soon be out of stock) or slower than expected (orders may have to be suspended immediately, otherwise it will face a cash crunch).

Tracking monthly sales figures is not as easy as it seems because some months have five Saturdays (the most important day of the week for sales) while others have only four, making comparison difficult. Some information systems correct this automatically using an algorithm. Many US trading companies do not depend on monthly statistics at all, but prefer to split the year into 13 periods of 4 weeks each. This is rarely the case for luxury companies, as sales is only a part of their business; everything else functions on a monthly basis.

Information systems are able to analyse current and expected stock shortages and recommend transfers. They can calculate theoretical OTBs and analyse delivery schedules to see if they are in line with expected sales or actual sales.

They can also process theoretical margins, theoretical inventories, and theoretical prices to analyse the variations observed as compared to this data. And this can be done by store or even by vendor.

In fact, in managing luxury outlets, the fundamental unit of observation is the store, and when one speaks to the general manager of Salvatore Ferragamo or Hugo Boss, it is always a bit unexpected to hear them announce the latest results from their main store in Chicago or their sales point in Shanghai. This simply means that they study these figures every day so that they can react very quickly if necessary.

To recap:

- *Distribution is a very precise and analytical sector.* Everything is measured and everything is controlled. It is therefore not surprising that, every day, managers track the turnover realised, the margins obtained, and at the least, the conversion rates (not forgetting out-of-stock situations) of all their stores worldwide. The cash register terminals connected to the central computer system can provide this information in real time from anywhere in the world.

- *The first reflex* should be to compare the differences between certain stores, certain countries, or certain categories of products to be able to compare them to the average.
- *It is also useful* to look at performance over the year and compare it to the previous year and also to compare one season to another.
- *In any case,* the day-to-day management of a sales point or several sales points is certainly an exercise that demands precision and an analytical mind.

Conclusion

In this book, we wished to provide all the necessary tools for senior executives of luxury brands seeking to organise and optimise the physical distribution of their products. This is why we have emphasised the choice and the organisation of the brick-and-mortar sales points (location, concept, logistics, identification and management of customer data, etc.), as well as digital distribution (online, offline, O2O, role of the Internet in physical distribution). Some readers may get to this point and say that all this is only of moderate interest to them because the specificities of their brand are different – either because of its size or its sector. We believe, however, that all that we have described applies to all sectors, and we would like to address this subject in this conclusion.

A first distinction should be made by sector of activity. Our remarks may have appeared to concern only the fashion, accessories, jewellery and tableware sectors. In fact, as we have shown, the trend for the past 30 years has been towards strengthening and developing single-brand stores, management of sales outlets and, by extension, that of digital alternatives, and is a daily concern and priority for management. All the brand managers we met told us how important it is for them to build a steady, trustful and profitable relationship with customers, which, of course, is either through a visit to a brand's store, or a unique, comprehensive and one-to-one contact on the Internet.

At first glance, it would seem that the beauty sector is less likely to use the exclusive and direct distribution system, and is also less interested in developing their own network of stores. However, in recent years, the brands have themselves developed stores exclusively dedicated to beauty (for brands as different as Chanel, L'Oréal, Dior, and Armani). In addition, the counters in department stores (very important sales points for beauty products) play by the same rules as those of directly operated sales outlets. More especially, in this sector, the creation of a direct customer database could facilitate closer relations with the market and invaluable opportunities for direct dialogue. In addition, as we explain below, the development of the niche perfume business places the creation of exclusive stores at the centre of the activity.

As we pointed out several times in this book, the watch industry is also evolving and the leaders of this sector also seem to consider brand-exclusive stores as effective tools for development.

As a result, for the vast majority of personal luxury sectors, managing sales points, in its broadest sense, and the simultaneous managing of online distribution channels are essential elements for development and an international presence.

Another distinction deserves to be made here: the size of the companies. For large groups, or for brands with a turnover of more than €500 million, prioritising the development of a worldwide structure of sales outlets of excellence, either with self-owned stores, shops-in-shops, or corners in department stores, is essential. Our book has detailed the rules of operation, set out the issues and outlined the conditions for success.

For smaller luxury brands, with turnovers of €30 million to €100 million, the priority in matters of creation and management of outlets is very different. Their strategy is very often to have a flagship presenting the entire collection of the brand with suitable marketing. Once the flagship is installed, the development of a global network of outlets will often call for creative solutions. Half of the turnover will be provided by multi-brand sales outlets, but in many countries, physical distribution will be handled by importers/distributors who will sometimes work with multi-brand retailers, and sometimes, with the blessings of the brand, open exclusive single-brand stores themselves.

In this very typical scenario, the management of the sales outlets, from the point of view of the brand, is not very different from the one we have described and explained in this book, but the system is slightly more complicated since it has to address several levels of additional stakeholders. The difficulty lies in the implementation of O2O: How can one build a distribution controlled by the brand while most of the offline distribution is controlled by third parties?

An entirely different sector is that of niche brands. This is a new and distinct category. These brands usually have a turnover that is generally lower than the other two categories (often less than €15 million a year), but this is not their only differentiating aspect. What characterises these brands in the world of luxury products is first and foremost the creation of handcrafted products which recognise the value of artisanal work, with limited series, and where the respect for creation and performance is their *raison d'être*.

Unlike medium-sized luxury brands, the niche sector encourages self-owned stores. These are usually small shops, not necessarily located in highly frequented areas, as if one had to make an effort to find them or rather discover them. For these niche brands, what counts most is the added value of exceptional products, precise and exclusive positioning and targeted customers.

Niche brands are most often found in the perfumery or cosmetics sectors, but they are likely to develop also in fashion, accessories, such as leather crafts, home decoration, watches and special wines and spirits.

How do these niche products grow to become global? Here too, some use intermediaries such as distributors or local importers, but they will no doubt seek to open exclusive stores both abroad and in their country of origin as soon as they are able to do so. That only goes to emphasise that the right reflexes and especially experience in sales point management will prove to be indispensable in this segment.

These niche brands have another specificity which we have not dealt with in this book: it is the intensive use of social media like Facebook or Instagram to build a constructive dialogue with their closely targeted customers mentioned above. This sphere, important in the marketing of niche products, is an integral part of online activities, but it is outside the scope of this book dedicated to the distribution and management of sales channels (offline and online). It is still worth remembering that the growth of niche luxury brands is largely due to personalised contacts with clients through social media, and is reinforced by bloggers and influencers. From that perspective, the two niche perfume brands developed independently by the two authors (*Dusita* and *Le Jardin Retrouvé*) are emblematic examples.

There is a third distinction that we need to learn more about here, which is the one concerning different types of customers. We dwelt at length on loyal customers, and mentioned occasional customers only in passing, though we did mention that they could represent at least 20% of the turnover for some luxury brands. In this book, we highlighted the importance of loyal customers who should be identified, catalogued and satisfied through targeted and well-organised digital operations, but we should not minimise the importance of occasional customers. These customers should in fact be won over and re-motivated with a view to turning them into loyal clients. In this domain, the use of social media is not very effective because many of these customers remain unknown and unregistered, just silent observers. To motivate them, one has to use tools that target the widest possible public, the 'old' medium of advertising. One should in fact create symbols that are immediately recognisable, such as the orange boxes from Hermès, or the label, also orange, of the Veuve Clicquot champagne bottles on a supermarket shelf that immediately attracts attention. It is necessary at this level to develop signs of affiliation[1] allowing these casual customers to identify the brand and make it part of the short list of brands they should buy. Alternatives to print advertising should also be developed in order to reach the maximum number of potential customers and thus renew the base of occasional buyers: this is clearly the role of online influencers today. They allow brands of any size and any sector to build a reputation and (sometimes) to sell. But this subject warrants a whole book in itself!

In the book *Luxury Brand Management* (Chevalier and Mazzalovo, 2020), it is said that many customers are excursionists who only buy once every two years. They are also the ones who have to be convinced,

---

[1] In this regard, we highly recommend the excellent work of Jenni Romanluk, *Building Distinctive Brand Assets* (2018).

and to do so, the best method is most probably the classic elements of a 'communications' marketing mix.

In these final pages, we have wandered far away from the subject of this book, 'distribution' and 'challenges of digital distribution', but we certainly do not want to give the impression that we have forgotten the basic rules of marketing.

We felt that it was important to provide the reader all the necessary tools for the direct and online distribution of luxury goods and to discuss the situations and issues that we will no doubt find on their agendas over the next ten years.

Bibliography

Amed, I. (2015) Karl Lagerfeld on the State of Fashion: It's a Mess. *Business of Fashion* (25 February), http://www.businessoffashion.com/articles/intelligence/karl-lagerfeld-on-the-state-of-fashion-its-a-mess

Amed, I. and Abnett, K. (2016) Burberry Aligns Runway and Retail Calendar in Game-Changing Shift. *Business of Fashion* (5 February), https://www.businessoffashion.com/articles/news-analysis/burberry-aligns-runway-and-retail-calendar-in-game-changing-shift

Aminoff, J. (2016) *Social Selling Luxury: Increase Sales by Engaging in the Digital World*. Jukka Aminoff.

A.T. Kearney (2010) *Achieving Excellence in Retail Operations*.

Atwal, G. and Williams, A. (2009) Luxury Brand Marketing: The Experience Is Everything", *Brand Management* 16 (5/6).

Bain & Co. (2012) *China Luxury Market Study*. November.

Bain & Co. (2017) *China Luxury Market Study*.

Barakat, M. (2019) *The Future of Luxury Retail: Hybrid Retail*. Lap Lambert.

Bastien, V. and Kapferer, J.N. (2008) *Luxe Oblige*. Eyrolles.

Batat, W. (2019) *Digital Luxury*. Sage Publications.

Bertelli, P. (2001) Foreword. In *Projects for Prada Part 1* (ed. R. Koolhaas). Fondazione Prada.

Blanckaert, C. (2007) *Luxe*. Paris: Le Cherche Mid.

Böck, I. (2015) *Essays on the History of Idea: Six Canonical Projects by Rem Koolhaas.* Jovis Verlag GmbH.

Cailleux, H. and Mignot, C. (2009) Is CRM for Luxury Brands? *Journal of Brand Management*, 16 (5–6): 406–412.

Capgemini (2008) Am I Being Taken? Inside the Dealership: The Impact of Consumer Negotiation Preferences and Strategies.

Chaffey, D. (2015) *Digital Marketing.* 6th ed. Pearson.

Chevalier, M. and Mazzalovo, G. (2015) *Luxury Management and Marketing.* Paris: Dunod.

Chevalier, M. and Mazzalovo, G. (2020) *Luxury Brand Management.* 4th ed., forthcoming.

Chevalier, M. and Lu, P.X. (2009) *Luxury China: Market Opportunities and Potential.* Hoboken, NJ: John Wiley & Sons.

Colloquy.com (2009) The New Champion Customers. *Colloquy Talk* (January).

Danziger, P. (2019) *Meet the HENRYS: The Millennials that Matter Most for Luxury Brands.* Paramount Market Publishing.

Danziger, P. (2005) *Let Them Eat Cake: Marketing Luxury to the Masses – As Well as the Classes.* Chicago: Dearborn.

D'Arpizio, C. (2017) 'Millennial State of Mind': The Tailwind Behind Consumer Behaviours and Winning Strategies, October. Bain & Altagamma.

D'Arpizio, C. and Levato, F. (2018) *Altagamma 2018 – Worldwide Luxury Market Monitor*, October. Bain & Co.

Davidson, W. (1999) *Retailing Management.* New York: John Wiley & Sons.

Davidson, W.R., Sweeney, D.J., and Stampfl, R.W. (1988) *Retailing Management.* New York: John Wiley & Sons.

De Boissieu, E. and Milleret, G. (2016) *Les Vitrines du Luxe : Une Histoire Culturelle du Commerce haut de Gamme et de ses Espaces de Vente.* Eyrolles.

De Châtel, F. and Hunt, R. (2003) *Retailisation: The Here, There and Everywhere of Retail.* European Publication Limited.

Diamond, E. (2006) *Fashion Retailing, A Multi-Channel Approach.* Pearson Prentice Hall.

Diaz, M. (2016) (Emaking), Experience. In: *Luxe et Digital,* Darkplanneur, Dunod.

Ellis, R. (2018) *Global Retailing.* CBRE.

Exane BNP Paribas (2016a) *The Dawn of Luxury CRM: E-mail Dos and Don'ts* (7 April).

Exane BNP Paribas (2016b) *The Dark Side of Digital Luxury.*

Exane BNP Paribas (2017) *The War for Talent.*

Exane BNP Paribas (2018a) *Luxuryland* (29 March), p. 155.

Exane BNP Paribas (2018b). *What's Hot and What's Not* (March).

Exane BNP Paribas and ContactLab (2015a) *Digital Frontier: The New Luxury World of 2020* (May).

Exane BNP Paribas and ContactLab (2015b) *Digital Competitive Map: Citius, Altius, Fortius* (July).

Exane BNP Paribas and ContactLab (2016a) *Digital and Physical Integration: Luxury Retail's Holy Grail* (March).

Exane BNP Paribas and ContactLab (2016b) *The Online Purchase Experience Ranking* (September).

Fernie, J., Moore, C.M., and Lawrie, A. (1998) 'A Tale of Two Cities: An Examination of Fashion Designer Retailing within London and New York'. *Journal of Product and Brand Management* 7 (5).

Fionda, A.M. and Moore, C.M. (2009) The Anatomy of the Luxury Fashion Brand. *Brand Management* 16 (5/6).

Frankel, A. (2007) *Punching In*. Collins.

Frasquet, M. and Miquel, M.-J. (2017) Do Channel Integration Efforts Pay Off in Terms of Online and Offline Customer Loyalty? *International Journal of Retail and Distribution Management* 45 (7/8): 859–873.

Gist, R.E. (1968) *Retailing Concept and Decision*. New York: John Wiley & Sons.

Glaser, J.E. (ed.) (2012) *42 Rules for Creating We*. Creating We Institute (28 September).

Gucci, (2016) A Journey of Desire, Gucci Day, 3 June 2016, http://www.kering .com/sites/default/files/document/gucci_day_presentation_03062016.pdf (accessed 20 April 2018).

Gutsatz, M. (2002) Luxe Populi/Developing Luxury Brands. Working Paper, July.

Gutsatz, M. and Auguste, G. (2013) *Luxury Talent Management*, Palgrave-Macmillan.

Gutsatz, M. and Auguste, G. (2015) *Luxury Talent Management*, Palgrave-Macmillan.

Gutsatz, M. and Schindholzer, B. (2011) Customer Experience Design for Luxury Brands. The Scriptorium Company, White Paper.

Harvard Design School Guide to Shopping (2001). Taschen, Köln.

Hebrero, M. (2015) Fashion Buying and Merchandising: From Mass Market to Luxury Retail. Create Space Independent Publishing Platform.

Heinze, A., Fletcher, G., Rachid, T., and Cruz, A. (2016) *Digital and Social Media Marketing: A Results-Driven Approach*. Abingdon: Routledge.

Hichman, D. and Marze, E. (2006) *The Affluent Consumer: Marketing and Selling the Luxury Style*. New York: Praeger.

Hirschberg, L. (2001) Luxury in Hard Times. *The New York Times* (2 December).

Hsieh, T. (2010) *Delivering Happiness: A Path to Profits, Passion, and Purpose*. New York: Business Plus.

IBM Institute for Business Value (2008) Why Advocacy Matters to Apparel Retailers.

Jones Lang LaSalle (2009) *Real Estate Transparency Index.*

Jones Lang LaSalle (2016) *Real Estate Transparency Index.*

Jones Lang LaSalle (2018) *Asian Research.*

Kansara, V.A. (2017) Inside Farfetch's Store of the Future. *Business of Fashion* (12 April).

Kapferer, J.N. (2015) *Kapferer on Luxury: How Luxury Brands Can Grow, yet Remain Rare.* Kogan.

Kapferrer, J.N. (2017) The End of Luxury as We Knew It. In: *Advances in Luxury Brand Management* (ed. J. Kemstock, T.O. Brexendorf, and S.M. Powell). Palgrave Macmillan.

Keller, E. (2007) Word of Mouth Marketing. *ARF (September).*

Keller, E. (2007) Unleashing the Power of Word of Mouth: Creating Brand Advocacy to Drive Growth. *Word of Mouth Marketing, ARF* (September).

Kingsworth, S. (2016) *Digital Marketing Strategy: An Integrated Approach to Online Strategy.* Kogan.

Knowledge@Wharton (2007) Are Your Customers Dissatisfied? Try Checking Your Sales People. Knowledge@Wharton (16 May). Retrieved from https://knowledge.wharton.upenn.edu/article/are-your-customers-dissatisfied-try-checking-out-your-salespeople/

Knowledge Networks (2009) How People Use Social Media. http://www.knowledgenetworks.com/news/releases/2009/052009

Koolhaas, R. (2001) *Projects for Prada, Part 1.* Milan: Fondazione Prada.

Kotler, P. and Keller, K.L. (2016) *Marketing Management*, 15th ed. Prentice Hall.

Kozinets, R.V. (1999) E-Tribalized Marketing? The Strategic Implications of Virtual Communities of Consumption. *European Management Journal* (June).

L2 (2010) *Digital IQ Report – Luxury* (October).

L2 (2013) *Digital IQ Index – Watches & Jewelry.*

L2 (2016) *Digital Index: Luxury China* (May).

Leadbetter, J. (2011) *Sales and Service Excellence: How to Stand Out from the Crowd.* Management Books.

Le Luxe est Vivant (2016) Tommy Hilfiger Pushes the Digital Borders of Fashion Week (23 February). http://www.leluxeestvivant.com/leblog/2016/23/2/tommy-hilfiger-repousse-les-frontieres-digitales-de-la-fashion-week

Lent, R., and Tour, G. (2009) *Selling Luxury.* Hoboken, NJ: John Wiley & Sons.

Levine, J. (1997) Liberté, fraternité but to Hell with égalité. Forbes. https://www.forbes.com/forbes/1997/0602/5911080a.html

Levy, M. and Weitz, B. (2004) *Retailing Management*. New York: McGraw-Hill Irwin.

Lockwood, L. (2015) NYFW Going Consumer? CFDA Studies Idea. *WWD* (14 December).

Lockwood, L. (2018) Chanel Shifts to Concession Model. *WWD* (8 November).

Luxury Institute (2010) *Leading Edge Insights into the World of the Wealthy*. Annual Note.

Marsden, P., Samson, A., and Upton, N. (2005) Advocacy Drives Growth. *Brand Strategy* 198: 45–47.

McKinsey & Company (2009) *The Promise of Multi-Channel Retailing* (October).

McKinsey & Company (2018) *The Age of Digital Darwinism* (January).

Michman, R.D. and Mazze, E.M. (2006) *The Affluent Consumer: Marketing and Selling the Luxury Lifestyle*. Westport, CT: Praeger.

Milnes, H. (2017) Farfetch CMO John Veichmanis: Data Is The New Marketer's Currency, *Digiday* (26 June). https://digiday.com/marketing/farfetch-cmo-john-veichmanis-data-new-marketers-currency

Moore, C., Doherty, A.M., and Doyle, S.A. (2010) Flagship Stores as a Market Entry Method: The Perspective of Luxury Fashion Retailing. *European Journal of Marketing* 44 (1/2): 139–161.

National Post (2013) Oprah 'Cannibalized' Me: Shop Clerk in Zurich Handbag Scandal Says TV Host Is Lying about Alleged Racist Incident. *National Post* (13 August). https://nationalpost.com/scene/oprah-cannibalized-me-shop-clerk-in-zurich-handbag-scandal-says-tv-host-is-lying-about-racist-incident

Nayar, V. (2010) *Employees First – Customers Second*. Harvard Business Press.

Oechsli, M. (2004) *The Art of Selling the Affluent: How to Attract, Service and Retain Wealthy Customers and Clients for Life*. Hoboken, NJ: John Wiley & Sons.

Okonwo, M. (2010) *Luxury on Line*. New York: Palgrave Macmillan.

Palmer, A. (2010) Customer Experience Management: A Critical Review of an Emerging Idea. *Journal of Service Marketing*, 24 (3): 196–208.

Pressman, A., Fisher, R., Koch, P.-A. and Rabenhorst, J. (2016) *Achieving Excellence in Retail Operations*, A.T. Kearney.

Reichheld, F.F. (2003) The One Number You Need to Grow. *Harvard Business Review* (December).

Rigaud, E. and Pini, F.M. (2018) New Luxury Management: Creating and Managing Sustainable Value across the Organization. *Palgrave Advances in Luxury*.

Romanluk, J. (2018) *Building Distinctive Brand Assets*. Oxford University Press.

Rosenthal, P. and Koller, L.D. (2002) *Faszination, Visual Merchandising*. Deutscher Fachverlag.

Sacerdote, E. (2007) *La Strategia Retail nella Mode e nel Lusso*. Milan: Franco Angeli.

Samoylenko, T. (2012) *The Role of Modern Architecture in Luxury Retailing: Architecture and Fashion*. Lap Lambert.

Shaw, C. (2007) *The DNA of Customer Experience*. Palgrave Macmillan.

Singer, J., Mathews, R., and Heggie, C. (2010) Socially Awkward Media. A.T. Kearney, Executive Agenda (December).

Socha, M., Conti, S., and Diderich, J. (2010) 'Retail Optimization' Is Luxury's New Buzz. *WWD* (25 May). https://wwd.com/business-news/business-features/retail-optimization-is-luxurys-new-buzz-3084951/

Solca, L. (2018) Retail Network Monitor website (January).

Som, A. and Blanckaert, C. (2015) *The Road to Luxury: The Evolution, Markets and Strategies of Luxury Brand Management*. Hoboken, NJ: John Wiley & Sons.

Spector, R. and McCarthy, P. (2005) *The Nordstrom Way to Customer Excellence*. Hoboken, NJ: John Wiley & Sons.

Srum, F. (2017) *Luxury Selling*. Palgrave Macmillan.

Stanley, T.J. (1991) *Selling to the Affluent*. New York: McGraw-Hill.

Strauss, W. and Howe, N. (2000) *Millennials Rising: The Next Great Generation*. Vintage Books.

Taubman, A. (2007) *Threshold Resistance: The Extraordinary Career of a Luxury Retailing Pioneers*. New York: HarperCollins.

Tepper, B. and Greene, M. (2016) *Mathematics for Retail Buying*. Fairchild Books.

Thomas, D. (2007) *Deluxe: How Luxury Lost Its Luster*. New York: Penguin Press.

Twitchell, J.B. (2002) *Living It Up: America's Love Affair with Luxury*. New York: Columbia University Press.

Ulrich, D. and Smallwood, N. (2008) *The Leadership Code*. Harvard Business Press.

Uncles, M.D., Dowling, G.R., and Hammond, K. (2003) Customer Loyalty and Customer Loyalty Programs. *Journal of Consumer Marketing* 20 (4).

Underhill, P. (2008) *Why We Buy: The Science of Shopping*. Simon & Schuster.

Value Retail News, November 2009.

Walk the Chat (2018) *China Digital Luxury Report 2018*. https://medium.com/walkthechat/china-digital-luxury-report-2018-a193d01314a9

Weathersby, W., Jr (2005) Chanel Ginza. *Architectural Record* (November).

Wetpaint & Altimeter Group (2009) *The World Most Valuable Brands: Who Is Most Engaged?* (July).

Wilder, C. (2001) No Time for Gloating. Informationweek.com (17 September).

Willeman, A. and Jary, M. (1997) *Retail Power Plays: From Trading to Brand Leadership*. New York University Press.

Winters, A.A., Fincher Winters, P., and Paul, C. (2003) *Brandstand: Strategies for Retail Brand Building*. New York: Visual Reference Publications.

About the Authors

Michel Chevalier is an expert in luxury brand management and in retailing.

He was Executive Vice President of Bluebell Asia Ltd, a group that imported luxury products and operated then 180 retail stores in Asia. He also managed the Paco Rabanne perfumes and Paco Rabanne fashion companies. He is now the president of Parfums Dusita, Paris, and visiting professor of Luxury Management at HEC Paris and the Universita Cattolica di Milano.

A graduate of HEC, Michel Chevalier holds an MBA and a DBA from Harvard Business School.

He is the author of *Luxury Brand Management* with co-author Gérald Mazzalovo and *Luxury China* with coauthor Pierre-Xiao Lu, both published by John Wiley & Sons.

Michel Gutsatz is an international expert in luxury brand management, based in Paris. He advises investment funds, luxury brands and retailers in Europe, China and the United States. He is a renowned speaker at international conferences on branding and luxury.

He is the president of a family Maison de Parfum, created in 1975 by his father, perfumer Yuri Gutsatz. Le Jardin Retrouvé is the very first Artisan Perfume Brand – the brainchild of Yuri's vision at the source of the niche perfume industry today. Le Jardin Retrouvé has been relaunched in 2016 with artist Clara Feder as its Creative Director (www.lejardinretrouve.com).

He is a visiting professor, teaching brand management and luxury retailing at major international business schools like CEIBS (Shanghai), Kedge Business School (Paris and Shanghai), and HKU (Hong Kong).

Prior to that, Michel was managing director of an image strategy agency and Human Resources and Internal Communication Director of the Bally Group in Switzerland.

Michel also created and developed the MBA in International Luxury Brand Management at ESSEC Business School, through partnerships with L'Oréal, LVMH, the Estée Lauder Companies, Cartier, Montblanc, Escada, Ermenegildo Zegna, and Firmenich.

Michel holds a PhD in Economics.

Index